In The Name of
God of Entrepreneurship

Serial Number: P2436120245
Title: Business Mastery
Author: Hossein Taheri
Translator: Dr. Mahshid Sanaeefard
Interior: Mehdi Ghasemi, Mahnoosh Javadi, Mehri Safari
Editor: Mandana Moradi
ISBN: 978-1-77892-206-0
Metadata: Business/ Managements/Entrepreneurship
Book Size: 6 By 9 Inches
Pages: 612
Canada Publish Date: March 2025
Publisher: Kidsocado Publishing House

Kidsocado Publishing House
Vancouver, Canada

Phone : +1 (236) 333 7248
WhatsApp: +1 (236) 333 7248
Email: info@kidsocado.com
https://kidsocado.com

Business Mastery

Creating Mastery in Business

Hossein Taheri

Translator: Dr. Mahshid Sanaeefard

Dedicated to the hardworking entrepreneurs of my homeland, Iran

Contents

Chapter 1: Understanding Potential

Chapter 2: Creating a System

Chapter 3: Creating a Value

Chapter 4: Strategic Superiority

Chapter 5: Branding

Chapter 6: Marketing

Chapter 7: Sales Creation

Chapter 8: Attraction, Interviewing, and Hiring

Chapter 9: Team Building

Chapter 10: Finance and Profit

Introduction

The journey of writing the Business Mastery book began with my ongoing concern to support Iranian businesses in every corner of the world. For years, I have studied numerous books, markets, industries, and organizations without pausing in my quest for knowledge and experience. I walked alongside each of them to uncover profitable ventures that stemmed from their own innovative thoughts and perspectives. During this time, I shared everything I learned and experienced through my personal media, believing it to be a form of giving back to a community that is innocent and dear to me. I felt it was my duty to empower the economy of my homeland.

However, as time passed and I pondered how I could have a greater impact, I decided to focus more on writing and crafting a thesis rather than solely relying on media. This medium, unlike media, has been largely overlooked and deserves more attention. I aim to write books that enhance my people's mastery in their businesses and enrich them for their efforts.

The Business Mastery Book **is about mastering the skills, strategies, resources, and positions necessary for the advancement of a business in any economy**. This mastery includes understanding the effective systems of a business, recognizing the potentials of the organization and market, creating impactful results, building a powerful brand, marketing value creation, achieving strategic excellence, mastering sales skills, forming winning teams, and managing finances for profitability.

This book was written to reflect the successes, profitability, and impact of a business on its customer community. It aims to help them identify and eliminate factors that disrupt the vital signs of their organizations so they can continue to thrive in any economy. It was written to empower organizational teams to turn market and economic changes into opportunities and launching pads for growth.

I wrote the Business Mastery Book to make ambitious visions accessible and to clarify uncertain paths as much as possible. This book was not written for me to take pride in it but rather so that my community can benefit from it, allowing me to take pride in them and my beloved Iran.

In closing, I would like to express my sincere gratitude to my collaborators, Mehdi Khalili, Afsaneh Rezayat, and Hanieh Danesh, who supported me with their insights and experiences in writing this book.

Hossein Taheri | 2023

Understanding Potential

Chapter 1:

Understanding Potential

"Fear is what prevents you from mastering your business."

Hossein Taheri

📖 **After reading this chapter, you will gain mastery over:**

- The four key elements of business growth and mastery (resources, opportunities, people, and partnerships)
- The importance of focusing on hidden assets.
- How to break free from the daily routines of business.
- The significance and process of developing competency.
- The skill of accepting criticism and raising your level of awareness.

All entrepreneurship wants to grow and improve their business, creating opportunities for development. But when we begin, despite all our efforts, things just don't work out. When we get stuck and something goes wrong, we take action to fix the issue, but after solving that problem, another part of our business faces a new challenge. It's similar to a house's pipe that keeps leaking despite one's best efforts to fix it. no matter how much we repair, water keeps finding its way out from somewhere else.

For example, when sales decline, we immediately spring into action and try different strategies to increase sales: we reconnect with past customers, advertise, create content, search for new leads and potential clients, participate in various exhibitions, organize conferences, and many other activities to boost our sales. Fortunately, our efforts pay off, and sales stabilize. However, soon after, we find out there's a problem in our financial or human resources system. It's like a constant cycle; after celebrating the resolution of one issue, we receive news of another, throwing everything off balance again. The taste of success never quite settles, and the growth of our business is hindered by sudden, subtle, and unappealing slowdowns. Many businesses reach a level of success, but few remain there, primarily because they haven't mastered their processes and operations. From my experience over the past 21 years, I've concluded that **a business that is in full control of its circumstances grows more effectively.** Mastery over the business doesn't lead to random successes; instead, it's a consistent process. We need a comprehensive plan for expertise and control over our business, enabling us **to identify and seize opportunities based on the available resources as we grow.** If I were to summarize the knowledge of business growth and mastery in two words, they would be **"resources"** and **"opportunities."** The key lies in the ideas and plans we create to make the most of opportunities using our resources.

When we focus all our resources on mastering one area of the business and believe there's nothing else left, true business mastery reveals untapped potential in that very moment. We can use these hidden capacities to stabilize other areas of the organization; this is where opportunity creation comes in.

At this point, we must also consider the third element: people. Who will carry out these plans? Do the programs we, as business owners, design, have the potential to be executed by our employees, stakeholders, and collaborators? After considering people, we need the fourth element, "willingness to collaborate." This enables us to bring together resources, opportunities, plans, and people in a participative framework to achieve growth. Mastering business growth, which involves resources, opportunities, people, and the willingness to collaborate, is a comprehensive tool that helps you increase production and grow your business, regardless of the current economic conditions. The truth is, there are specific models that lead people to success in business and life, pushing them toward greater control and growth. When you learn how to apply strategies and principles that have worked for others, you compel yourself to follow in their footsteps. We've learned from the best in various businesses and distilled these lessons into smaller, actionable pieces that can be implemented with "measurable results" in your own business.

▶ Understanding Potential for Energy and Activity

I have always used concepts from physics to develop my business. We've often heard that everything in the universe is related to energy. Energy can be defined as "stored work" or "the ability to do work." In other words, when we talk about the energy of a substance, we're referring to that substance's capacity to perform work. Simply put, whenever work is done, energy is being converted. Life itself is meaningless without energy. In many cases, whether in life or in business, we exert a great deal of energy, yet our efforts do not yield results. For example, if you invest a significant amount of energy into moving an object, but that object doesn't move, all you've done is waste your energy. So, simply **expending energy does not always result in progress.** In every business, there is a lot of hidden energy that can be unleashed. By releasing this hidden energy within our business, we can accelerate our momentum and activities.

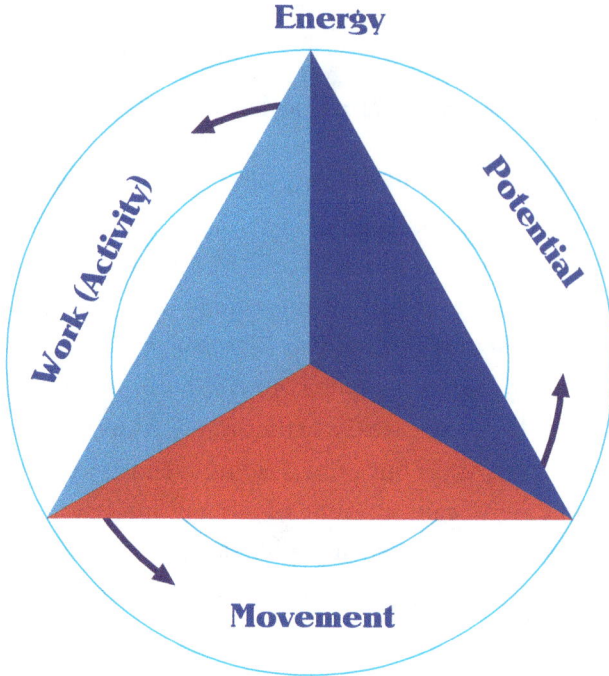

Given the principle of **"energy conservation,"** which states that "energy cannot be created or destroyed, only transformed from one form to another or transferred between substances," our approach to designing effective and impactful movements must focus on uncovering hidden potentials to utilize untapped energies for generating effective activities within the organization.

Every individual, organization, or business possesses growth potential. This "growth potential" is what I seek when I enter an organization as a coach. Rather than adding costs and responsibilities, I aim to identify the hidden potentials within that organization. In essence, without our consumption, these resources lack the power to create opportunities, and discovering these hidden resources can become the driving force and motivation for the organization. Your potential or that of your business is determined by the skills and knowledge you possess.

▶ Potential Means Focusing on Hidden Assets

Potential refers to abilities that have not yet been realized. Studies from the Harvard Business Review indicate that, based on conducted surveys, 98% of organizations recognize their potential. However, practical assessments reveal that many existing potentials within organizations remain underutilized and are not being leveraged. It's akin to being a skilled archer with the best bow and arrows, knowing precisely which target to aim for, yet failing to shoot because you're complacent with the resources at hand. This complacency does not equate to high potential. What truly matters **is performance; high efficiency is not necessarily linked to potential.** Mastery in business depends on executing that performance, not just knowing and understanding it. Many companies have an extensive list of clients they no longer work with and have not even reached out to once. This can exemplify hidden potential in sales and marketing. Numerous team members possess knowledge and skills that we are unaware of, and even they may not realize how their seemingly obvious skills could be impactful for the organization's effective initiatives. This represents an opportunity to harness the potential of human resources.

In one of the organizations, I worked with, there was an employee who was very calm, quiet, and introverted, making it difficult for me to engage and communicate with him. He was deeply focused on his work and did not involve himself in side conversations. One day, while preparing a PowerPoint presentation, I needed to convert some Excel data into a chart. I asked my colleague, Mr. Amirkhani, if anyone on the team was proficient in Excel because I wanted to create a chart for my presentation. He promptly replied, "I can do that for you right now," and within less than a minute, he completed the task for me. He was well-versed in Excel and many of its formulas and functions essential for managing the financial aspects of an organization, such as calculating salaries, cost accounting, and profit margins, skills that we were unaware of. **In fact, neither was he aware of our needs nor were we aware of his expertise.**

This is a simple example of uncovering hidden potential. Hidden potential can be a skill, a connection, or knowledge that someone else around you or within your organization possesses. Recognizing and utilizing this can greatly enhance the progress of your organization. You can learn from the experiences of others even more than from your own.

I encourage you and your colleagues to complete the table below to identify your hidden potentials and those within your organization. Take the time to do this. Reach out to your customers, key partners, and anyone you have collaborated with in the past for assistance.

Individual Potential

Knowledge and Skills:

....

....

....

....

....

Teamwork Skills:

....

....

....

....

....

....

Motivations:

....

....

....

....

....

....

Interests:

....

....

....

Wishes:

....
....
....
....
....
....
....

Specialization and Experience:

....
....
....
....
....
....
....
....

Social Services:

....
....
....
....
....
....

Organization Potential

External Relationships:

....

....

....

....

....

Financial Resources and Assets:

....

....

....

....

....

....

Non-Financial Resources:

....

....

....

....

....

....

Customer Responsiveness and Loyalty:

....

....

....

....

....

Marketing Channels and Media:

....
....
....
....
....

Partnerships and Organizational Relationships:

....
....
....
....
....
....

Documentation of Records:

....
....
....
....
....

Brand Power:

....
....
....
....
....
....

The more potentials you discover and understand, the faster you will accelerate your growth and mastery, gaining insights that you may have previously overlooked. By identifying and comprehending these potentials, you will free yourself and your team from the daily grind of business operations. You should always seek to uncover existing potentials to utilize them and make the best decisions. **Now, let's explore the most significant factor that hides and limits these potentials, preventing growth, success, and mastery in your business: repetitive mistakes and recurring events.**

If you find the courage to take a moment to sit down and take a superficial and detailed look at your business, you will clearly see how many repetitive feelings, thoughts, and, most importantly, mistakes and recurring issues are there. As a general and accurate rule, the more these repetitions occur, the more they indicate a lack of growth in a business system. **Is your business painfully caught in a cycle of repetition?** People often lack the courage to take bold steps to end the disastrous repetitions in their lives. You should be wary of this cycle and not accept it, even for a single day. Whenever you notice that repetition has become prominent in your business or that discussions and problems are recurring, you must pay attention to what you need to learn and implement that you haven't done yet. Essentially, the only way to end repetition is through heightened awareness and increased consciousness regarding our current situation. You may have felt that you have the necessary potential to achieve your dreams and know what actions you should take to reach them, yet you hold yourself back from moving forward on this path. There may be barriers preventing you from utilizing all your potentials to improve your quality of life. Many people know what they want to do but do not take the necessary steps to achieve their desired outcomes. This largely depends on your mental conditions and the design of your thinking. Therefore, the more you can understand yourself, the more you can excel in sales, management, marketing, finance, human resources, branding, and business strategies, which will also help improve your management and interaction with customers and employees.

▶ Strategies for Discovering and Increasing Potential

To achieve better results, everything hinges on the outcome. However, changes must first occur within ourselves, as improving our skills and abilities requires a commitment to change. The release of potential has a direct relationship with the creation of competencies, which is the path that can lead us to higher positions. My advice to you is to start by assessing your current standing; essentially, identify where you are in your life. Next, specify the goal or position you wish to achieve, and finally, develop a plan that will effectively help you reach your objective. This goal can vary based on your business context; for example, you might recognize your capability and desire to capture a larger market share, or feel that your business has the potential to achieve greater profitability. To do this, be honest with yourself.

How Can I Achieve Better Results and Returns Using My Potential?

....
....
....
....
....

What do I do well? Where do I need to be to feel successful, happy, and satisfied?

....
....
....
....
....
....

What goals have I been striving to achieve?

....
....
....
....
....
....

In which areas do my potential and abilities for advancement lie?

....
....
....
....

What is the quality of my daily efforts and activities?

....
....
....
....
....
....

How do I feel about my current position, and what have I achieved so far?

....
....
....
....
....
....

Where do I currently stand in life, and what goals do I want to achieve?

....
....
....
....
....
....

Step One: Cultivating a Competitive Spirit

A child, driven by a competitive spirit, can achieve everything they desire. In this pursuit, all their hidden potentials are discovered, which is a significant factor in reaching their goals. **Competition is a reality of life, and you can see its effects everywhere:** among athletes, in businesses, in schools and universities, between political parties, and many other contexts. **We are inherently competitive, as old as the history of living beings.** I know you are not a child, but you should strive to enhance your competitive spirit and that of your organization, remaining relentless until you achieve your goals. If you don't see competitiveness within yourself, try to foster it. Challenge yourself daily to facilitate progress and get closer to your objectives. Without challenging yourself, you can expect no progress, and without progress, there will be no change.

Professional athletes or Olympic champions cannot discover and unleash their hidden potentials without elevating their competitive spirit. Competition isn't just about striving to win; it's about improving upon your previous self and becoming the best version of yourself, raising your standards. An important point to remember is that you should never fall into a scarcity mindset. **Competitiveness is about clarifying our resources to create opportunities and discover hidden assets, not about focusing on what we lac.** We all possess an inexhaustible source of energy within us that compels us to act and complete our tasks. This powerful force comes from within and allows us to examine everything that diverts us from our goals. This is the essence of competitiveness and determination. **Competitiveness drives us to do things we fear.** Sometimes, we must undertake tasks we are reluctant to tackle because we know they are time-consuming; like contacting a stranger, staying up late to back up a company's server, or restarting a project. The most successful individuals know that in such moments, the best action is to start immediately. Every moment spent in fear pulls you further from success. **Overcoming false fears facilitates the discovery of potentials.** According to research by Dan and Brad Street, two prominent researchers, **organizational**

productivity, a lack of marketing knowledge, and an absence of a fighting spirit and competitiveness among company leaders are the main reasons behind more than eighty percent of business failures. This statistic clearly indicates that having a competitive spirit against other companies is the most crucial aspect of business leadership in a world where competition is increasingly intensifying.Striving to quickly, deeply, and better understand the needs, wants, challenges, and aspirations of customers compared to competitors is the best program you can implement to discover your organization's potentials. Fostering this spirit will help you sell more products at higher prices than your competitors, leading to years of growth and sustainability in the market.

Successful leaders focus not only on their current competitors but also on potential rivals, as they understand that most of yesterday's successful companies failed due to neglecting potential competitors, not because they lagged behind current rivals. For example, Nokia, once the undisputed leader in the mobile phone market, did not lose to competitors like Alcatel and Siemens; instead, it was overtaken by potential rivals like Samsung and Apple, who focused on smartphones, unlike Nokia, which concentrated on basic phones. This is why great leaders always consider this crucial question: What competitors might enter the market in the next five years and completely render our products obsolete with offerings or technologies fundamentally different from today's products and technologies?

To achieve this, we must answer the following key questions:

Who are our competitors?

....

....

....

....

Which of them are direct competitors and which are indirect competitors?

....

....

....

....

....

What are the strengths and weaknesses of each of our competitors?

....

....

....

....

What skills, resources, and tools do we need to overcome our competitors?

....

....

....

....

....

....

What methods can we use to acquire these resources?

....

....

....

....

....

....

How can our competitors harm us?

....

....

....

....

....

What actions can we take to address our weaknesses?

....

....

....

....

....

Why should our customers choose to buy from us instead of our competitors?

....

....

....

....

....

....

Are these reasons compelling enough?

....
....
....
....
....
....

Can we rely on these reasons for the long term?

....
....
....
....
....

What expectations do customers have from competitors that they have failed to meet?

....
....
....
....
....

How can we fulfill these expectations?

....
....
....
....
....

Successful leaders not only focus on their current competitors but also pay attention to potential competitors. They understand that many once-successful companies failed due to their lack of awareness regarding these potential rivals, rather than merely lagging behind their current competition.

For instance, Nokia, which was once the undisputed leader in the mobile phone market, did not fail due to competition from companies like Alcatel or Siemens. Instead, it was overtaken by potential competitors like Samsung and Apple, who focused on the smartphone market while Nokia remained focused on basic phones. This is why great leaders continually contemplate this important question:

In the next five years, what new competitors might enter the market and offer products or technologies that could completely render our current products obsolete?

You will not fully realize your capabilities unless you break your boundaries and move forward. Choose a new challenge and discover something you haven't done before. When you start something new, the challenge becomes harder, and that's when you uncover your true abilities.

Weakness is strong. I must be stronger.

Jocko Willink

Step Two: Embracing Criticism and Feedback

To fully utilize your potential, it's essential to pay attention to another critical point: embracing criticism and feedback from others. You can leverage this feedback to improve your circumstances. In fact, you should be your own harshest critic. Even negative and envious criticisms can serve as motivation. We often have a misconception about criticism; it is not merely about finding faults or blaming others. **In fact, criticism means distinguishing good from bad or listing pros and cons.** Unfortunately, our understanding is often shaped by the belief that criticism is solely about negative aspects. Criticism can be a source of awareness and intellectual growth, regardless of whether it is constructive or destructive. It can act as a protective factor for our resources. **One of the most significant outcomes of criticism is the reduction of human errors.** Being open to criticism is a catalyst for change, revealing genuine opportunities within these shifts. **Criticism serves as a form of feedback** in the workplace, aimed at improving individual performance. Typically, people criticize one another to assist each other in achieving better results. If you understand what it means to be open to criticism, you won't feel negatively towards others' feedback; instead, you will view it as an opportunity for your own growth.

Naturally, we all seek affirmation and appreciation in our relationships with others. Some of us even obsess over what others think of us. This is why, when someone criticizes us or we receive feedback that we perceive as unfavorable, we spend a long time pondering its cause and what emotions it might evoke in the critic. These thoughts, stemming from our inability to accept criticism, lead us to develop mistaken feelings about ourselves and others. *Is there a way to prevent this feeling? Why do we fear criticism, and how can we become more receptive to it?*

Criticism is often used to assess competency or lack thereof and to judge based on that. It is an evaluation aimed at identifying errors or problems in a behavior or performance. In contrast, feedback involves transferring valuable information regarding an action, process, or event to the original source or controller. Criticism also involves communication skills, while feedback enhances your performance. **If you are always satisfied with your performance without anyone offering their perspective, you cannot be sure of its quality, as that is merely your opinion,** and no one else has shared their thoughts with you.

Despite the fact that criticism can often be uncomfortable, it is important to recognize that many of these opinions, when expressed constructively, can provide suggestions for professional, social, and ethical growth. Failing to accept them deprives you of the chance to hear further constructive criticism.

People who are resistant to criticism not only fail to use this feedback positively but also frequently experience emotions such as depression, anxiety, anger, shame, hatred, defensiveness, and a decrease in self-esteem. Moreover, those who are unable to accept criticism may become obsessive, repeatedly examining their performance, self-criticizing, and blaming themselves for everything.

▶ What is Destructive Criticism?

Destructive criticism occurs when a critic aims to undermine your character and diminish your performance without any intention of fostering improvement. Those who understand what it means to be open to criticism can control their responses to such behavior and ensure that unfounded opinions do not negatively impact their motivation. Thus, by effectively distinguishing between constructive and destructive criticism, we can better manage our time and energy. **Spending time on destructive criticism is futile and can harm our sense of self-worth.**

So, how can we recognize destructive criticism and enhance our receptiveness to feedback? Below are some important points related to openness to criticism that practicing and focusing on can make it easier for you to receive feedback.

▶ View Criticism as a Type of Vitamin

Consider that you, like all other humans, are not perfect and have your shortcomings. Recognizing your strengths and weaknesses can help you progress with a more open mindset. One way to discover hidden potential is through the perspectives of others. Therefore, it's important to understand that the critic is not against you. **Always keep in mind that the critic has your best interests at heart and intends to help by offering constructive feedback.** You can think of criticism as a vitamin supplement that, despite its unpleasant taste, ultimately benefits you. Criticism provides more opportunities for growth and allows us to learn more so that we can perform better. Someone who offers you constructive criticism has good intentions and wants your efforts to lead to success.

▶ Evaluate Whether Criticism is Destructive or Constructive

Before reacting hastily to criticism, consider a few important points. The skill of being open to criticism can help you distinguish constructive feedback from destructive remarks. Destructive criticism targets your character and can be harmful, whereas constructive criticism focuses on your behavior and performance, aiming to draw your attention to how you can improve your work.

Here are four characteristics of destructive criticism:

- Delivering criticism in front of a third party or in a group setting.
- Using derogatory and disrespectful language.
- Criticizing the person's character rather than their incorrect behavior.
- Relaying the criticism to someone other than you.

When receiving criticism, ask yourself the following questions to help you assess the nature of the feedback and discover effective responses:

- Is the critic genuinely concerned about you?
- Does the critic have expertise in this area?
- Is the critic your manager or a colleague?
- What is the tone of the critic?
- Is this criticism based in reality and applicable to you?
- Is the critic's goal to help you grow, or do they intend to undermine your self-esteem and credibility?

After reflecting on your answers to these questions and gaining a better perspective on the criticism you received, try to view it as a dialogue. If you feel comfortable, discuss your feelings about the feedback with the critic. Instead of focusing on the tone, pay attention to the suggestions and critiques provided. Remember that some individuals may not have learned how to control their emotions and communicate appropriately.

So, it's best to focus less on people's tones and more on the substance of their comments. **Separate the tone from the suggestions and concentrate on what will help you improve.** It's essential to review these criticisms multiple times. While not every piece of criticism directed at you may be true, they often contain valuable insights for your growth, so take note of them and use them effectively.

▶ Avoid Emotional and Defensive Responses

It's natural to feel emotional upon hearing criticism. It's also common to want to defend your decisions. However, you must set aside this mindset. **Constructive criticism can lead to your professional development, so there's no need to justify your actions or defend your decisions.**

▶ Embracing Constructive Criticism

As soon as you understand the critic's good intentions, set aside any distracting thoughts and actively listen to their feedback so you can make effective changes. **When someone criticizes you, focus on the points they raise without letting your emotions take over, as you will thank them for their insights in the future.**

Therefore, after receiving feedback and understanding what being open to criticism means, concentrate on the expressed points and work on improving your performance. Being open to criticism means expanding your worldview. The broader our perspective, the better results we can achieve. It's important to recognize that we are the ones determining our path forward. By being receptive to criticism, we learn to think critically. Criticism is a form of honesty that allows us to gain a new viewpoint, so there's no reason to be defensive against differing opinions. Identifying blind spots and focusing on them gives us a greater chance of success.

In psychological techniques related to criticism, being open to feedback is an essential skill for growth and development. Openness to criticism consists of five key steps:

- Listening carefully and managing your emotions.
- Thanking the critic for their feedback.
- Expressing regret and accepting mistakes.
- Asking questions about the reason for the criticism.
- Explaining or apologizing as needed.

You can ask the critic the following questions:

- What suggestions do you have for improving my work?
- How can I manage my projects better?
- If you were in my position, what would you do?

Sometimes, Valuable Feedback Comes from Unqualified Sources at times, you might receive valid criticism from someone who lacks credibility or who presents it in an inappropriate manner. In these situations, maturity and awareness help us distinguish between constructive and destructive feedback.

Step Three: Cultivating a Mindset of High Risk-Tolerance

One essential factor in harnessing your full potential is having a high-risk tolerance. Nothing in life is certain, and sometimes the outcomes of your decisions may differ from your expectations. Many successful individuals have been willing to take risks and have not shied away from difficult situations, which is why they have achieved high status. However, it's crucial to note that taking risks is completely different from acting recklessly. While successful people embrace risk, there are many who act impulsively, diving into situations without careful consideration. For example, some may suddenly quit their jobs or invest all their savings in a single venture. If you want your company to grow, you must be prepared to take action, not just talk and plan. While planning is important, commendable, and necessary, those who achieve results tend to prioritize action over planning.

Step Four: Enhancing Awareness Through Deep and Continuous Learning

Begin every endeavor with awareness. The idea of trying everything to enhance your potential and capabilities is futile and time-consuming. Life teaches you new things every day, and you gain more experiences. Learn as much as you can, as learning is about benefiting from others' experiences. Attend classes, seek help from a coach, and expand your studies.

Determine what educational resources and skills are necessary for your field. This might include training courses, practical experiences, online learning, new technologies, management skills development, or improving communication skills, among others. Use credible educational resources based on your time and financial constraints. Connecting with individuals in similar fields can significantly enhance your learning speed. These individuals can provide valuable insights and help expand your network. Discipline in learning facilitates experience acquisition.

When new learning opportunities arise, remember that not everything is worth learning. Sometimes you may receive irrelevant advice or incorrect information from others, and it is your responsibility to discern what is worth keeping and what should be discarded. Additionally, remember that growth and change never stop over time, whether you notice it or not. The more knowledge you acquire, the more you will grow. Learning is an endless journey.

Step Five: Developing an Adaptable Mindset

Having an adaptable mindset is a key element in increasing your potential, particularly intellectual potential. This is the work your brain does behind the scenes to help us learn from mistakes, embrace failure, find solutions, and move forward. This flexibility cannot be underestimated in entrepreneurship. The survival of a business depends on the ability to learn and overcome challenges. An inflexible mindset hinders learning from mistakes, while an adaptable mindset empowers you to view mistakes as learning opportunities. We must accept that we sometimes fail in our jobs, careers, businesses, or relationships.

Failure does not define our character; rather, it reflects our performance in response to unexpected events. I had a friend who lost all his assets (over five billion tomans) in a business deal. Shortly after this incident, I called him, and as expected, he was very depressed and considering declaring bankruptcy and halting all his activities.

The only advice I gave him was: **"Never equate your self-worth with the net value of what you've lost."** I told him, **"Was that amount really your worth that you now want to stop everything?"**

Unexpected events can occur, altering or delaying your plans. This is completely fine. You can adjust your plans according to these events. These occurrences are part of all our lives, so embrace them willingly and continue striving to enhance your adaptability.

Although failures can be heartbreaking, embarrassing, and demoralizing, it is essential to keep moving forward. Dedicate time to process these emotions and reflect on them. Then, let them go. Holding onto negative feelings keeps you in a fixed mindset. Remember that your goal here is to operate at your full potential and move ahead. Overemphasizing past mistakes and failures is the surest way to halt your progress. Allow failures to be a learning opportunity.

I know this sounds like a cliché, but let me clarify something here: maximizing your abilities or potential does not mean you have to be a perfect, flawless person. The truth is that no relationship, skill, or job ever reaches perfection, and there is always a higher level to achieve. Every record will eventually be broken, and you cannot expect everything to be perfect and without flaws all the time. So, while striving to utilize your maximum capacity and abilities, remember that you cannot be flawless and mistake-free in everything.

Every mistake you make is, in fact, a step toward realizing your potential because it highlights your weaknesses, showing you what you need to work on. Learn from your mistakes, grow, and adapt to every situation.

The primary barrier to achieving your full potential is your mindset and what resides in your mind; it begins in childhood and can accompany you throughout your life. Don't let public perception deter you. **Have you ever heard of the "Bannister Effect"?** For years, it was believed that a human could not run a mile in under four minutes. However, on May 6, 1954, Roger Bannister ran a mile in three minutes and 59.4 seconds, achieving what had always seemed impossible.

Roger Bannister did not let public opinion block his path and demonstrated that this prevailing belief was merely a mental barrier. Following his achievement, others continued to break records. Currently, the record holder is Hicham El Guerrouj, with a time of three minutes and 43.13 seconds.

Living to your full potential requires stepping out of your comfort zone and expanding your boundaries. Average people do average things, achieve average results, and lead average lives. Extraordinary individuals perform extraordinary actions, achieve extraordinary results, and live extraordinary lives.

Success in life, while utilizing your full potential, means embracing uncomfortable situations. When trying new things, allow adequate time to pass. Many of us, while experimenting with a new task or skill, tell ourselves, "I've found my calling" However, determining whether something truly suits you takes time.

No one can perform flawlessly from the moment they start a task. So, have realistic expectations of yourself and allow time to reveal what areas are best for you. When you give yourself the chance to experience new things, you often relieve pressure from yourself and avoid the expectation of quickly mastering a skill.

If you are a perfectionist, you have likely experienced this pressure and understand how stressful and anxiety-inducing it can be. So instead of checking on the first day whether you have failed or succeeded, give yourself time and postpone judgment. Think of it as practicing, not more than that. This is similar to working out; after a few practice sessions, you might feel a dip in your confidence or optimism simply because you are not yet proficient. However, you must be realistic and wait before reaching the desired level. Surely, you observe all the movements in new workout videos or successfully implement weightlifting techniques. There is nothing wrong with taking the necessary time to learn how to do new things. In the end, your efforts will yield results.

Step Six: Overcome Your Fears

If you do not confront your fears and find a way to navigate through them, they will hold you back from living fully. Fear is what prevents you from stepping outside your comfort zone.

Your comfort zone is a place where you don't need to muster much courage, and you can live this way. However, your maximum potential lies beyond that safe zone. Therefore, you must step out of this area. Your greatest abilities will emerge when you embrace risks, face challenges, and leave your fears behind.

You may find that your abilities relate to the business world or to being someone who manages a charitable foundation or a grassroots organization. You might experience some social anxiety or be terrified of speaking in front of a crowd when you enter these fields. To reach your maximum potential, you must confront and overcome these fears.

Fear is something that often does not completely disappear. Thus, it is crucial to learn how to manage it. Sometimes, it might be beneficial to consult a therapist or psychologist to help you overcome your fears. In some cases, with time and gradual exposure, you can also learn to cope with these fears. One of the biggest barriers to personal growth and development is fear. Fear keeps you in your safe zone, preventing any progress. Therefore, first, identify your fears, and then take action to eliminate each one.

Remember the first time you wanted to ride a bicycle? Did you do it with total courage or with absolute fear? How do you ride a bike now? Let's go a bit further. What was it like the first time you sat behind the wheel of a car? Did you drive confidently or with total fear? How about the day you started your own business?

As you became more aware of the processes you were undertaking, your fear diminished. The nature of fear is based on "the unknown." If we gain more knowledge and understanding about the phenomena around us, our fear lessens. We are always presented with opportunities to confront our fears, but we often stay behind those fears and avoid seeking understanding and awareness to move past them, just like learning to ride a bike or drive a car.

▶ **Write Your Five Key Takeaways from This Chapter:**

1. ....

2. ....

3. ....

4. ....

5. ....

▶ **Three Steps I Will Immediately Start:**

1. ....

2. ....

3. ....

▶ **One Golden Lesson to Share with Others:**

....

....

....

....

Download all the tables and exercises of this chapter from the following website.

https://hosseintaheri.ir/bmg/

Creating a System

Chapter 2:
Creating a System

"The fruit of creating a system is organizational transparency."

📖 **After reading this chapter, you will gain mastery over:**

- The concepts and objectives of systemization

- The needs and steps for creating a system

- Optimization and leveraging

What is a system, and why is systemization necessary? How can we create an efficient system? Does a system require the presence of a manager? What happens if we don't have a system? This section will address these questions.

A system is a collection of elements with defined inputs and outputs. In this section, I want to focus on *creating a system*, not just the system itself. Without a system, you cannot manage or control people effectively. However, when a system is in place and everyone knows what they are supposed to do, productivity gradually increases.

A system is a clear method for performing tasks and activities within an organization to achieve a specific result. **It's not about delegating tasks, but about delegating outcomes.** Tasks must serve the result.

Products, services, and human resources are potential assets for a business. All three generate income, but it is the system that creates wealth. Without systematization, you can't evaluate your employees' activities. By systematizing, you can understand how your employees collaborate and achieve results. In fact, you must accept that your work environment is shaped by systems.

If you don't have a system, you will go bankrupt. A bankrupt company is one that works only to cover its costs, and over time, when it can no longer keep up with expenses, those costs accumulate and turn into debt. The nature of costs and debt is essentially the same. A "cost" is a "small debt" that you pay, but if you can't pay off these small debts, they grow into a larger debt that you can't manage, and eventually, you'll go bankrupt.

A business that can only cover its expenses without generating any surplus is bankrupt, even if it's still operating and putting in effort! Do you know why? For the same reasons mentioned in Chapter One: **exerting energy doesn't always translate into progress.**

Bankruptcy doesn't necessarily mean closure; many bankrupt companies are still open. A company that closes and faces creditors is already destroyed. **If you're only working to cover your costs, you're already bankrupt** because there's nothing left for you. In reality, you haven't built a system that generates growth and progress for you. It's like a car that's running but not moving, just burning fuel.

The power of a **system** is directly related to its financial capacity. In other words, you need to plan and manage the system in such a way that, in addition to covering ongoing expenses, you also have a surplus for savings and investment. Just covering costs is not enough.

A car is a perfect example of a **system.** It has suspension, movement, and many other advanced systems. However, if the car doesn't have a driver, it won't move. Some people think that once a system is created, no one needs to guide it. That's not true. You don't create a system so you can step away from it; someone still needs to drive it. The driver must operate in a way that avoids accidents and keeps the car safely on the road. How does the driver follow rules and guidelines to avoid crashes? Get rid of the illusion that **"we create systems so we don't have to be there ourselves."** You need to be present to see results and help the team achieve its goals. You create systems to eliminate unnecessary tasks for yourself, your employees, and your customers. You create systems to prevent burnout. Therefore, creating a system means managing both operations and performance.

Operations relate to the car itself, but performance is tied to the driver.

So, you need both. Managing operations is about what the hardware of the system does, but the person guiding the system will always impact how efficiently the system performs.

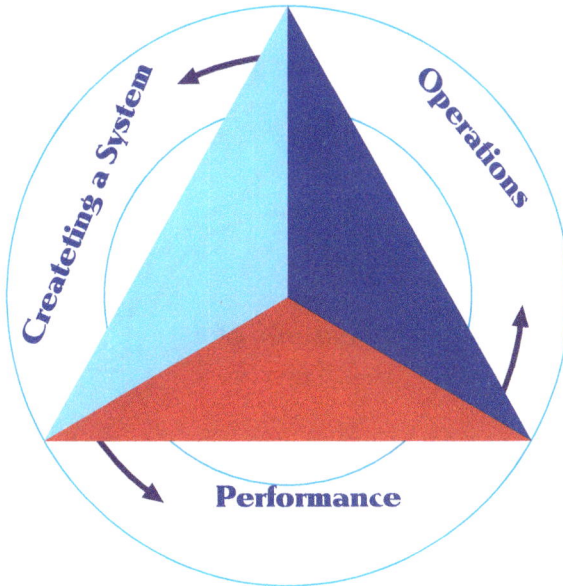

Systems are repetitive processes that operate regardless of the size of the business. The actions and tasks that drive business growth are processes that, after being created, are replicated and modeled throughout the organization, much like the tailoring process. When a tailor wants to make clothes, they use both the knowledge of sewing and their work experience. Experience means knowledge that has been put into practice. The tailor first learns how to sew, then turns that knowledge into practice, then into skill, and finally into **expertise**. So, when you want to create a system for doing something, you must first have expertise in that area.

In the second step, you need **tools.** For example, a tailor needs a sewing machine, needles, thread, and scissors. Tools are the resources you need to apply your expertise. Tools are essential in any system. If you want to have specific software to communicate with customers, you will need tools like a computer. After tools, you need **ideas** and **planning.** You have to use your expertise and tools in a way that produces optimal results and ensures that the resources, costs, and time you invest are balanced with the money, credit, and experience you gain in return.

▶ Features of a System

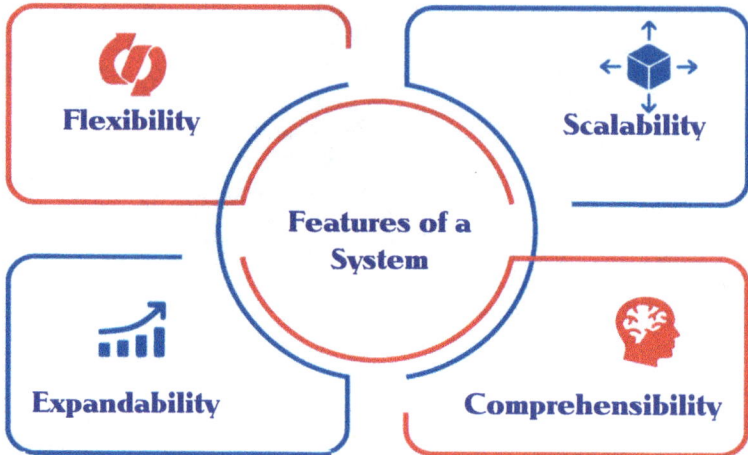

1. **Scalability:** This means that the system can be scaled up or down in size. It is measurable and adaptable to different levels.

2. **Expandability:** A system must be expandable so that it can grow. With expandability, the system has the potential for development.

3. **Comprehensibility:** A system should be understandable. Both its users and employees should be able to grasp how it works. For example, think of ATMs. They consist of hardware and software. Banks load them with money and connect them to the accounting system. They rely on account data, networks, and branches. All of this serves a clear outcome; when someone inserts their card into the machine, they get cash. Every part of this process is comprehensible to the users. When you want to expand the system or change its scalability, you simply copy the same process and implement it elsewhere. We once aimed to implement a system for a company that struggled to understand financial processes. The

lack of comprehensibility in their system led to errors. I advised the CEO that everyone in the finance department should take a finance and tax course, so they could understand why they were using the tools and could provide valid reasons to tax authorities.

4. **Flexibility:** Imagine a tailor who lacks flexibility; they would make clothes in one size for everyone. A tailor must make what fits the customer, not just what they personally prefer. Similarly, when you are systematizing your business, you need to be flexible. Systematization means delegating results, not just tasks. You provide employees, managers, or customers with the tools, knowledge, and ideas they need to make decisions and take action.

As I mentioned earlier, if you don't build systems, you will face bankruptcy. You will waste time and resources on ineffective actions that only allow you to break even, covering just your costs. In this situation, you are already bankrupt.

It's important to have a clear perspective on systematization. In systematization, you need to focus on the roots. Imagine an apple tree; you expect it to produce apples, not pears or figs. The outcome is predictable. Now, imagine that one of the apples you harvest has a bad taste, and so does the second one. Why do I use this example? Because often the "fruits" you gather in business are the result of your actions or those of your team. For instance, one of your employees might complete a task in a way that produces a poor outcome. If you blame the employee, it's like focusing on the fruit rather than the root. You throw the fruit away and reprimand or even fire the employee, without addressing the root cause. System-building is a root-focused, long-term process. Once the roots are established, what happens? The tree grows and begins to bear fruit. The problem with bad fruits starts at the root. Too often, we mistakenly think that by changing the outcome (the fruit), the cause will also change. However, once the roots are established, the system will bear fruit naturally.

This is exactly like system-building. Once you establish a system, you don't need to worry about how tasks are being completed, because you've delegated the result. However, if the result doesn't meet your expectations, you need to go back and examine the root cause.

When you face problems within your organization, don't immediately blame the employees. Sometimes the root of the issue lies in the organization itself. If you can't train employees to understand the system and work within it, maybe the issue is that you yourself haven't fully understood the system yet. When working in a system, if any part of the process takes longer than expected or if the results deviate from the goal, the issue will quickly reveal itself and become obvious.

The purpose of system-building is to reduce unnecessary dependence on the business owner or manager. This is a two-way relationship. The fruit is dependent on the root. Managers who focus on micro-managing are unable to create systems, as they are constantly looking to delegate and control tasks, not results. First, you need to focus on the outcome. If the desired outcome is not achieved, then investigate the cause. However, if you constantly interfere with every little detail and try to dictate every step, it's clear you don't have a well-defined system or clear outcomes.

Once you define the outcome and build a system, you can easily create organizational transparency for everyone involved. **I can confidently say that the "fruit" of creating a system is organizational transparency.** This means that every part of the business knows what its role is and what it's responsible for. In a well-structured system, each component knows its job and does not interfere with the responsibilities of other components. If you organize your work from the roots up, you can confidently say that your business is running in a systemized way.

▶ What Are the Goals of Systematization?

We have already defined what a system is and listed its characteristics. Now, let's examine the goals of a system. The goals of a system can be summarized as follows:

- Meeting the needs of users and customers
- Reducing operational costs
- Increasing savings
- Streamlining data flow
- Accelerating the execution of results
- Defining appropriate methods for managing business activities
- Eliminating redundant, contradictory, and unnecessary services

First and foremost, a system must meet the needs of users and customers. If you implement an idea but find that your customers are still not satisfied and you aren't attracting enough new customers, this means you haven't properly systematized the process. A system should also reduce operational costs. When creating or improving a system, calculations are made. For instance, if you plan to establish a training center, and the process takes six months instead of two, it indicates that there is no system in place, which increases your operational costs.

A system increases savings within the organization, creating reserves. It also ensures that resources are used efficiently. With a system in place, you can understand how each task or product is completed, how long it takes, and the costs involved.

Systems are created to streamline or improve data flow. Your organization holds information or data that you need to share with your employees. First, you categorize and determine who should have access to which information. For example, you might say, "We are working to create a system that ensures customer satisfaction." If you have a dissatisfied customer, when they contact customer service, there must be systematized documentation; both in terms of software and behavior; that addresses the issue. This allows for optimized use of data and ensures you achieve the desired results.

If you don't have a financial system, extracting profit and loss, receivables, payables, income, expenses, and debts will take a lot of time. Most importantly, a system improves how your business activities are conducted and prevents repetitive, contradictory, or unnecessary tasks.

▶ Basic Requirements for Creating a System

What do you need to create a system? What resources are necessary to build one? The basic tools required to create a system include software, hardware, thought frameworks, and emotional frameworks.

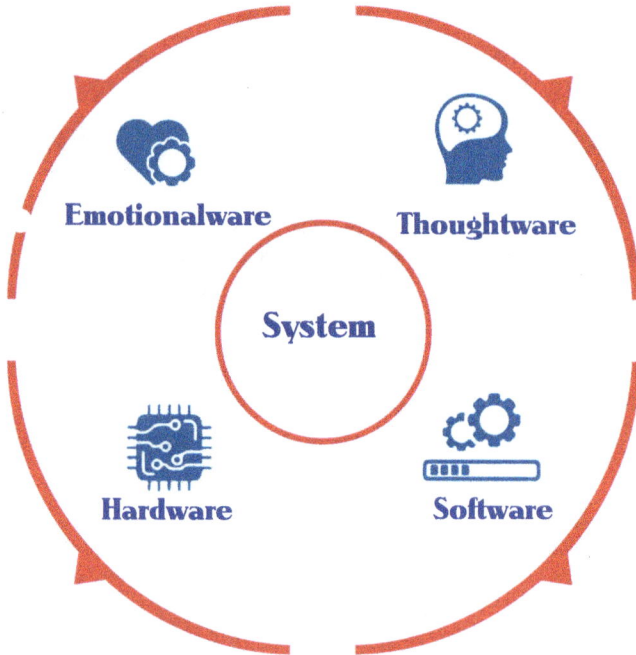

The existing **software and hardware** in the organization are defined. Prepare a list of them and then consider which ones can be updated and optimized. If you only focus on software and hardware, the system will fail because there is no driving force behind it. It's clear that, like a car with a gearbox and engine, it won't move if there's no operational power.

Thoughtware means that before you create a system, you first need to think about what kind of system you want to establish. In my opinion, often there is no need to create a new system; rather, it can be easily discovered. Currently, there are certain tasks and activities being carried out in your company, and the processes of some tasks are clear. Identify these and improve them. Additionally, you should find the software and hardware related to that system.

Emotionalware means that individuals should want to perform their tasks with interest, diligence, and loyalty. Every system consists of several "subsystems." For example, the financial system includes subsystems for payroll, inventory, record-keeping, and ledgers, among others. What's important is that the systems and subsystems must work diligently and commit to their responsibilities. Even if you have the best computer and the most up-to-date financial software, if records are not correctly maintained by individuals or if your accountant lacks the motivation to register documents, this system will not yield the expected and acceptable output.

▶ Where can systems be implemented?

We have referred to the necessary tools for creating a system. Now we want to know where these tools should be used. Where should systems be created? Now is the time for implementation, and we want to create systems with the tools we mentioned.

But you must systematize the customer production line. Create actual customers for yourself. In fact, we want to create a lead generation system. One of the things some companies do is look for actual customers at exhibitions. They provide beautiful forms and business cards, but later find that it was not effective. Why? Because there was no system behind this work, and the execution method was not systematic either. There are issues with both the method of execution and the follow-up process. For example, they might say they collected a thousand phone numbers at the exhibition so that after the exhibition, the sales team can call these numbers and find ten good customers among them. In this way, one number covers the costs of the exhibition, and the other nine are profit. However, this does not happen because the customer creation system and the customer production line are flawed.

What's the solution? First, think about what system you can implement. One way is to give out a catalog instead of a form and design a QR code on it so that when interested potential customers seek more information about you, they can scan it and easily familiarize themselves with your products by visiting your website. After that, by placing useful supplementary content on the site and obtaining customer information like email or mobile number through a simple form, access to that content can be activated for them. In this way, you not only obtain a real customer number but also gauge their interest and enthusiasm for the information provided. Most importantly, this information is automatically recorded in your system and SMS panel.

Alternatively, you can define the system in such a way that they can enter the site via the same QR code and download the price list. When they click the download button, a message can be sent to them saying that they will receive a discount for their first purchase within ten days after the exhibition. These are just examples, and you can create your systems in a more creative way.

The important point to remember is that **not everything can be systematized.** For example, management cannot be systematized; it's just like driving a car. The car is a system, but how a driver operates it is not part of the system; the method of driving is part of the system, while the driver is the controller and observer of the system.

You can define a system for the production line as well. In services, for instance, consider a restaurant that must produce, package, and serve pizza in a systematic way. Order reception should also be systematic. Snapp food gained power by creating a system for order registration. Additionally, there are employees who control that created system. Many companies go bankrupt because they do not have a system. The profit production line must be systematic. A simple idea is to ask your bank to deposit ten percent of your balance every day into an account that is tied to your expenses. This is something the finance department can define to be done in cooperation with the bank, and someone should check whether this is done or not. **This is a capital production line system**. The work of investing and creating capital is a systematic job. With the capital production line, you will create capital from the profit you earn. It doesn't matter whether it's in the currency, gold, or housing market. What's important is to create capital.

In the production line and the recruitment of human resources, one of the systematic tasks is to keep the recruitment section of your website active if you have one. You've posted job advertisements and want to systematize this process. You assign someone to review the resumes. My experience shows that most people who use prepared resumes lack the creativity to design a resume for themselves. Based on my experience, do not call a person with a bad resume. That person will either not show up or will come late, and even if they do come late, they are not the right fit. So, you can filter people and invite those who are suitable for an interview. Once they accept, they enter the hiring system. Tell them to work for a month to observe the work method and the way to interact with customers before proceeding to sign a contract.

A specific system can also be established for liquidity management. Many companies perform well and generate good income, yet they do not make a profit because they do not manage their expenses correctly. Since they only make money to spend, they end up bankrupt. **They lack a system to preserve and manage their expenses regarding**

their resources. They also do not have a system for liquidity management and cannot manage their cash flow. Purchasing management can also have a system so that coordinating with the manager for purchasing supplies and raw materials is not necessary. First, you need to correct your perspective on systematization, and then take action to systematize. Until you align your perspective on a topic correctly, how can you understand and execute it properly? You must first gain a proper view of the system before implementing it. **You cannot solve a problem without understanding it.** Avoid wasting your resources by eliminating some unnecessary and repetitive activities, and learn to **work within a subsystem.** "PPD" refers to: "P" (Production), "P" (Preservation), and "D" (Development). We will call it the "PPD System.

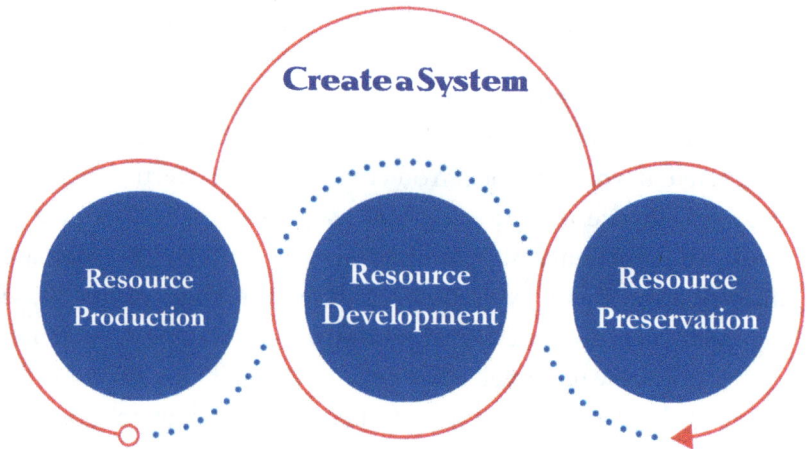

Create a System

Resource Production

Resource Development

Resource Preservation

- **Customer Production Line**
- **Product Production Line**
- **Profit Production Line**
- **Capital Production Line**

- **Investment**
- **Skills Training**
- **Development and Communications**
- **Implementing Changes in Work Patterns**

- **Cost Management**
- **Liquidity Management**
- **Customer Management**
- **Human Resources**

▶ Five Stages of Systematization

To carry out a systematic task, you must go through five stages. In fact, you need to provide the conceptual tools, hardware, software, and motivational tools for these five stages of systematization. It is important that these stages are understandable within your system. You should know how to produce, preserve, and develop resources.

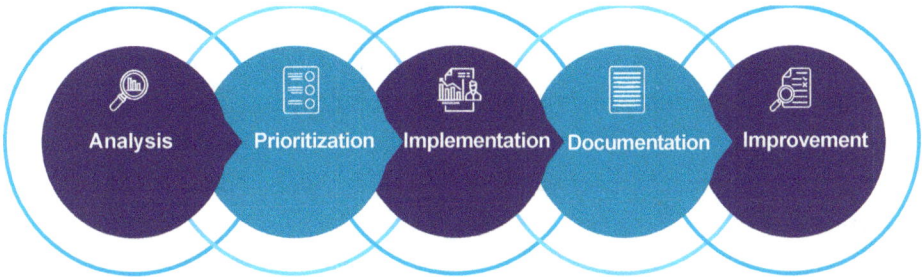

Analysis · Prioritization · Implementation · Documentation · Improvement

To accomplish this, you must analyze and list repetitive **tasks and errors.** Then, create a system. Every task you want to perform in the system must be analyzed beforehand. In resource production, some tasks can be optimized through analysis. Therefore, when you analyze, you should focus on the production line of the product, customer retention, and so on, and identify where your repetitive errors are occurring.

The next step is **prioritization.** There are certain errors and mistakes that jeopardize the entire system. Not all problems are equal, nor are they equally bothersome. To understand how to resolve issues, you need to acquire knowledge. Having knowledge helps you in prioritizing. **Don't make systematization a daunting task for yourself.** Prioritization means understanding what is important. What should you do first? Among these problems, which one poses the greatest risk to the system? After prioritization, we move on to mapping. I want to explain the digital marketing system. Does creating a website mean internet marketing? So, we have a website. We need to create engaging content for that website to generate traffic, meaning we want visitors, just as every store needs customers. To increase visits, we need SEO and advertising. We need to ensure that visitors convert into actual customers, calling us for information about our products. How do we facilitate their access to information? The landing page must attract customers. The way I interact with customers should have a format that is appealing. If they register their email, send them educational emails; if they provide their phone number, add them to a WhatsApp group for training. After three training sessions, share a product introduction video. This way, you begin to create a process.

If during the implementation of this process we notice a sales team error in sending information to customers based on our analyses, we can easily correct just that part in the system. When we analyze in parts, we will fix the root cause once and for all, yielding healthy and fruitful results.

To enhance the value of the system you create, document all the execution methods. How you marketed, how you designed labels and stories, how you communicated with customers, how you led your team during a crisis, etc. Crisis situations are the best time for systematization, as errors reveal themselves during crises. That's why when a task takes too long, it indicates that something is amiss.

Whenever your employees have many questions, it means you need to build a system. Then implement it, and after implementation, make improvements. If you don't make improvements after implementation, your efforts will be fruitless. A task that isn't **improved** upon hasn't been executed at all. You need to repeatedly execute and refine processes.

After executing the processes, replication takes place. **Replication means having a system; it signifies scalability and development.** It means that I have done something correctly and replicated it, resulting in exponential growth. This is the essence of creating a system. Replication means that as a manager, after twenty years of activity, what have I replicated? Have I managed to cultivate five individuals like myself so they can perform the same tasks? Replication is the output of the system. If a system cannot be replicated, it indicates that one of the five stages; analysis, prioritization, implementation, documentation, and improvement; has not been executed correctly.

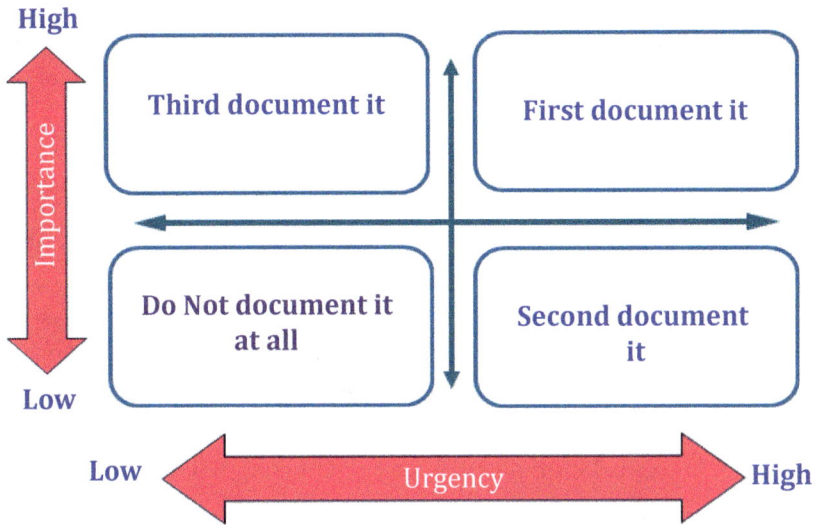

High

Importance

Low

| Third document it | First document it |

| Do Not document it at all | Second document it |

Low **Urgency** **High**

Tasks are examined from two perspectives: importance and urgency. Tasks with low importance do not require documentation, as they are pointless and hinder proper systematization. Such tasks create problems within your system. Based on priority, the first task to document is one that has high importance but low urgency. Next, document tasks that have low importance but high urgency. Finally, address tasks that are both important and urgent.

In creating a system, the myth of automating and executing all processes automatically is bound to fail. **Systematization does not equate to automation.** The hardware, software, and frameworks you have do not imply that everything operates without your involvement. Additionally, **systematization is not the same as documentation.** Documentation is not merely the creation of records. Some people mistakenly believe that obtaining an "ISO" certification means they have established a system, when in fact it might not qualify as one. **Systematization requires discovery.** Many tasks you perform right now should be analyzed, prioritized, visualized in terms of their roles, and then executed. After execution, these tasks require correction and improvement, which leads to replication. For example, taking a cutting from a plant and replanting it elsewhere is a form of replication. This is the essence of a system. You should continuously work on improving your processes. In a system, everyone must enhance their own processes. **A system is about managing operations and performance; it's like driving a car.** Even if you have the best vehicle, if you cannot steer it correctly, your system will encounter problems, potentially causing damage to your resources.

A system should be capable of improving its own performance. In creating a system, set aside any managerial pride. Try to demonstrate accountability and commitment by actively seeking feedback from others. You must define the ideal state within the system. An effective system must have a goal. **This goal represents the ideal state:** Where do you want to go? How should the production, preservation, and development of resources be carried out? In a system, strength and capability lie in collaboration. When everyone works together, you are powerful. The engine of an airplane is powerful, yet it cannot take off unless it is properly installed on a framework. **A system is a coherent assembly of specific elements working together for a defined purpose.** No part of the system is more important than another.

Delegation of authority is crucial in creating a system, as a system is not dependent on any single individual. We are an organization. Without delegation, replication does not happen. Out of 100% of my work, I perform 30% myself and delegate the rest piece by piece to others. You must gradually delegate some of your tasks. Delegation involves empowering individuals to use and allocate resources effectively. When we grant someone the authority to utilize organizational resources for pursuing tasks, this constitutes delegation. However, authority must align with responsibility. **You cannot assign responsibility without granting authority.** Responsibility refers to the duty of completing a task and the mission for which the individual has been given the power to utilize resources to achieve a specific outcome.

The most important aspect of responsibility is accountability. **Being accountable means being ready to explain any deviation from established expectations.** If I have granted someone the authority to use resources for a specific goal, they must also be accountable. For example, if they were supposed to reach point A but have now reached point P instead, they must explain why. This exemplifies the concept of delegation, and this can also be systematized.

It is essential that in creating a system, both understanding and completion exist. This means understanding how to perform tasks and ensuring they are completed. Many people know they should do something but do not finish it, resulting in the system not achieving its intended outcome. Creating a system means starting a task correctly, continuing it correctly, and finishing it correctly. We systematize tasks to enhance the power and speed of completion within the organization.

As I mentioned earlier, during the execution phase, it is crucial to document methods and processes, which signifies a significant advancement. How can we achieve substantial progress? Dedicate thirty minutes each day to documentation. **Until you write it down, you won't own it.** Take time to document your execution methods and what you have discovered and addressed in your organization. For instance, if you have a sales team, ask the sales manager how a successful task was accomplished today and how company resources were utilized efficiently. Record this. Through systematization, you free the minds of your team members. A mind preoccupied with repetitive tasks, constant errors, and trivial matters cannot operate at a high level of focus. Systematization liberates thought and enhances mental processing power. That's when creativity takes shape.

Systematization does not mean eliminating your presence from your business. An old proverb states, **"The best fertilizer for the farm is the farmer's footprint."** A farmer can create an irrigation system and harvest crops systematically, but they cannot be absent.

Don't think that if I systematize, I can just relax and check my bank account on my laptop. Systematization does not eliminate human errors; it minimizes them. **Your role in systematization is to reduce errors, not to eliminate them completely.** Let go of idealism and perfectionism. Systematization is a condition that allows you to develop your operations and performance. Do not attempt to systematize overnight; systematization is the pinnacle of glory and power in a business. When Walmart, McDonald's, Digikala, and Snapp systematized, their glory and power increased. Customers recognize they are dealing with a thoroughly systematic, strategic, and powerful organization with a plan for every aspect. Systematization is a time-consuming and ongoing effort. Building a system and then abandoning it is like leaving the garden hose running while you walk away; it will damage the garden and the fruits. Therefore, systematization is not about abandonment.

▶ Optimization and Leverage

The entire story of a business boils down to two key elements: layout and scheduling. If these two aspects fall out of alignment, all our resources will become chaotic. Everything we have discussed teaches us how to establish proper layout and scheduling.

You may have heard the phrase, "Work smart, not hard." **This statement is misleading.** While it is indeed essential to work hard to achieve goals, it must also be done intelligently. For instance, do you remove a nail from wood with your fingers and call that working hard, or do you use a proper tool like a crowbar? This simple example illustrates the distinction between hard work and smart work. Both intelligence and hard work are necessary for success.

In business, the goal is to avoid unnecessary exertion. Excessive effort often leads to disastrous outcomes. For example, **if you apply**

too much force while tightening a screw, you risk breaking it. Excessive force results in waste and loss of productivity. If you push too hard on the gas pedal of a car, eventually, you risk damaging the engine. **Excessive effort is a sign of mismanagement.** A business owner who understands their enterprise effectively creates systems to avoid unnecessary exertion. They build a brand that avoids excess, work on the organization's agility, and adopt superior strategies that minimize wasted effort.

Optimizing and leveraging a business is based on this principle. To achieve an effective layout and scheduling, you need to combine four key elements:

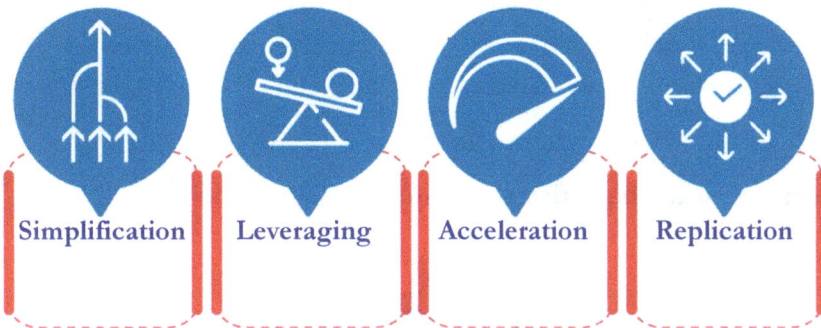

| Simplification | Leveraging | Acceleration | Replication |

In the first step, **simplify** your business as much as possible. This means focusing on clear communication, transparent organizational strategies, and selecting ideas that can bring customers closer to you. Large companies like Google, YouTube, Instagram, and even Walmart have worked extensively on simplification, eliminating unnecessary and redundant elements and activities from their operations. This requires both intelligence and hard work; you need to endure pressure and invest time.

The second step is **leveraging,** which involves knowing how to use leverage to achieve results within your desired timeframe. What is the role of leverage? It acts as a tool, idea, or method that helps you avoid unnecessary strain. Excessive effort can be dangerous; effective managers learn to distribute the load rather than carry it all themselves.

Next is **acceleration,** which focuses on how to make your business move faster. Acceleration means that when you successfully execute a task, you determine how to do it quicker, better, and more agilely the next time.

Most importantly, there is **replication.** In the previous section, we explained replication in detail. **What is leverage?** It refers to any tool or method that makes achieving results easier for you while maintaining those results. Sometimes, you may use certain tools that simplify tasks but do not yield the expected results, especially in communication. You may establish a business connection and think it is leveraging your resources, only to find that it consumes them without delivering results. If leverage is not used correctly, you end up exerting effort without any return. Leverage should always yield the results you desire from your business.

Leverage must have three essential characteristics:

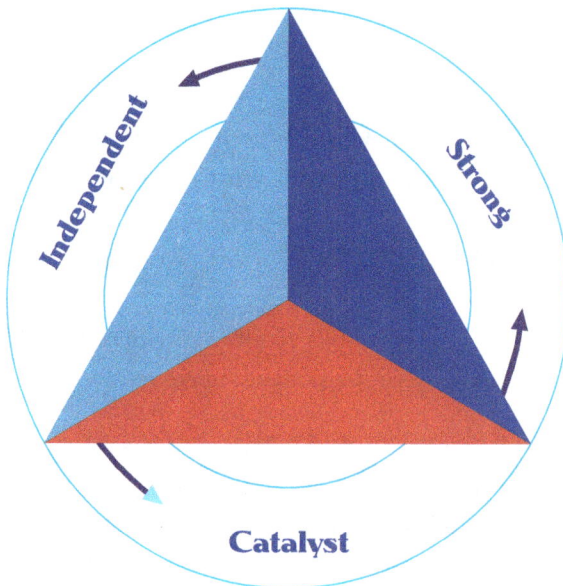

1. **Independence:** This means you shouldn't have to constantly spend resources to utilize this leverage. You should be able to use this leverage whenever you want and put it back when you don't need it. Some people use leverage so extensively that it becomes an integral part of their operations. For example, they might say, "We established a working relationship with someone, and now we feel beholden to them," or they might have created a system but now don't know how to disengage from it. Leverage should remain independent.

2. **Catalyst:** Leverage should accelerate your progress toward the goals you've set.

3. **Strength:** When you apply force to leverage, it should not bend or break. When building your leverage, focus on the strength of the leverage and the work you intend to accomplish with it. For instance, if you're relying on your human resources and team, and when it comes time to move a heavy burden in the market, you find your leverage is weak, the team may falter midway. Another example is if you've established a connection but later realize that this person is unmotivated and lacks support, leading to disappointment. Similarly, if you purchase financial software only to discover it doesn't provide many necessary reports, these issues arise because your leverage isn't strong enough.

One of the most effective forms of leverage that is independent, catalytic, and strong is passive income. Some individuals invest a portion of their active income to generate passive income. This allows you to focus on your work while investing in a maximum of two or three areas. You can achieve passive income in these three domains:

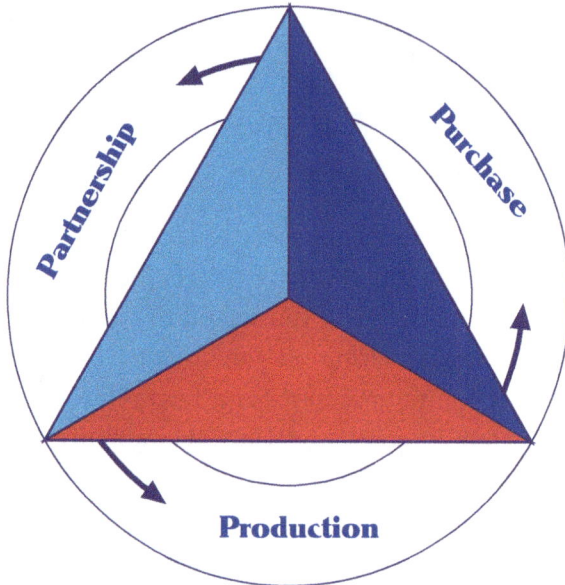

For example, my work is in education, but I invest a portion of my income in a restaurant. I do this because I need cash flow generated every night. I delegate the execution and planning entirely. I am the investor, and I periodically oversee to ensure my investment is being properly maintained. Alternatively, I might provide liquidity for a construction group and invest there. I also generate passive income through production by collaborating with a manufacturer. I create passive income through purchases (such as real estate, gold, raw materials, etc.), production (producing something other than what I personally create), and investment (in manufacturing activities or joint projects). It is preferable for wealth to be converted into capital, which, in turn, generates wealth and then assets for you.

Four Main Levers in Business:

Economies of Others		Knowledge of Others
	Four Main Levers in Business	
Resources of Others		Experience of Others

1. Knowledge of Others

The first lever is the knowledge of others. This includes explicit knowledge, such as what you have learned in university or through various training programs. The expertise of everyone who works with or for you can serve as a powerful lever. When you find yourself deeply engrossed in a topic and your mind feels exhausted, you might say to yourself, "I should go read a book." Often, as you read, you discover answers hidden within the lines, alleviating your mental struggle. In this sense, the knowledge of others becomes a crucial support for your own understanding.

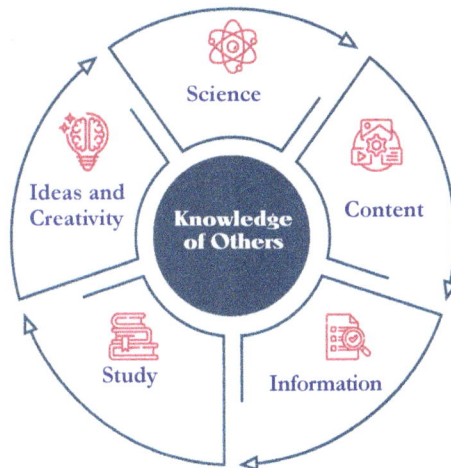

Science

Content

Information

Study

Ideas and Creativity

Knowledge of Others

Knowledge serves as an additional lever, and its foundation can include science, content, information, study, ideas, and creativity.

Part of the knowledge of others can be the content they have created. Reading books by experts in your field not only adds to your resources but also aids you in understanding, utilizing, and applying that knowledge effectively. The content produced by others serves as a foundation for your own understanding.

Another key aspect of leveraging knowledge is the information others possess. This includes data regarding their expertise, the market, and your business. What valuable information do they have that can assist you? Even a child can possess insights that prove useful. By utilizing this information, you can manage your timeline and expedite your progress. The burdens you can't lift without knowledge, content, and information can be alleviated through the insights of others.

Studying others' experiences is another effective lever. When someone has a book in hand, ask them to summarize its main point in one sentence. Reading can significantly contribute to your understanding of others' knowledge. Personally, I enjoy examining the bookshelves when I visit someone's office to see what they read most often. Sometimes, their readings may reflect a problem I currently face or one that may arise in the future.

The ideas and creativity of others can also serve as a lever. You can utilize an idea or creative solution from a team member or draw inspiration from the internet.

Additionally, you can borrow concepts from others' advertising slogans. Ideas do not emerge in isolation; they often start as vague and nebulous concepts. You can easily use an idea from advertising, recruitment, or marketing as a lever for your own endeavors.

2. Experience of Others

The next lever is the experience of others, which can be broken down into several components: skills, consultation, and collaboration.

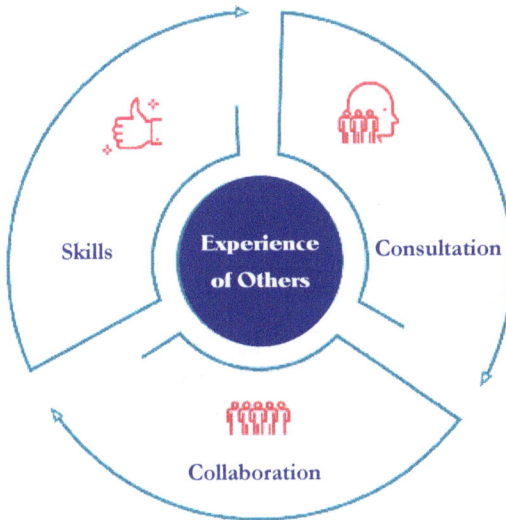

Skills are one of the key experiences of others and are often referred to as "tacit knowledge." While explicit knowledge consists of what you learn in university, the skills gained through experience represent the insights individuals acquire during their practical endeavors. These skills serve as a vital point of leverage. Skills embody the "tricks of the trade" that you can utilize. Why not take advantage of this rich source of experience? If someone is more adept at a task than you are, why not learn from them? These tricks not only serve as a lever but also act as catalysts, making them independent and powerful assets in your toolkit.

When you recognize the levers available to you, you realize that you can also serve as a lever for others, and you will never undervalue yourself. You won't engage in casual interactions with just anyone; instead, your relationships will become more meaningful and valuable.

Consultation is a form of experience. When you seek advice from someone, you benefit from their knowledge and experiences, helping you understand what actions to take. **Create a checklist and proceed based on it.** Some individuals excel at certain tasks due to their expertise, while others may be better at different tasks because of their unique experiences. This knowledge and capability of individuals serve as levers; those who are independent, catalytic, and strong. The essence of a lever lies in these characteristics. Whenever you wish to utilize a lever, check if it possesses these three qualities. Whether you're reading a book or seeking advice, ensure that it embodies these attributes. **Consult the best individuals in your field.** As Rumi said, "Working with the generous is not difficult." These individuals have established their positions and are not threatened by your growth; they recognize that your success does not jeopardize their own. If they fear this, they may be merely pretending to be successful. A truly successful lever is not concerned about being used by others. Its strength lies in its ability to absorb excess effort and create momentum.

Partnership is another way to leverage the experiences of others. There's a saying: "If partnership were good, God would have a partner." But why compare yourself to God? We are servants of God. In Surah Tawhid, we learn that He has no need for a partner. We often resort to such sayings because we struggle with managing expectations, origins, relationships, and partnership interactions. When you want to engage in a partnership, ensure you trust your partner, sign a clear contract, and move forward together.

Most successful businesses worldwide are built on partnerships, both internally and externally. They establish strong collaborations within their teams and then invite others to buy into their success. People recognize that these businesses are "riding the winning horse," and they invest accordingly.

3. The Economy of Others

The third potential lever is the economy of others. You may have a plan, idea, or project that you can implement using the wealth of others. Leveraging the resources and investments of others can serve as a powerful tool. For example, a brand itself is an asset. Some individuals become representatives of that brand, transforming it into their own capital.

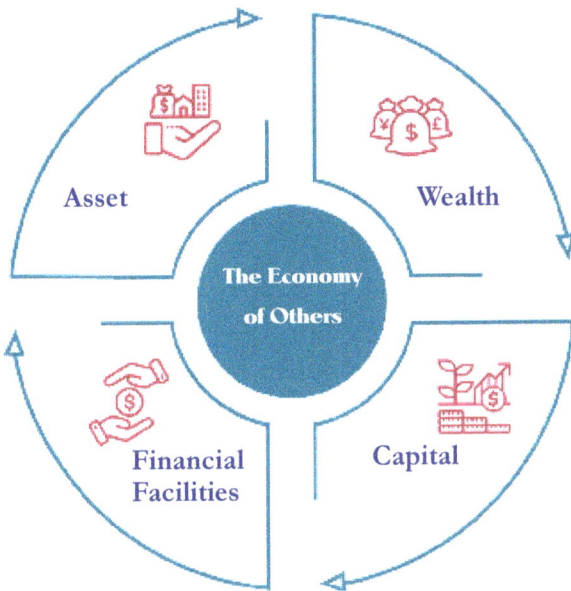

Attracting an investor can also act as a leverage; however, avoid attracting a depositor instead of an investor.

An investor is different from a depositor. A depositor is someone who, when granting you financial facilities, says that if I deposit this money in the bank, I will receive a certain amount of interest. How much will you give me? This is depositing, and it doesn't yield much return because the basis of this investment is interest-based lending, which can bankrupt any business. An investor says, "I will put my capital into this project, and we will share in the profits and losses together." If someone is willing to work with you under this model, it means they are a person of action. Otherwise, they become an additional burden, just like interest-bearing money that imposes a financial and cost burden on you. Thus, the capital of others can also serve as leverage.

Assets can also be leverage. Suppose you want to establish a restaurant. Your grandfather owns a commercial property that has been vacant for a long time. You ask him for permission to set up your restaurant in that property and create value using his asset as leverage.

Financial facilities are also leverage. Many people ask how we can take out loans. I always have an explanation about loans: If a loan is for capital production, it's good; however, a loan for creating debt leads to disastrous results. Some people only take out loans to pay off their overdue debts. It's like tying a weight to someone who is struggling to swim in a sea of waves. Some take out loans that, after a while, lead to bankruptcy. Financial facilities can be a lever for capital production, like those who take out loans to purchase raw materials or property.

4. The Resources of Others

Other people's resources can also be leverage. Suppose you want to create content, and your friend has a well-equipped studio. Many of the actions you need to take for the development of your business do not require an injection of money and capital.

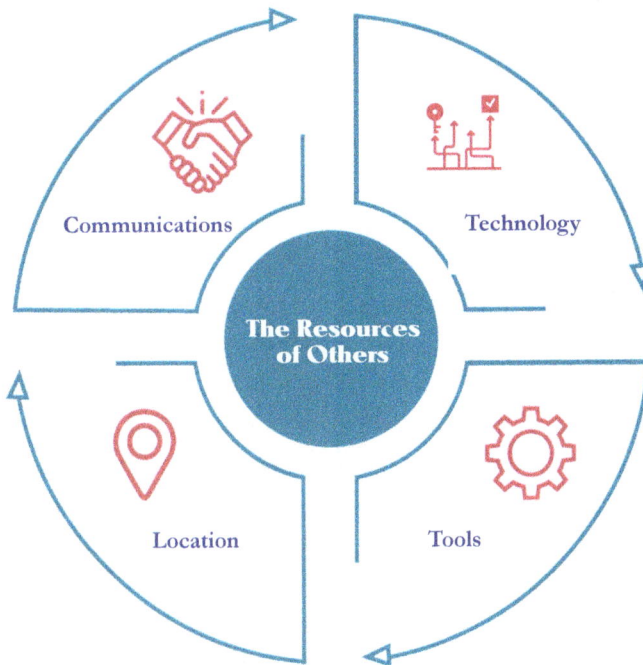

For example, a company is exceptional in marketing and sales and says, "I currently have high demand in the market and want to expand my production line." I suggest, "First, raise your standards. Then, either produce your products in a factory that has human resources, research and development, and production line, or ask a certain factory to produce them but package them under your brand." iPhone, Oila, Famila, and Softlan produce without having their own factories. Their products are manufactured in factories where they have no ownership. Digikala and product sellers on this site use each other as leverage. They don't have the time or patience to create a site and produce content, so they easily list a product on Digikala and find a suitable supply chain for it. In fact, they leverage digital resources, and Digikala leverages their productions and warehouses.

Communications are another lever and one of the resources of others. When you go somewhere, you first look to see if you can find someone you know. This is the leverage of communications. You utilize that person's communication leverage by saying, "Call so-and-so and place my order with them." You use this resource to expedite your work.

Leverage means not exerting unnecessary effort and not wasting energy. If you waste energy, you will not achieve growth, profit, credibility, experience, and a sense of satisfaction. What resources do you have from others? Knowledge, experience, economy, and resources are the four main levers. Everything else we mention falls under these levers. Now, I ask you to write down a series of ideas and levers that come to your mind for yourself. You can always create situations to use levers in the best way. Pay attention to whether it is a catalyst or not, whether it is strong or not, and whether it can help us while maintaining results. A lever is a tool or method that makes your work easier and simpler while maintaining results.

▶ Important Points in Leveraging

Leverage is not a ladder that you climb up. This means do not exploit the knowledge, experience, economy, and resources of others. A person who has taken money from others and run away has not leveraged; rather, they have built a ladder. When you leverage, everyone must benefit. Your team and human resources are part of the levers, and everyone should benefit from them. Those who are like ladders are not strong levers.

In leveraging, you should eliminate unnecessary elements as much as possible. Successful companies in the world adopt a moderating mindset in leveraging; **instead of adding useless elements, they seek to eliminate inefficiencies.** You want a lever and a support; the rest is extra. You want to connect with one person, but you inform fifty people, and in the end, the event you wanted doesn't happen, and you lose the benefit you were seeking. So, adopt a moderating mindset. You must know that not every round thing is a walnut; sometimes, it might be a potato.

From this moment, let's create a database of levers. Every day, to maintain the quality of your levers, create a potential lever. One of the levers we mentioned was the knowledge of others. Ideas and creativity are one of the subcategories of the lever of the knowledge of others. I have a file on my laptop where I store interesting images, materials, and videos that I come across while browsing, and I use them to create campaigns or gather ideas. I also keep all the regulations and legal provisions in a separate file.

Do not rush. Some levers can withstand only a little pressure, and if too much pressure is applied, they may break, and your work won't reach a conclusion. You rush to expand the market, and thus you break that lever. Rushing causes your lever not to be independent and powerful. I have a friend who works at a bank, and he says that anyone who is in a hurry to get a loan has a problem somewhere. It means they have debts and can't pay their installments, and eventually, they become bankrupt.

Lastly, document everything. Document every experience you have in leveraging, systematizing, and making the system agile, because this documentation prevents others from repeating the same experiences and, over time, will become a powerful lever itself.

▶   **Write Your Five Key Takeaways from This Chapter:**

1. ....

2. ....

3. ....

4. ....

5. ....

▶ **Three Steps I Will Immediately Start:**

1. ....

2. ....

3. ....

▶ **One Golden Lesson to Share with Others:**

....

....

....

....

....

....

Download all the tables and exercises of this chapter from the following website.

https://hosseintaheri.ir/bmg/

Creating a Value

Chapter 3:

Creating a Value

"Generosity is invaluable and cannot be priced. "

📖 **After reading this chapter, you will gain mastery over:**

● The concept of value and how to create it

● Organizational agility and how to establish it

Five Steps to Create a Value Proposition

If you consider a business as a system, you will encounter three determining factors through which you can differentiate your business by creating change in one of them. Any conflict, whether within the organization among employees or externally between competitors or customers, occurs in one of these three factors. **These three factors are benefit, structure, and the prevailing mindset within the organization.**

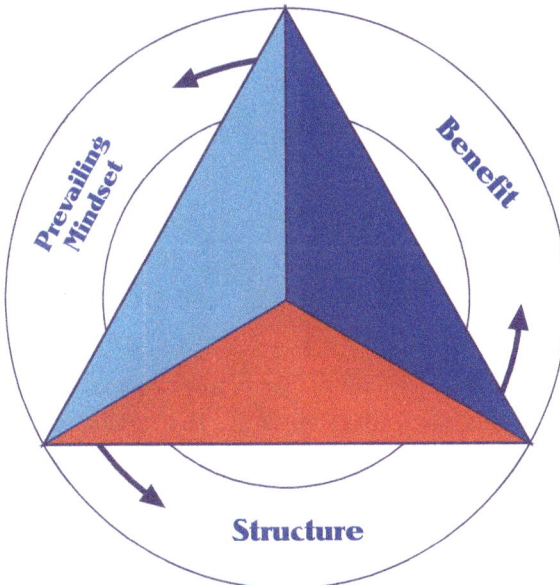

The first factor is benefit. The benefit of a business is the intrinsic and created values that impact the lives of its members. In fact, an organization must have an answer to how it can grow itself while also fostering the growth of its stakeholders. These stakeholders are not just customers; they include intermediaries, employees, suppliers, key partners, shareholders, and all individuals associated with the benefits derived from value creation in the business. Your benefits depend on your audience. To clarify the benefits of your business, you must answer the following three questions:

What change do you bring about in the lives and businesses of your customers?

....

....

....

What are the benefits of collaborating with you?

....

....

....

How do you create benefits for your customers?

....

....

....

The second factor is structure. Structure consists of software, hardware, and human resources (people) that create a system for implementing programs. How are the activities that create benefits and the mission for which the organization was established carried out? What methods are used? How is the system structured? What software and hardware are used to accomplish tasks? Does the system operate according to a program? How does it create ease? Structure represents the distinguishing feature. The structure of Snapp and Tapsi in terms of software and hardware is different, and whichever performs better has an advantage in the internet taxi market.

The third factor is dominant thinking. Who runs the business? How are the red lines determined? In a business, a unitary judgment is required for decision-making. You need governance for yourself, your organization, your market, and everyone who works with you. Your red lines must be clear so you can define certain principles; "In the home, if there is power, one word suffices." With dominant thinking, you can operate better. You must establish governance for your team, product, brand, market, stakeholders, intermediaries, distributors, suppliers, and even your competitors. You determine which competitor will contend with you. When you have a strong competitor, your power increases, you are motivated to grow, and you are challenged to improve and address your weaknesses. People trust those who have established governance in their work.

You must design the governance, and before designing, you should know what it is.

Benefits are the selected activities executed through the utilization of knowledge, skills, and missions within the system. Structure specifies the types of activities. The governance determines how activities are interconnected and in what order. It defines who will execute the activities, how, and according to what principles. These three factors are essential for enhancing value.

▶ What is Value?

"Value" means adding something to the world of customers that did not previously exist or was not offered, and it facilitates their life and business. "Increasing benefits" means adding something to the product that the customer will find useful and unique. **In fact, value is the balance between the cost incurred for a product and the satisfaction**

derived from its use by the customer. Therefore, do everything you can to establish this balance and equilibrium in the customer's mind through all available resources, and this means spending resources to create opportunities.

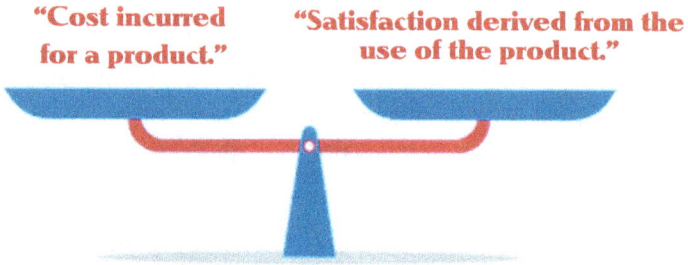

"Cost incurred for a product."

"Satisfaction derived from the use of the product."

They do not review whether there is a correct balance between the value created by some organizations and the customer satisfaction achieved. For this reason, businesses that focus solely on growth will not have stability in profit and continuous benefit. Although they may grow, they will only remain at the top for a short time before declining.

Every product consists of three key elements for creating value. None of these three are value themselves; rather, they are the expected fundamentals of a product.

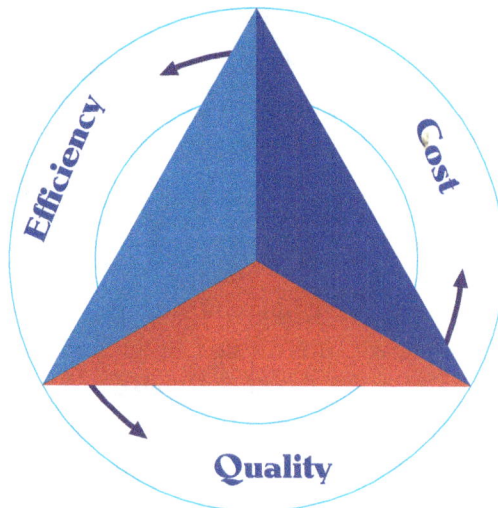

Efficiency

Cost

Quality

The first element is cost, which refers to the expense a customer pays to receive the expected and acceptable performance. Sometimes, a customer pays only the price of a product without it having any actual value. This occurs because there is no real balance established. Value is what a customer is willing to fight for, investing necessary resources and making efforts to obtain it, as they seek satisfaction and benefit. **If you have created a valuable product, the customer will undoubtedly be willing to pay for it.**

The second element is quality, which encompasses the needs, expectations, and preferences of the customer. Therefore, quality alone is not value.

The third element is efficiency; it refers to the specific and expected function of a product to address the concerns, needs, and desires of the customer, shaping customer demand.

$$\text{Value} = \frac{\text{Efficiency} + \text{Quality}}{\text{Cost}}$$

In your business, you have costs that are paid by customers. On the other hand, you also have quality and functionality, and the sum of these divided by the cost creates value.

Value is an asset that is constantly growing and enhancing itself. A business adds value every day through benefits, structure, and the dominant thinking that governs it, as well as the rules and red lines it follows. Therefore, anyone in the organization who acts against the value expected by the customer is damaging the asset. Value is an intangible asset.

Value involves eliminating unpleasant feelings. Have you achieved customer satisfaction when they use your product? Is there a balance between customer satisfaction and the cost they paid? Has the customer expressed their satisfaction to you and showcased it to others? **Have you utilized all your resources to create value?** Have you liberated the customer from feelings of deficiency and the lack of a need?

In today's world, numerous needs exist that can be addressed through creating value and providing innovative solutions. I suggest you look for a problem you believe you can solve with a creative solution. This approach will help you create unique value. Creating value generates profit. When you create value, you first generate profit for the customer, which in turn leads to profit for you. Remember, value creation is primarily for the customer, not for you. The key point is to focus on various customer needs. The narrative should not revolve around you and your product; it should center on the customer and their needs. If your offering lacks benefits for the customer in terms of value, structure, or guiding principles, then you have wasted your effort.

Therefore, you need to redesign your product, services, and value proposition. If you have not created value that benefits both the customer and yourself, prioritizing value for the customer is the first step toward achieving profitability. In economics, "value" refers to the monetary worth of a product, which means the goal of any business is to create value for the customer first and then convert that into profit. To build a successful and sustainable business, you must first provide benefits to others and then expect rewards based on the value you have delivered. **A valuable product sells itself.** The greater the value you create, the higher the price customers are willing to pay, resulting in a win-win situation. If you position your business based on the value desired by the customer, they will seek more services and, consequently, greater satisfaction, leading to increased purchases. The progress of a business, much like any form of social interaction, requires building trust. The value of your business should aim to improve the lives of others (the customers) in a way that earns their trust and satisfaction. If you achieve this goal, you can attract more customers and retain and engage them effectively.

Value supports teamwork because everyone understands what they are working toward and how to enhance both their own and their customers' performance. By creating value, you can reduce the complexities of teamwork. Complexity serves as an obstacle to creating value. When you eliminate unnecessary elements from individual and group functions, the time needed to coordinate product production and delivery decreases, which helps reduce resource waste. By focusing on customer needs, enhancing satisfaction, motivating employees, optimizing work processes, reducing costs, and increasing competitiveness, you can effectively create value.

Value is the key driver of profit and customer growth, and it can contribute to customer development in three areas:

- **Customer Perceived Value (CPV)**
- **Customer Lifetime Value (CLV)**
- **Customer Equity (CE)**

▶ Customer Perceived Value (CPV)

When you create value in your business that is recognized by the customer, it is referred to as CPV. How does a customer perceive and evaluate the value created by a seller or company? Perceived value refers to the value experienced and felt by the customer. Customer satisfaction and loyalty depend on the balance between the costs incurred and the satisfaction derived from the product or service.

If you only advertise and claim that your offering is excellent, but the customer does not perceive it that way, it will not yield any benefit. How can the customer understand that the value created aligns with what they wanted? How can they trust and accept this perception?

When a customer accepts this, they become accustomed to the value designed by you. When you manage to instill belief and understanding in the customer, it indicates that you have generated interest in them. Once they are interested, they develop a habit. Companies like iPhone, Uber, and Amazon condition individuals to the feelings they experience from using their products and services, thereby increasing what is known as Customer Lifetime Value (CLV).

Three Components of Value

Customer Equity

Customer Lifetime Value

Customer Procived Value

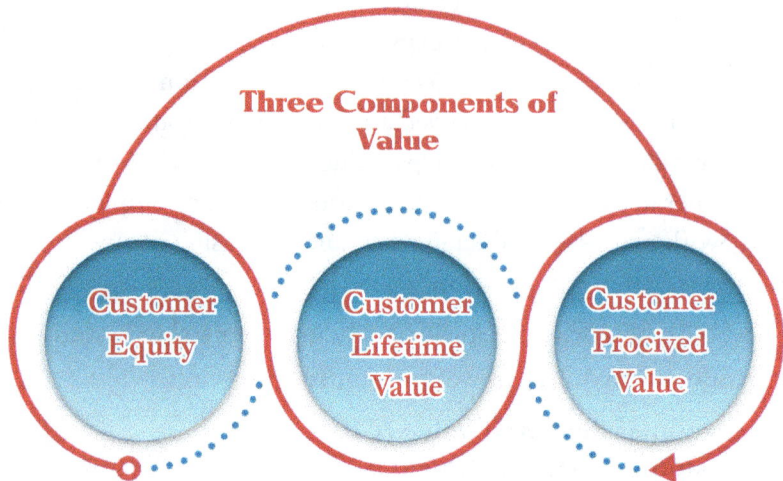

▶ Reflects the importance of the customer as an asset with a financial reservoir that possesses the potential for growth and development.

▶ Value, financial aspect, customer, business aspect.

▶ The total profits generated from all transactions and interactions of a business with a specific customer throughout their lifetime.

▶ How does a customer perceive and evaluate the value created by the seller?

▶ Customer Lifetime Value (CLV)

Customer Lifetime Value refers to the total profit generated from transactions with a customer over their lifetime, divided by their duration as a customer. Essentially, the value of loyal, long-term customers is much greater than that of new or one-time buyers. This formula turns customers into profitable assets and is a critical metric in evaluating a business.

Often, you don't need a large number of customers; instead, you need high-CLV customers. This means you've built enough loyalty and understanding so that these customers continue to bring you value. It doesn't matter whether you receive payment from ten customers or a hundred; if you generate more profit from fewer customers, your workload decreases significantly while your efficiency and growth improve. Those who want to buy from you should both like you and be able to afford your products.

While some people might lack the ability to pay, if they perceive the value, they will find a way to make the payment. For instance, if your roof is leaking, you'll do whatever it takes to repair it. Similarly, if a product holds value, the customer will find a way to pay for it. Everyone seeks a path to attain what they perceive as valuable. Many of you likely own things that were difficult to afford at the time of purchase, but due to the value, you made it work.

When you create CLV, you gradually build Customer Equity, which has a direct relationship with Brand Equity and reflects the long-term importance of a brand. In economics, this is referred to as "**Symbolic Capital**"; meaning that your name often precedes you. People not only want your product or service but also your brand. They want to associate with you, and the credit your brand gives them creates value for them. This reflects the importance of a customer as an asset or a "financial reservoir with potential" in your business. As a result, companies with high brand equity also tend to have high customer equity.

Customer Equity (CE)

Customer equity consists of three key elements:

1. **Customer Acquisition:** The ability to attract new customers to your business.

2. **Customer Retention:** The ability to maintain and keep customers loyal over time.

3. **Customer Development:** The process of nurturing customers, encouraging them to increase their engagement and spend more with your business.

Customer Equity

Three key components

$$(AS+CR+CA)=(CE)$$

Ad-on-selling
AS

Customer Retention
CR

Customer Acquisition
CA

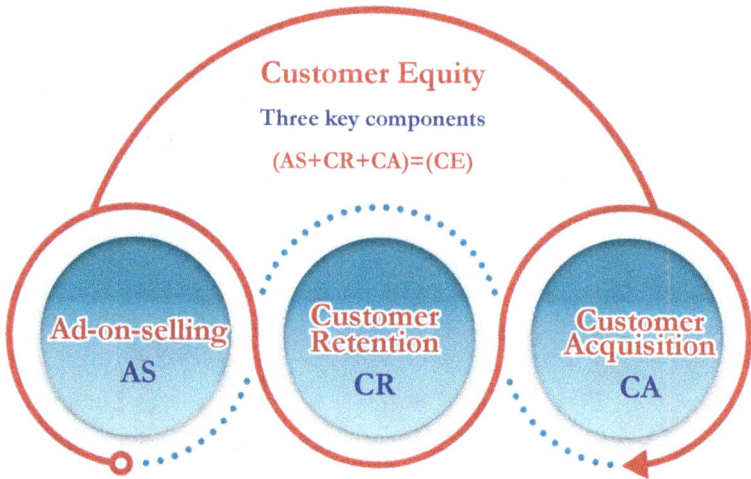

- ▶ Programs for selling additional products to existing customers (without extra risk or cost).
- ▶ Complementary products for growing customers

- ▶ How can we gain their satisfaction?
- ▶ How can we go beyond the boundaries of satisfaction?
- ▶ What strategies should we implement to turn a customer into a long-term business partner?

- ▶ How to select customers
- ▶ Identifying profitable customers from unprofitable ones
- ▶ Where can you find leads?

▶ Customer Retention

After acquiring a customer, how do you strengthen your relationship with them? How do you achieve and increase their satisfaction? **Customer satisfaction is different from simply making customers happy.** You need to adopt strategies that transform customers from mere service recipients and consumers into long-term business partners. Although acquiring customers is a lengthy, costly, and energy-intensive process, retaining customers is more challenging than acquiring them. We aim to ease these challenges by creating value. When you create value, you identify its position in your business and ensure that no one diminishes that value. Evaluate all of these aspects in your business. Business experts either create models or make the best use of successful ones.

▶ Customer Development

Once you have retained a customer, how do you nurture them? What strategies do you have for selling to existing customers without incurring additional risk or cost for them or for you? How can you present complementary products to them? A business should be able to sell more to its existing customers without imposing additional risk and costs. Certainly, when selling based on customer needs, both the customers and you benefit, eliminating the need to seek new customers and incur those risks and costs since you have reached a mutual understanding with your audience.

▶ Value versus Purchase Risk

Your money is in the customer's pocket. Fill the customer's pocket so that yours fills as well. When you want to fill the customer's pocket, you must consider the balance of benefits. During each purchase, the customer has a secret checklist that weighs their potential costs and risks against the benefits they expect. In fact, they constantly ask themselves what they will gain in return for the resources they will lose. There are three types of risky costs associated with every purchase:

- **Financial Costs**
- **Time and Energy Costs: The time and energy spent searching.**
- **Emotional and Psychological Costs: The stress and mental burden resulting from others' judgments.**

Shopping can be a very stressful and frustrating experience. false prices, shopping in unfavorable weather conditions, and the risks that arise in relation to costs. There are also performance risks when the customer is uncertain about the product's performance, and physical risks when there is a possibility of damage to the product. The customer is worried about potentially damaging the product because they don't know how to use it. This has emotional and psychological costs.

What is financial risk? The customer feels that their financial situation, job status, or social standing is at risk. When the customer perceives all these risks and dangers, they try to minimize them in any way possible. Therefore, they seek suppliers who have considered these risks. When a customer compares two products, they will choose the one that has fewer risks.

Value and value design mean providing a sense of security to customers, stakeholders, intermediaries, suppliers, distributors, and the team that works with you. When there is security in collaborating with a company, everyone lines up to work with that company. When you create security, the customer will have no concerns about working with you, and reaching growth and control in your business will no longer be a dream.

Values are supposed to respond to the customer's risks. If you cannot plan based on values, the customer will retreat due to the risks and postpone their purchase. If you haven't created a strong value for them, they will buy from other businesses. You have prepared the customer, but they will purchase from someone who provides more information and better security. Help the customer overcome their fear of decision-making.

Social		Performance	
Branding		Expected Product Performance	
Social Proof		Financial Cost	
Purchase Acceptance		Alignment with Customer Issues and Pain Points	
		Quality, Efficiency, and Effectiveness	
		User Guide	

Physical		Financial	
Packaging		Discount	
Product Design		Payment Terms	
Transportation Method		Facilities	
Instructions for Use		Purchase Guarantee and Product Authenticity	
		Perceived Value of Financial Efficiency and Profitability	

To complete the customer risk canvas, ask your current customers. One of the most important questions I encounter in consulting and training sessions is: "How can we provide better services to our customers?" My answer is always that you need to understand your customers' needs and establish a clear system to meet those needs. Do you know the best way to understand those needs? **Ask them.**

You can use these questions in surveys and communications with customers before and after their purchase:.

What do you like about our products/services?

....

....

....

....

....

If you were to recommend our business to someone, what would you say?

....

....

....

....

What suggestions or ideas do you have to improve the product sales process?

....

....

....

....

....

....

Rate the quality of the following from 1 to 5. 5 means the best, and 1 means the weakest. (Use each number only once.)

Description	1	2	3	4	5
Price					
Ease of use					
Packaging					
Delivery and shipping method					
Sales team guidance and consultation					
Location					
Website performance (if applicable)					
Product up-to-date status					
Support team					

Do you, in addition to purchasing our products/services, also buy from similar businesses? (Yes/No/Sometimes)

....

....

....

What other services/products would you like us to offer

....

....

....

▶ Designing Key BusinessValue

A company without its customers is nothing. You live through the values you create and the values perceived by your customers. Customers expect value from your business in several areas.

▶ Expected Value from Products

Companies make products, but customers do not buy products, they buy solutions to their problems. They purchase benefits.

- **What are the customer's expectations from your products and services?**
- **What satisfies the customer's needs?**

Products are tools that help customers achieve their goals based on their needs and desires, not the goals you set for them. Therefore, you must design products that specifically address the needs and demands of customers. Products that offer better solutions to problems create value for customers. Better solutions mean greater value. A better solution balances benefits and risks. How? It's quite simple. Many companies offer the same benefits to compete with one another, but which solution is better than the rest? In reality, competition is not over the products of manufacturers, but rather over the value these products create. This value manifests itself in packaging, services, advertising, customer consultation, financial facilitation, innovation, delivery, warehousing, and other factors that enhance the customer experience. How does the presentation of goods and services, from packaging to advertising and branding, play a role in a competitive space?

What impact does naming, labeling, and positioning compared to competitors and branding have on the customer experience? How can the relationship between the core product and other ancillary benefits increase the perceived value of the product in the eyes of customers?

Three Important Customer Issues and Their Solutions

Issue 1: ....

Our Solution: ....

Issue 2: ....

Our Solution: ....

Issue 3: ....

Our Solution: ....

Designing Three Quick Actions to Address Discovered Issues: ....

After identifying the solutions, it's time to design actions to address the customer issues. This means finding the biggest problem for your customers. Perhaps your failure is due to not delivering products on time, so focus on that issue. Update your customer service and response approach. Shorten your response time as much as possible. Find out what your customers' "if only" wishes are. Explore their needs, desires, demands, and dreams.

Human nature seeks greater benefits, and we discover more profit by answering the questions in the table below.

Evaluation of Claim	How likely is it that your product or service will do what you claim it can do?
Evaluation of Benefit	What does your product or service do to change or improve the lives or work of your customers?
Evaluation of Care	What does your product or service add to the customer or preserve for them?

Evaluation of Value	What does your customer consider valuable and is willing to pay for?
....	....

Evaluation of Popularity	Which of your products or services are easily sold and are popular?
....	....

Evaluation of Differentiation	What sets you apart from your competitors?
....	....

Evaluation of Evolution	If your best products were considered flawless by customers, how would they differ from today?
....	....

Evaluation of Advantage

....

....

....

....

What are the main reasons your business excels, allowing you to offer high-quality products and services?

....

....

....

....

Evaluation of Resources

....

....

....

....

What skills, abilities, and capabilities will you need in the future to create excellent products and provide top-notch services?

....

....

....

....

Evaluation of Conflict

....

....

....

....

Which of your products or services should you stop producing or offering?

....

....

....

....

Evaluation of Methods

....

....

....

....

What can you do right now to make your customers say, "This product is outstanding"?

....

....

....

....

The market only rewards superior performance. Identify the areas of operation where you can be the best and excel.

Product	Our products are superior to our competitors in the following ways:
....	....
....	....
....	....
....	....

Services	Our services to customers excel in the following areas:
....	....
....	....
....	....
....	....

Employees	The active individuals in our company are superior to those working in other businesses in the following ways:
....	....
....	....
....	....
....	....
....	....

Location	The places where we provide our services to customers are superior in the following aspects:
....	....
....	....
....	....
....	....

Ease of Use

....
....
....
....

It is easier for customers to purchase from us because:

....
....
....
....

Facilities

....
....
....
....

Our facilities can be superior if:

....
....
....
....

Communication

....
....
....
....

Communication with us will be easier for our customers if:

....
....
....
....

Response Time

....
....
....
....

We respond to customer needs faster than our competitors because:

....
....
....
....

Speed of Response

....

....

....

....

We can increase our response speed to our customers if:

....

....

....

....

Price

....

....

....

....

The prices of our products and services are better than our competitors' because:

....

....

....

Pricing Valuation

....

....

....

....

....

Our prices can be superior if:

....

....

....

....

....

Quality

....

....

....

....

The quality of our products/services can be superior to our competitors in the following ways:

....

....

....

....

Quality Improvement	We can improve the quality of our products/services if:
....	

Sales Methods and Product Introduction	Our sales and production/services introduction are superior to our competitors in the following aspects
....	

Sales Method Improvement	Our sales methods can gain superiority over our competitors if:
....	

Processes	Our methods for advancing and managing the business, processing purchases, and responding to customer needs and feedback are superior to our competitors in the following aspects:
....	

Process Improvement	We can significantly improve our processes and customer interactions if:
....	....
Credibility	Our credibility in the market is superior to our competitors in the following ways:
....	....
Credibility Enhancement	Our credibility can even surpass that of our competitors if:
....	....

▶ Expected Value from Services

According to statistics and research from the past ten years by the International Monetary Fund regarding developed economies, approximately 70% of the gross domestic product in these countries is attributed to service organizations. This indicates the expected value from services, which can be categorized into five key areas:

- Organizational Agility
- Responsiveness
- Guidance and Training
- Timely and Complete Delivery
- Follow-up

▶ Organizational Agility

Organizational agility refers to an organization's ability to rejuvenate itself and adapt quickly in a changing, chaotic, and uncertain environment. **It reflects how a company responds to changes,** emphasizing that this quick response must also be stable.

The business world is constantly changing due to rapid and extensive shifts in the economy and production. Both the economy and business influence each other. If you design a resilient, adaptable, and agile business, it will endure economic fluctuations. While the economy may be struggling, a business can still perform well. This means you can separate the two; most successful businesses have quickly adapted to environmental changes in volatile economies.

When you encounter an obstacle while driving, you react quickly, but you must ensure that this quick reaction does not cause your vehicle to tip over. Thus, stability is also necessary. The combination of stability and speed of response creates agility. Examine how your speed of change compares to that of your competitors.

When something happens in the market that affects the economy, if your speed of change is low while your competitors' is high, and they possess greater resilience and adaptability, they will have more agility than you. This is why they can perform better in that situation. Sometimes, an event occurs in the market, and some companies easily grow while others stagnate. The main factor affecting agility is the readiness for action. You must be mentally and skillfully strong enough to be ready for appropriate, timely, rapid, and stable movement, enabling you to act more agilely. This action requires three components:

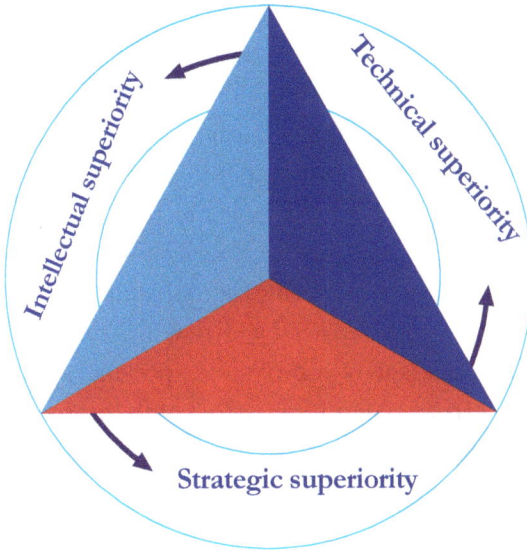

You need to act quickly in terms of your thinking, technique, and strategy. It's like martial arts or wrestling competitions, where in just a few seconds, the positions of the winner and loser can switch. This happens because one competitor has managed to act more swiftly and change the outcome. Both wrestlers are engaged in the competition, but one acts faster, indicating they have better readiness for movement. If you have speed but lack stability, you are not agile, as that speed could throw you off balance. Speed, combined with readiness for movement, creates stability, which is a crucial factor for progress. To enhance agility, you must improve your mental performance and activities to increase your speed. Additionally, you should engage in practices and adopt attitudes that help you maintain your balance.

Balance = Stability + Speed

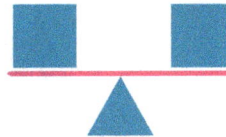

Today, agility is not optional for businesses; it is mandatoryThe agile economy and production force everyone to be agile in various areas. Agility is not just a quick reaction to environmental changes; it's about responding at the right time to those changes.

Agility produces a clear and tangible outcome. When you plant the seed of agility in the field of your business, it takes root, grows branches and leaves, and eventually bears fruit. The fruit of agility is responsiveness and accountability. I am certain that companies that are more accountable are also more agile. These companies act responsibly towards themselves, their employees, and their market.

Accountability means combining the right mindset and skills within an organization in such a balanced way that it fosters agility. During the COVID-19 pandemic, many companies experienced reduced customer access to their services. However, for some, accountability dictated that they maintain their interactions with customers through online platforms. Take a look at your business under a microscope and ask yourself: Have you truly moved towards accountability to create agility?

The strength of a business lies in the level of trust that flows within it. A business that does not foster a safe and trusting environment within and between its employees cannot be agile. This is because people cannot trust one another and grow. Likewise, a business that does not provide a safe environment for its customers cannot be agile.

Accountability is the foundation of trust.

In organizational agility, there are three main models:

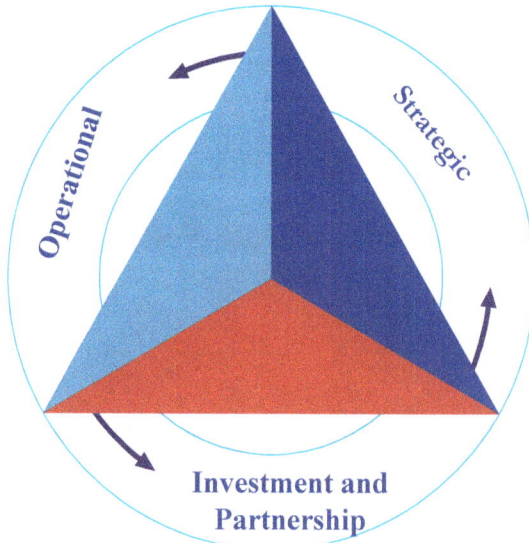

▶ Operational Agility

Operations refer to an organization's ability to quickly direct resources toward creating opportunities to improve the business. How many resources do you currently have that you are unable to turn into opportunities?

In many organizations, resources are not used properly because the operations have issues. For example, you may have organized three or four conferences, prepared several videos of satisfied customers, attended exhibitions, created a lot of content, and carried out many other activities. Yet, you still haven't become the top choice for your customers. You continue to face problems in content production and marketing operations because you have not been able to fully utilize the resources or assets you already possess. You have the raw materials, but you cannot use them optimally to produce the final product.

For example, in the financial sector, if you are unable to quickly transfer issues to your company, your business will suffer. If you do not have a proper financial system and do not prioritize financial discipline protocols, it means that the organization's ability to quickly allocate financial resources to improve your business is compromised. This indicates that the financial claims process lacks agility; it is neither fast nor stable. It lacks balance, and when this balance is disturbed, it shows that you have not performed well in this area.

Sometimes, in my consultations, I suggest that now is the time to buy raw materials. Some people listen and respond, while others resist and say, "How could so many changes happen so suddenly?" The reality is, yes, they can. The only constant in business is change itself.

Change doesn't change, but it forces us to change in many areas. Many people see the changes, but they don't take the necessary actions for those changes.

If an organization notices that the prices of raw materials are fluctuating, but its operations aren't strong enough to quickly adjust financial processes, it will eventually be pushed out of the market. Communication is one of the most important resources in business. Why do you establish communication? To gain benefits and provide benefits to others. If an organization cannot leverage its extensive network to improve its business and increase customer return rates, it loses the agility of its communication operations.

Many organizations lose customers due to a lack of agility. This lack of agility cannot be compensated for by other services. When a customer is looking to fulfill their needs, you cannot offer them something else because they want their needs met in the quickest and most stable way possible. There must be balance within your organization so that the customer knows what to expect.

▶ Investment and Partnership Agility

The second model is investment and partnership agility. **Sometimes, improving and developing a business requires collaboration with new individuals or other businesses.** Business exists to serve the market. Some organizational activities, such as production, marketing, research, development, and branding, must be operationally effective. Once production is complete, you should be able to commercialize it, meaning turning raw materials and goods into wealth. Therefore, you need an agile organizational model focused on attracting investments or forming nonprofit partnerships.

Nonprofit partnerships mean you share a market with another company, but you do not share services. For example, imagine I have a shared market with a company providing accounting education and consulting services. We both intend to offer quality and comprehensive services to managers and business owners. To enhance my offerings, I collaborate with that company, which contributes to the agility of my organization. For instance, food industry producers, such as those in dairy, often interact more with their distribution networks, urging them to deliver products to customers faster. This way, they operate with agility. They invest in enhancing their operational capabilities, creating a distribution network that allows them to get their products to retailers more quickly, which in turn fosters their growth and development. Thus, investment agility pertains to how you invest in various areas and create more partnerships for your employees.

▶ Strategic Agility

The third model of agility pertains to strategy. With strategic agility, you can gain a competitive advantage because strategy only makes sense in a competitive context. An organization with a better strategy can compete more effectively, understanding that planning is essential for outperforming its rivals, plans that must be executed quickly and with stability. Strategic agility can rapidly create a competitive advantage through new innovations. Success in a competitive landscape requires recognizing and capitalizing on potential opportunities while mitigating or avoiding threats. This necessitates speed, stability, and balance in strategic agility. Developing strategic agility empowers leaders and creates conditions for them to discern market changes effectively. **Once market changes are identified, organizations must pivot quickly and take action with both speed and stability. Some changes can be beneficial for businesses, while others can be detrimental.**

Therefore, in situations where the pace of change is high, it is crucial to quickly implement new ideas to maintain a competitive edge. A winning organization prioritizes addressing concerns and meeting customer needs above all else.

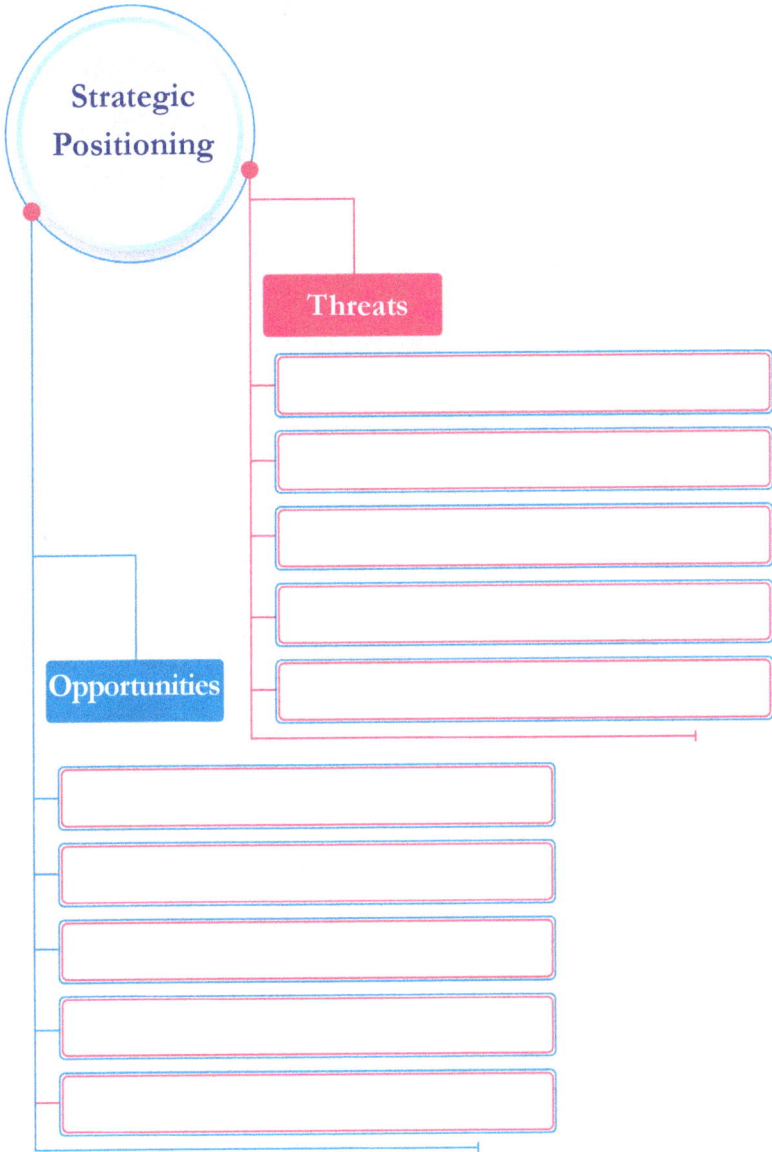

▶ How to Build an Agile Organization?

1. Choose the Right Mindset

Culture and structure must evolve together. Therefore, choose a mindset that fosters agility, allowing not only for agile thinking but also for practical agility in action. This agile mindset should be present at all managerial levels, not just among senior management. Everyone should think, plan, and act with agility to ensure that it is reflected throughout the organization.

2. An Agile Organization is Always Changing

An agile organization is in a constant state of change and is focused on addressing challenges. If you do not initiate change yourself, you will be changed by customers and the market. In a dynamic organization, growth is a continuous process. This means that growth is sustained, and the organization provides and plans for the necessary resources to facilitate this growth.

3. Share the Vision

The vision means that all parts of the organization understand what they are working towards and what they aim to achieve. The vision breaks down into goals, meaning that the overarching vision is divided into smaller objectives, which in turn become actionable plans.

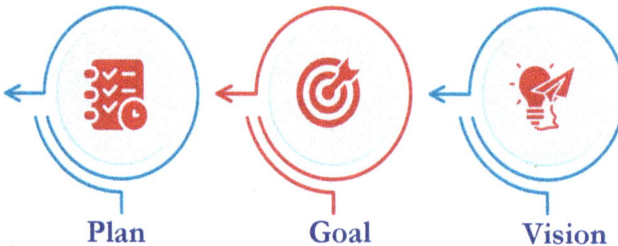

Plan   Goal   Vision

For example, your organization's vision could be to increase the current number of 1,000 customers to 1,800 in six months. To add 800 new customers, measurable goals are necessary. Another organization's vision might be to respond to customers in under five minutes. For instance, all the agents of Snap (drivers, support staff, platform supervisors, etc.) know that their competitive advantage lies in speed and stability. The driver must reach the passenger in under five minutes, and if they don't, the passenger will contact support, who must respond immediately and quickly resolve the passenger's issue. This is a vision. The more you clarify your organization's vision for its members, the more alignment with management increases and the less ambiguity they have. **When coordination improves and repetitive tasks decrease, the agility of the organization increases.**

4. Develop actionable guidelines

The vision, goals, and plans shape operations. Operations refer to activities that must be carried out correctly and according to plan. For example, if you aim to add 800 customers in the next six months, you must contact several potential customers daily and convert them into actual customers. Therefore, you must act according to specific guidelines. The clearer and more precise the contents of these guidelines are, the better you can operate, and your organization will become more agile. However, be careful that these guidelines are not overly idealistic.

5. Monitor opportunities

The more you monitor opportunities in the market environment, the better you understand your competitive advantage. If you see flaws in your competitors' products, this is an opportunity for you. If another competitor is not providing good services to customers, this is also an opportunity. Chinese automakers have grown significantly due to this. They monitored the Iranian automotive market, identified existing opportunities, and understood where Iranian manufacturers were weak. With agility, they managed to capture the Iranian market and introduce their cars because they recognized environmental opportunities. Paying

attention to environmental opportunities, such as technological changes and customer needs, allowed them to grow in the competitive space.
When an individual or a group is responsible for creating agility in
the organization, they should ask different sections and units of the
organization to report market changes so that they can plan to deal
with these changes and prepare support and services in the best way.
When the market is always changing, it is better to be aware of these
changes as early as possible. It's like being warned of an impending
flood, you will save yourself if you learn about it a few hours earlier. If
you become aware of market changes more quickly, you will save both
yourself and your business.

6. Be Flexible in Resource Allocation

The sixth point is flexibility in resource allocation. In an organization,
there are scarce resources and key resources. For instance, financial
resources and cash flow management are considered scarce resources.
Time and the leader's availability are also limited resources. Sometimes,
we tend to be excessive in this area. When a manager is told that many
companies perform significantly better than us in content production,
they might respond, "Well, just use the mobile phones you have to
create content." However, content produced with a mobile phone may
not be of sufficient quality, and producing high-quality content requires
cameras, tripods, computers, and other equipment. Ignoring the need
to adapt production methods and being overly frugal in resource allocation can result in losing agility, allowing competitors to overtake us.

Act proactively before a disaster occurs. When faced with change,
if you don't utilize your resources effectively and demonstrate agility,
competitors will capture a larger market share. You need to identify
your competitive advantage in a timely manner and allocate a budget
accordingly. Timely budget injection into the business is crucial. A
budget for a company is like medicine for a patient. Don't say, "This
medicine is too expensive" or "Let's try herbal remedies from the local
apothecary to see if that works." Sometimes, due to uncertainty about

our plans, we fail to allocate budgets in a timely manner.

7. Organizational Units Must Be Accountable

The seventh factor in organizational agility is creating accountable units. Make sure that for any rights and opportunities granted to individuals or teams, they are held accountable for their performance. By doing this, you won't have concerns about resource allocation or budget management. Train your teams to be accountable to other parts of the organization and to customers. When you establish small, self-managing groups and encourage team participation where individuals take responsibility for their work, this contributes to the organizational culture.

Each part of the organization must be accountable for its performance. The production department should not say, "The product failed because we didn't have a research and development team." The sales department shouldn't claim, "The customer is dissatisfied because the supply chain didn't deliver the product correctly." If you don't hold your organizational units accountable to each other, their time will be wasted, leading to a culture of blame and harming your collective resources. Furthermore, if they cannot resolve issues collaboratively, they will undoubtedly impede agility, leaving you caught up in problems that do not contribute to growth.

8. An Agile Organization is Result-Oriented

For organizational units to prioritize accountability, you need to build an organizational culture based on results, not just activities. Communicate to your employees that the results of their work should speak for themselves. They have the necessary resources, time, energy, and credibility; however, if they do not deliver the expected accountability and results, this is a problem. Establish performance measurement indicators for individuals, teams, and units. This means having metrics that can showcase and compare performances. For example, "Today, I negotiated with fifty customers, and ten of them made purchases. Why did your unit only ship products to seven customers?" This is what result-orientation looks like.

In Nigeria, every barrel of oil sold is tracked transparently from the moment of sale until the money is deposited into the treasury. In result-orientation, you speak with numbers. Some companies only incur costs without generating income. Agility defines the boundary between costs and revenues. Given your resources, workforce, and ideas, you should aim to achieve your objectives within a specific timeframe **because the economy is a science of conversion.**

You convert your life, thoughts, and experiences into a product. This product has a cost, and you sell it to the customer considering your profit. Now imagine if the product is not delivered on time, the customer is dissatisfied, and you get paid late or not at all. This means the company cannot maintain a competitive advantage in marketing and sales. What happens then? The phenomenon of **"imperfect conversion"** occurs, where you end up with nothing. You have worked hard but received no results, leading to exhaustion without achieving your goals because there was no culture of result-orientation within the team.

9. Ensure Information Transparency

Information transparency within the organization enables you to operate more agilely. Provide your team with enough unfiltered information related to products, customers, and processes, categorized and readily accessible. Sometimes, people don't even share the combination to their safe with the finance manager. If you're occasionally unavailable or difficult to reach, should everyone wait for you to continue their work? Or you may have brought in an expert for customer relations, but haven't provided them with sales records.

10. Embrace Rapid Experimentation

Quickly put your ideas into practice and test them to gain rapid experience. This is agility. The flaws in your processes will only become apparent when they reach the customer. If a customer has a question or adds a point, that form needs adjustments for better clarity. This is a structural task within the organization. By fostering rapid experimentation, you sustain learning within the organization. One of the valuable features of agility is embedding continuous learning into your organizational culture.

Share what you learn to improve operations with others. Document your learnings to create implicit knowledge and establish a "knowledge management" system. A knowledge management system means documenting organizational experiences. When a new person joins the organization, you can provide them with this documentation to read and benefit from the organization's experiences. This practice is extremely beneficial and promotes agility.

Years ago, I recorded my expectations for my employees in a video on a CD, which I would give to new hires so they could familiarize themselves with their responsibilities. This approach was similar to holding an hour-long orientation session, but I only invested ten minutes. For tasks that can be standardized, you shouldn't waste the manager's time or the organization's time on repetitive activities. Instead, develop solutions for frequently asked customer questions.

To better understand rapid experimentation, consider the example of police operations in hostage rescues. The first step in a hostage rescue operation is gathering a comprehensive set of information and analyzing it to see if it resembles previous cases. Then, appropriate strategies are devised. Knowledge management plays a critical role here.

Another example of rapid experimentation is fire-fighting operations. If a fire is caused by electrical wires, the approach to extinguishing it differs from a fire caused by a gas leak. Organizations like police and fire departments, which must operate with agility, focus heavily on rapid experimentation and knowledge management.

11. Establish Systemic Integration

The chain of tasks and activities must be coordinated. Often, we introduce a technology, system, or tool into the organization without ensuring proper coordination. Many organizations change their financial systems due to increased assets but later find that despite the expenses, they haven't acquired suitable tools. This may be because the individuals working with that system were not trained, or the connections and network communications were not properly executed, resulting in a lack of agility. Without systemic integration, the financial system remains disjointed. Thus, all activities must be synchronized to produce a clear output.

12. Build a Strong, Specialized Team

Agility is unrelated to the size of an organization or the number of its employees. Today, we don't categorize companies as large or small, but rather as successful or unsuccessful. Success is measured by the speed of response to environmental changes and the balance they achieve.

You need a strong, specialized team capable of fostering agility, which means improving organizational culture and structures. Identify individuals eager for change within your organization and form a robust, specialized team with them. Assess where your weaknesses lie and what factors hinder your coordination speed. Identify where you lack tools and equipment and understand what dissatisfies customers. This team can use a magnifying glass to pinpoint the obstacles your organization faces.

13. Plan for Unexpected Events

This concept is referred to as "flood management" or **"bench management."** Imagine a team that has a player like Ronaldo, and the coach says the team's performance depends on this player. Therefore, he must be in good condition to perform well on the field. Now, suppose the opposing team's coach instructs his players to stop Ronaldo by any means necessary, even if it requires injuring him. If this occurs, the entire strategy of the team that has Ronaldo falls apart. This means they were not prepared for an unexpected event.

The first principle of agility is that the market environment is always changing and full of unforeseen events. Therefore, with flood management, you should allocate some of your ideas, resources, and energy for unexpected events. Create decision-making resources or reserves based on your experiences. These may never be utilized, but if Ronaldo gets injured, who will replace him? Economic conditions or customer preferences may shift, leading them to say they no longer want in-person shopping but only online purchases. If a business is unprepared for this change, it will be caught off guard. You need to know how to convert your investments to avoid losses in the event of currency fluctuations. Be aware of what to do if businesses shut down again due to circumstances like a pandemic. This is the essence of flood management.

14. Focus on Fewer Priorities and Eliminate Uncertain Options

Agility means finding the right path by prioritizing fewer options and eliminating uncertainties. When you are faced with multiple options during decision-making, you may end up overwhelmed with as many as a hundred choices. This can lead to "decision fatigue," where you quickly skim through the last priorities because you want to make a choice more swiftly.

Why should you eliminate uncertain options? These are the choices that often require significant resources, time, and energy to pursue. Start with smaller tasks. When you remove uncertain options, your decision-making speed increases. The sooner you make a decision, even if it's wrong, the quicker you will realize you need to correct it. This is far better than continuously postponing decision-making. When the brain consistently makes quick decisions, it gathers information and discards ineffective data, allowing it to reach conclusions faster from a limited set of options.

Imagine you want to get internet service for your company. Would you act more quickly with two options or fifty? When you have fewer priorities on the table, you eliminate uncertain options faster and take action. The alignment of thought and action is one of the essential tools for agility.

15. Ensure Alignment of Thought and Action

Think big but act small. If you always want to think big while also acting big, you'll fall behind and lose your agility. Start moving by re-acting swiftly to environmental changes and creating stability through balance, along with establishing an appropriate culture and structure.

16. Create Automated Processes

Some actions in progress are routine and repetitive. To save customer time, you need automated processes, such as responses to frequently asked questions from customers that you've already prepared. For example, you can use automated email and SMS response systems to send price lists, and so on.

17. Make Agility Programs Transparent

Agility is not a process that achieves success behind closed doors. When you want to implement agility programs within your organization, hold meetings to explain your plans. Solicit feedback from your team to re-fine these programs. Agility is a team effort, not an individual one, and it must be operationalized at all levels of the organization. For instance, if you want to reduce customer response time from half a day to one hour, this directly relates to your vision. Communicate to your team that we need to achieve a one-hour response time and that everyone must participate, given the ideas and resources at our disposal.

18. Support Agility Advocates

When you implement agility programs in your organization, do not expect everyone to support agility. Only a few individuals will champion this change. Therefore, eliminate anything or anyone that hinders agility. You must enforce organizational agility due to market changes; it is not optional. Some individuals, habits, processes, and organizational programs act as speed bumps. Identify these obstacles and remove them as much as possible. Supporting your agility advocates can greatly assist you.

19. Establish a Cycle of Repetition and Improvement

Always seek ways to repeat successful actions within your organization, as this is the key to your progress. Often, when you articulate your vision and publicize your agility programs, some team members who are speed bumps do not understand this necessity. Timely change requires agility and an appropriate response to market conditions and your business. Therefore, emphasize your organization's vision, continually repeat it, and strive for improvement.

▶ Guidance and Training

One significant concern for customers during the purchasing process is how to use the product. This concern can be mitigated through guidance and training. Create instructional videos or brochures for them, and provide training on how to use the product when you deliver it.

▶ Follow-Up and Monitoring

Follow-up is not an annoyance; rather, it is a crucial competitive nature. Companies that do not consistently monitor their status or that of their customers often lose market share to competitors. Many of us misunderstand the concept of follow-up. It is one of the most valuable traits a company can possess. Follow-up makes sense before and after a sale, ensuring that customers do not feel abandoned. Treat this as a fundamental principle in creating service value; the more diligently you follow up after a sale, the more valuable you will be perceived by the customer.

▶ Expected Value from Processes

What is a process?

A process is a systematic series of activities that transforms one or more inputs into an output. It defines how tasks are carried out and demonstrates how to create more value. Processes are tools that enable efficient competition and value creation, including:

- Production processes
- Research and development
- Marketing
- Talent development and human resources
- Business growth
- Financial management

Some companies may have large processes made up of smaller ones. For example, the production process encompasses numerous inputs, materials, technologies, labor, etc., all converging to create a single product.

If you view processes as resources, you can create a more efficient competitive advantage. To achieve organizational agility, you need to refine your processes, as agility becomes your competitive edge. Additionally, strategic superiority, teamwork, and team management transform into competitive advantages.

In services, this is also true. How do insurance companies sell? How do accounting firms operate and provide financial and tax services? By streamlining processes, you can create value. Allow customers and audiences to reach you more quickly. Establish a process for talent development and human resources. As a manager, you must invest time in growing your business.

▶ Expected Value from Employees

Alongside products, services, and processes, the individuals who collaborate with you are also key differentiators from your competitors and a source of value creation for customers. **To create value, you must enhance these individuals' skills and equip them with the necessary tools and technologies.** By building a knowledge base and facilitating internal experience sharing and customer service skills training, you can elevate their operational effectiveness and performance. The closer you bring employees together, the closer you bring customers to the organization. If you ignore the market, the market will ignore you as well.

▶ Expected Value from Communication Channels

A communication channel is where you provide information and services. As much as possible, smooth the pathway for customers to access your product and simplify the ordering and purchasing process. One value you can create in the distribution channel is responsiveness before a purchase or providing content. Inform customers that if they don't make a purchase, it's okay, as you can offer them a guide or a checklist to help them make a more informed decision. **What online platforms can you create for order registration? Part of this new value arises from online capabilities and software, and part comes from direct sales that eliminate intermediaries.**

Enhance the way you deliver products to customers to strengthen the value you provide. If you package or ship the best product in the worst way, you create a countervalue. Improve the quality of your packaging. You must consider everything that is important to the customer. Some businesses have created ordering incentives. For example, if you buy earlier, this is the price, and if you buy more, this is the price. Digikala has produced content extensively and has thus reached the top. In the last two to three years, this company has hired 4,700 new employees because it educates people before they buy, creating trust. A company that creates value builds security, and it is this security that increases sales.

▶ Expected Value from Generosity

Generosity cannot be valued and has no price. The more generous an organization is, the more valuable it becomes. Don't think that providing customers with information about products and their benefits will lead to a loss. No, that's not the case. Generosity in providing information often fosters customer loyalty. Prioritizing employee welfare is among the values of a successful business. Don't view your employees merely as tools; if you have a utilitarian view, they will see you as a tool to earn their wages as well. In that case, they will not value the company; instead, they will focus on the pay they receive. Elevate your employees' recognition generously and listen to their concerns and worries. Invest in their improvement and create an environment for growth and advancement. This creates value for you. Welcome anyone who wants to stay in this environment, and don't worry about those who wish to leave because everything has meaning with you. **Employees always seek a pleasant and safe work environment.** If managers can provide suitable working conditions, employees will transfer these values to customers, and the generosity you bestow upon your employees will be gifted to your customers. Nothing can replace generosity and honesty.

▶ Expected Value from Fairness

What does fairness mean? Fairness means justice and equity. It means being in a position where everything is fair and mutually beneficial. Everyone should gain from a transaction. Fairness creates value. A product's high price is not related to fairness. **We don't have expensive or cheap products;** instead, we have valuable and non-valuable products. Is a Benz expensive, or does it deserve its price? A Benz is valuable compared to its cost and the features it offers, so it is fair. **Fairness means not charging customers more than the actual value, and for every amount you charge, provide services that make the customer feel it was fair and worthwhile.** If your company is renowned for maintaining fairness in business dealings, it will undoubtedly attract strong investors. Those seeking higher profits are chasing success, clearly demonstrating the meaning of fairness in their businesses. Fairness should be designed. Among the elements that lead to the design of fairness are charitable contributions. Bill Gates has been quoted as saying that he intends to step off the list of the richest people and return the money he has taken from people through charitable partnerships.

To promote this idea, not for show but to foster a culture, recently, I allocated a budget for painting the classrooms and walls of a schoolyard in a village near Isfahan. I derive joy from visiting there occasionally to see the children studying in that school and enjoying their education. I studied in a suitable environment, and I believe these children deserve to study in a good environment as well. Who knows, among these students, there may be future leaders of the country. What could be better than this? Charitable contributions are a form of fairness, bringing both spiritual and material blessings. Additionally, you will experience a better sense of well-being. Until now, you may have noticed that most companies, in their pursuit of profit or greater success, should actively participate in improving the quality of life for people and society. This is a duty. You make money from the community, so return it to the community. See how much value is created by doing this. Some large companies allocate a specific budget for this purpose every year. This goodwill is not just for the community; it's also for yourself. Some of your employees may have suggestions for you in this regard.

The value of a business is directly related to how it creates an environment for individuals.

► Expected Value from Innovation

Innovative companies are always on the lookout for new customer needs. A valuable company is always several steps ahead of its customers. **Innovation means improving the functionality of a product.** By fostering innovation, you create a dependency between customers and your products and services, gradually developing a sense of loyalty. When you innovate, others may imitate you and grow as well.

Innovation, by creating practical value, helps save customers time, money, and energy. Your innovation might allow customers to meet their needs with less effort. One common issue in the marketing strategies of some companies is that they promote their products and services instead of the values behind them. When you market your values, customers will seek you out. If customers come in but you cannot respond adequately, it indicates a lack of organizational agility. Without organizational agility, you cannot defend your values.

To enhance innovation and create more value, you should focus on three important factors:

- Improving the quality of customers' lives
- Solving a persistent problem
- Enhancing product functionality

▶ Four Essential Categories in Creating Value for Customers

We will examine the effects of each of these four categories in the table below:

Functional	Emotional
Time-saving	Sense of worth
Simplicity and ease of use	Personalization
Wealth creation	Motivation
Risk reduction	Sense of ownership
Organization of tasks	Aesthetics
Cost reduction	Sensory appeal

Change in Life	Social Impact
Ideal lifestyle	Attention-grabbing
Anxiety reduction	Social responsibility
Physical and mental health	Gaining credibility
Entertainment and happiness	Reduction of social anxiety
Building new behavioral habits	Membership in a group

▶ Building a Value Proposition in Five Steps

Step One

Identify the primary need of your audience. Until you understand what people need and what their main problem is, you cannot create significant value. This requires initial research, a comprehensive understanding of the target community, and knowledge of the audience persona. To understand the needs and main challenges of individuals, you should talk to buyers, consumers, customers, and intermediaries in your field. The information these sources provide will give you important clues for designing the value proposition in your business model. Now, you write:

What does your audience need?

....
....
....
....

What plan do you have for discussing with buyers, consumers, customers, and intermediaries?

....
....
....
....
....

What information have you gathered from them that helps in designing your value proposition?

....
....
....

Step Two

List the advantages of your products or services. Write down each advantage or specific feature that your products have. Briefly write these advantages, focusing on customer needs. Additionally, avoid including overly obvious or inherent features of your product. Now you write:

What is the unique feature and advantage of your product?

....

....

....

....

....

....

....

....

....

....

....

....

....

....

....

....

Step Three

Write down the reason why each feature is valuable. At this stage, you should explain in one or more short sentences why a specific feature of your product is valuable. For example, if the advantage is the variety of color options, you should explain here why this is considered a value. Does your customer really need this wide range of colors? Now, write down your thoughts:

Why is this advantage considered a value?

....
....
....
....
....
....
....
....

How does this advantage benefit the customer?

....
....
....
....
....
....
....
....

Step Four

Connect the value to the audience's problems. In this stage, you need to intelligently link the audience's problems and needs to one or more of the values mentioned.

- Example: Appliance repair company.
- Customer Problem: Transportation and time-consuming repairs.
- Advantage: Repairs at home in the shortest possible time.

What needs of your audience do you recognize?

....

....

....

....

....

....

....

....

Which of the values you have created can you connect them to?

....

....

....

....

....

....

....

....

Step Five

Emphasize your value proposition. Now that you have established the basis of your value proposition in the business model, you need to refine its appearance a bit and introduce yourself as the sole provider of this outstanding service. Of course, it's not necessary to be the only one providing this benefit. Now you write:

....

....

....

....

....

....

....

....

....

....

....

....

....

....

....

....

....

....

....

....

At the end, six fundamental questions for creating value in business re-creation are provided:

Have you ever found yourself engaged in an activity without knowing the reason behind it, simply because someone asked you to do it?

....

....

....

....

....

....

....

....

What problems do the activities that are performed help solve for individuals? Do these activities resolve the confusion and complexities present in your organization?

....

....

....

....

....

....

....

....

....

....

Does performing this activity create any benefits? Does what you create and present in your organization convey a sense of usefulness due to the enthusiasm you have for it?

....

....

....

....

....

....

....

....

....

....

Are the activities being undertaken transformative and do they genuinely change something? Is there a simpler way to carry out these activities?

....

....

....

....

....

....

....

....

....

Do these activities lead to value creation?

....

....

....

....

....

....

....

....

....

....

Have you ever found yourself engaged in an activity without knowing the reason behind it, simply because someone asked you to do it?

....

....

....

....

....

....

....

....

....

....

....

....

....

....

▶ **Write Your Five Key Takeaways from This Chapter:**

1...

2...

3...

4...

5...

▶ **Three Steps I Will Immediately Start:**

1...

2...

3...

▶ **One Golden Lesson to Share with Others:**

....

....

....

Download all the tables and exercises of this chapter from the following website.

https://hosseintaheri.ir/bmg/

Strategic
Superiority

Chapter 4:
Strategic Superiority

The strategy is the path to achieving a goal, not the goal itself.

📖 **After reading this chapter, you will gain mastery over:**

● The concept of strategy and strategist

● Effective elements in business superiority

● Strategic thinking, action, and product.

Napoleon Bonaparte was a skilled warrior, a conqueror, and a man of the battlefield. Although he always believed that as the commander of the army, he implemented effective war strategies, he thought he must be present in battle himself. You might ask why he held such a belief. He thought that if he were present, his army would win, and if he were not, his army would suffer defeat. After a while, the number of battles became so great that it was no longer possible for him to be present at all of them. Consequently, small defeats gradually turned into larger defeats, simply because he couldn't be at multiple fronts at once. In the end, he faced the same fate that spread across the world.

Yes, Napoleon Bonaparte was a good warrior, but he was not a good strategist. Strategy is supposed to work instead of us, not for us. The strategy of a manager, a leader of an organization, or better yet, a business master, should be designed so that the same processes and outcomes can be achieved even when he is not present. Ask yourself: **Am I a good warrior or a good strategist?**

Most of us are good warriors; we achieve significant victories and create effective results through the emergence of multiple markets and battlefields. However, with the pressure from competitors, this ever-victorious warrior becomes weary. His victories fade, and as a result, his desired outcomes no longer occur. Without strong leadership and excellence, he loses the market. Strategy is the arrangement of resources in such a way that you have an advantage over your competitors. This advantage is not about the quantity or quality of resources. If we ask why some companies have an advantage over others in the market, the answer is that merely having a strategy is not enough; what matters is having a superior strategy.

You need a strategy so that even if you are not present, your thoughts, plans, and experiences continue to work. So far, we've learned that:

- **Strategy requires thought, planning, and experience.**
- **Strategy requires action, movement, and correct execution.**
- **Strategy is the essence of your leadership toward the goal.**

In the field of business mastery, we need mastery not just in strategy but in the execution of that strategy. You want to reach a goal, and to get there, you must follow a path. For instance, if you want to go from Isfahan to Tehran, the route you will take is clear. You have a strategy for your journey to Tehran. This is why you must consider which path will shorten your journey, which will be more enjoyable, and which has better signposts. The answer to these questions enhances your strategy in choosing this route. Superiority is always created with a distinctive feature, where you can create sustainable competitive advantages (continuous abilities to perform better than competitors).

▶ What is strategic superiority?

When your competitive advantages and the value you've created in your business allow you to consistently perform better than competitors, you have strategic superiority. Therefore, you should combine competitive advantage with your business strategy to achieve competitive superiority. Businesses must have a strategy that stands out, as they are part of the economy. To have a superior economy, you need a superior business. A superior business requires value creation, branding, and professional, targeted marketing, all of which are embedded in strategy.

But where exactly does strategy fit in? Consider it this way: you have goals and plans. The overlap between goals and plans is what constitutes strategy. In other words, strategy is what transforms our goals into plans or aligns our plans with our objectives. So, a plan is part of the strategy. Previously, we mentioned that strategy means a pathway. A pathway is the route that guides you. Going back to our earlier example: you are in Isfahan and want to go to Tehran. There are multiple routes to take. Deciding which route to take is the strategy, while determining how to traverse that route is the plan.

How? = Plan

| Plans | Strategy | Goals |

Which route? = Strategy

To achieve your goal, you must have both a different strategy and a different plan. You should also be able to easily adjust your plans and ideas when necessary. From the perspective of business mastery, strategy is the action that elevates your business. Constantly ask yourself: Is what I'm doing helping to grow, advance, and improve my business?

What is a marketing strategy? It's the actions in marketing that will help you grow. What is a branding strategy? It's the actions that will strengthen your brand. What are human capital development strategies? They are the **actions that will bring you peace of mind regarding your human resources.**

▶ Who is a Strategist?

A strategist is someone who advances a business. They decide which path to take and how to proceed. They study, learn, and gain experience to achieve this goal.

A business master is someone who is highly skilled in business. They not only decide which path to take (what actions to take) but also how to take it (how to create an advantage). It's the act of "creating an advantage" that makes them a master.

1. Start with "Why":
Why should you take this path?

2. The 'Why' Behind the Why:
Why do you want to take this path? The "why behind the why" helps you focus on the "how." As Nietzsche said, "He who has a 'why' to live can bear almost any 'how'." I say, anyone who has a 'why' in business can handle any 'how.' Why do I want to become a business master? Because I can achieve at least five to seven times more with the same effort. That's the power of a business master. A business master can achieve more because they design superior strategies with the same resources (time, human, financial, etc.).

The three key factors for success in business are:

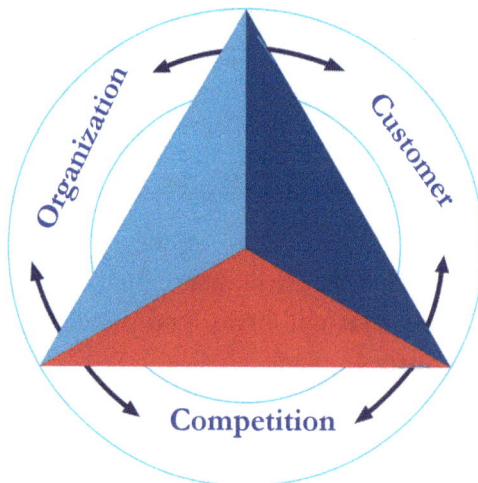

Competition

Getting better before getting bigger. When you improve, growth follows. One of the key factors in business success is competition. Analyze the current state of competition in your industry and identify the key factors that lead to victory or failure. Determine what areas you need to strengthen in order to outperform your competitors.

Organization

To survive in the industry and market where we compete, we must understand and enhance the strengths and competitive factors of the organization. Focus on the core strengths of your organization, as these are essential for survival. Simply put, concentrate on the critical elements that ensure the survival of the organization. Tell yourself, "I need to succeed in the market, so I must succeed in competition. And to do that, I must first succeed within my organization."

Customer

The most important key to a business's success is the customer. The success of an organization depends more on customer satisfaction than on satisfying shareholders or employees. When assessing a company's success, I often ask: Does the company have a clear vision? Does it understand its competitors? Can it recognize how competitors attract customers? For example, in a city like Isfahan, there may be around a hundred pizza shops. If a hundred and first shop opens tonight, it won't necessarily add more customers to the market. Instead, the new shop must compete to attract a share of the existing customers.

By improving any of these three factors, competition, organization, and customer, you will experience more effective growth. Therefore, focus on them in your strategy. Why do you need strategy? To win the competition. Why do you need strategic advantage? To ensure your strategies outperform those of your competitors

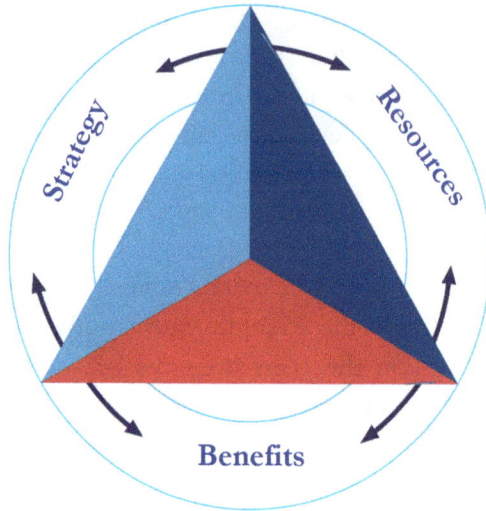

The three elements of resources, benefits, and strategy are influential in business

Resources

In business, you have a set of resources, such as money, human capital, social capital, credibility, connections, and other assets common to all businesses. The competition is always over resources. However, it's important to note that the customer is not a resource; the customer is the result of your resources. This means you've used money, human labor, experience, and connections to produce a product or service that attracts customers. Everything you use to produce your product or service is referred to as your resources.

Benefits

The second element is the benefits you gain in the market. You are seeking profit and advantage, both for yourself and for your customers. But the question is: where are these resources and benefits positioned? Where can you obtain this benefit? The answer lies in your strategy. You have a benefit in mind, but how can you achieve it? What path do you need to take to reach the point where you can obtain that benefit?

Strategy

The third element is strategy. Many times, your strategies may fail because you are unsure of what you want, you don't have a clear vision of your destination, you're unaware of the benefits, or you don't know where to find them. For example, a seller of exclusive mobile numbers needs to find places where they can sell a $5,000 line for $50,000. Their benefit is clear, but where should they go to make it happen? Knowing where to position yourself to gain this benefit is your strategy. Now, a set of resources is required to help you achieve those benefits faster and more effectively, and this is what gives you strategic advantage.

The goal is to do what others are doing, but with more optimized resources. Both you and your competitors have defined resources, and everyone wants to gain benefits in the market. Strategy is about using your resources more efficiently and effectively than others to gain more benefits. This is what we mean by having a superior strategy compared to your competitors. In any case, these resources must be used to achieve your benefits, but the key is which organization uses its resources more efficiently and effectively. The main game is between resources, benefits, and positioning. Positioning is where the benefit exists. The company that positions itself correctly in the market and finds the right place will attract the best customers.

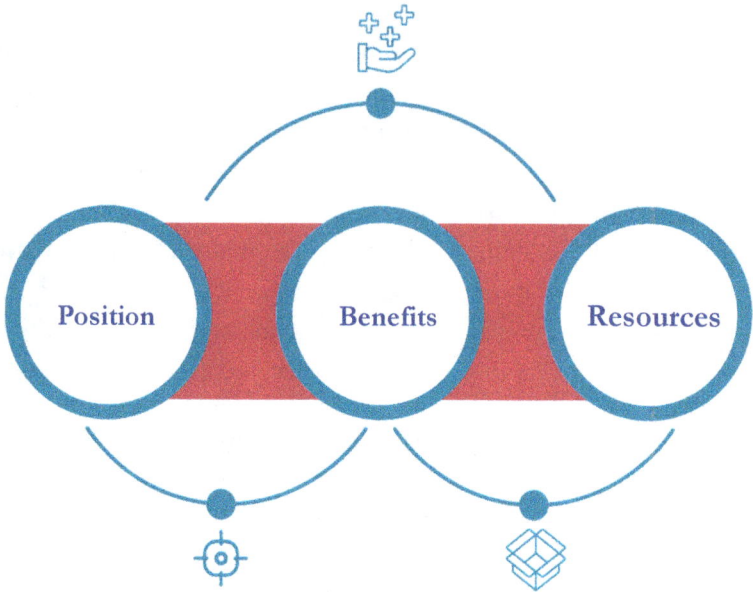

Doing What Others Do, but with Fewer Resources (More Efficiently)

Do your employees fully utilize their capabilities to support the organization's resources?

When the word "strategy" is mentioned in the market, many people think they need to grow larger and become more complex, believing they require hundreds of pages of plans and expensive consultants. However, in many cases, it's enough to simply think about the path, the reasons behind it, and how to take that path. You don't need to keep trying different strategies over and over. Sometimes, just one or two well-implemented strategies are enough for a business to get ahead of its competitors. It's important to consider your own position, the resources you have, and the benefits you seek. **To reach a unique and specific position, you need special and specific resources because you want to achieve a unique and specific benefit.** But the question remains: among resources, benefits, and position, which is the most important? The answer, without a doubt, is resources. This is because everyone wants the same positions and benefits. So, are your employees using all their abilities to protect,strengthen, and grow your resources?

Strategic resources possess specific characteristics. Essentially, a resource must create value. This means it should either reduce costs or increase the price of a product. For example, you participate in a course to gain knowledge, which can be considered part of your strategic resources. You can draw on the experiences of a consultant, read books, or hire someone to create value, either by lowering costs or by increasing the product's price. Here are a few examples:

- Imagine two hospitals with specific resources. One of them has specialized departments and well-known physicians, and this resource enhances the hospital's reputation and attracts more patients. In other words, their resources have generated value and increased the prices of the services offered by that hospital.

- Consider two restaurants that have the same resources and both purchase ingredients for cooking at the same price. However, the quality of the food differs because of the chef they hire. The restaurant with the more skilled chef prepares better dishes and can sell them at a higher price.

A chain store that eliminates intermediaries and sources its products at a lower cost creates value, resulting in reduced expenses for both itself and its customers.

A strategic resource characteristics

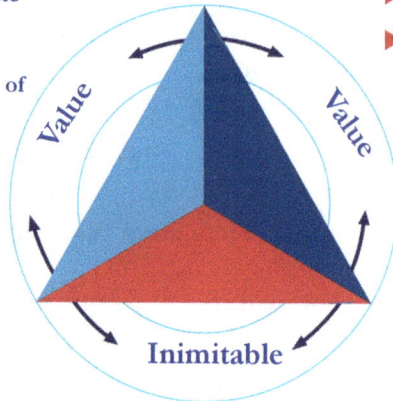

▶ A resource must create value

▶ Or reduce costs

▶ Or increase the price of goods

▶ Valuable resources are scarce

▶ should not be available to everyone

▶ Create barriers to prevent the discovery of benefits.

▶ Prevent copying or substitution of outputs.

A strategic resource must have three characteristics:

1. Create Value

The resource must create value. Valuable resources enable an organization to implement strategies that enhance efficiency and effectiveness. Such resources can help create opportunities or neutralize threats. Resources that reduce company costs or positively impact revenue enable a company to maintain financial balance easily.

2. Be Rare

A strategic resource must be rare. Valuable resources should not be readily accessible to everyone. If competitors can easily access a valuable resource, it loses its rarity. Having a rare resource provides a strategic advantage.

3. Be Difficult to Imitate

A valuable and rare resource should be difficult to imitate. Create obstacles to prevent others from discovering your resources. A strong system often designs complex strategies that work simply. Many successful organizations have strategies that remain uncopied because their resources are valuable and rare. Have a unique approach or "trade secret."

The resources you hold are core to your business strategy. As mentioned before, to build competitive advantage, focus on having unique resources. Perform the same work as others, but with better and more efficient resources. Strategic resources create strategic advantages. Sometimes your resources are your experience, knowledge, or connections. When benefits and positioning are similar to those of competitors, resources make the difference.

Questions to Consider:

- Are your resources strategic?
- Do your resources create value?
- Are they rare?

Make a list of your resources in your business. Anything that contributes to the production of a product is a resource. Are your resources valuable, rare, or difficult to imitate?

With careful consideration, you can place yourself in a position

Inimitable	Rare	Value-Geneating	Resources

to grow your business effectively, especially when current methods aren't working as they should.

As I mentioned, Napoleon was an excellent warrior but not a great strategist because he did not choose a successor. Essentially, he failed to delegate strategic thinking, action, and outcomes essential to achieve desired results.

A strategy requires the "TAP" approach:

- **"T" for Strategic Thinking**
- **"A" for Strategic Action**
- **"P" for Strategic Product**

TAP

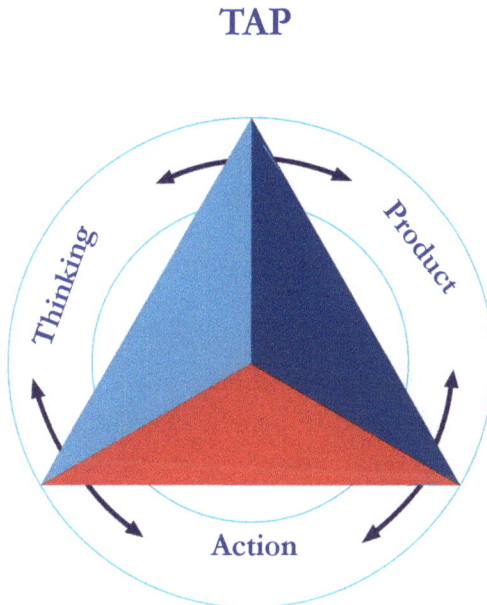

▶ Strategic Thinking

Strategic thinking is the most critical task you need to undertake. The quality of your strategic thinking, focused on the key elements of your business, has a significant impact on your success. Strategic thinking involves directing your decisions based on the potential outcomes they may yield. What position do you want to reach? For what benefit? Using which resources? Think, envision, and guide. What decisions need to be made? What resources should be allocated to achieve the desired position and benefit?

Strategic thinking is both the highest-value and most essential activity in your role. This differs from strategic planning, which is a process, while strategic thinking is a skill that you need to cultivate. Planning involves steps on how it will be written and executed, but thinking sits above the plan.

Today's fast-paced world requires agility, economical considerations, and market awareness, making strategic thinking essential. If you fail to analyze core issues accurately, you may impose undue physical and mental stress on your employees, resulting in confusion and failure. Without strategic thinking, opportunities and advantageous positions are lost one after another.

In strategy, a position means placing yourself where opportunities exist, as opportunities lead to benefits. Potential benefits arise from the underlying factors that create opportunity, even if they are yet to materialize. Where are these benefits? Often in difficult places, like the peak of a mountain. Without accurately defining your position in the market, potential benefits cannot be realized. Be aware that not every idea is worth pursuing. Strategy acts like a line, guiding you. Through strategic thinking, you can calculate the costs of each action, as every expense consumes resources.

| Ordinary Thinking Process | { | ▶ **Stimulus** ▶ **Reaction** | Superior Thinking Process | { | ▶ **Stimulus** ▶ **Thinking** ▶ **Reaction** |

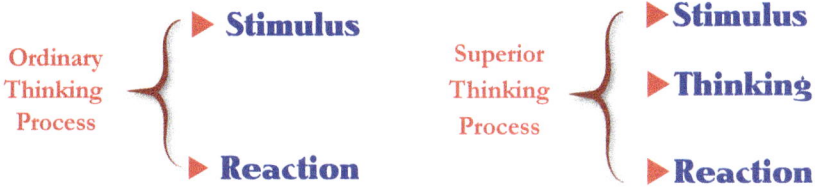

▶ Difference Between Strategy and Tactics

Learning the basics of chess, how the pieces move and the rules, takes just five minutes. However, mastering the game requires much more. This difference illustrates the distinction between tactics and strategy. While tactics are the specific methods for implementing a strategy, strategy itself demands time and continuous thought. Tactics are about execution, whereas strategy requires consistent strategic thinking to find growth levers, which help a business make leaps in progress.

Napoleon, for instance, could have achieved lasting success if he had used strategic thinking to develop leverage, nurture capable successors, and create a resilient empire.

The reasons why strategic thinking is essential are as follows:

- Identifying opportunities and vulnerabilities
- Filtering out ideas that lack value
- Considering probabilities and risks
- Calculating the costs of each action
- Assessing the feasibility of effective tactics
- Avoiding mental and experiential biases
- Detecting business discontinuities

Strategic thinking helps transform chaos into order. For this reason, strategy is a continuous path.

A true traveler is not one who occasionally rushes or feels tired; rather, a true traveler is one who moves slowly and steadily.

▶ Strategic Thinking Skills

There are 9 strategic thinking skills. Above all else, a good strategy requires the skill of strategic thinking.

1. Analytical Skills

Strategic thinking differs from planning. While planning is a process, strategic thinking is a skill, and all skills are acquired and learnable. To enhance strategic thinking, you must first develop analytical skills. This will enable you to analyze various inputs and outputs. For instance, consider how much return I have gained for the ten million tomans spent on social media advertising, not just financial returns but also what I have achieved overall. For the salary I pay monthly, how much sales and revenue am I generating?

2. Communication Skills

The second skill in strategic thinking is communication. Regardless of the size of your company, strong communication is essential. By establishing the right connections with your team, clients, and partners, you can generate sound ideas and build powerful collective wisdom. Good communication allows you to learn from successful individuals and experts. Whenever I see a successful entrepreneur, I try to model my system after them, even if they are in entirely unrelated industries. Sometimes, when I go to buy trousers, I notice how excellently the salesperson provides service. After the sale, they call me to check if the trousers were good and if I had any sizing issues. I think to myself, if a trouser salesperson does this, I can use this idea for my customers as well. I can ask customers if they have used my product, if it was satisfactory, and if they were pleased. The customer feels that once the product was sold, I didn't forget them; instead, I became their friend. The next time they want to purchase this product, they will come to me first. This is what strategic advantage looks like. Businesses that can grow their internal and external communication skills can enhance the quality of their services.

3. Systemic Thinking

Systemic thinking is not limited to a single unit or department within an organization; it involves thinking holistically about the entire organization and system. Consider this example: while I am driving, my car suddenly shuts off. I call a mechanic and tell him my car has stalled. He arrives, checks the vehicle, runs diagnostics, and says thankfully that the engine isn't damaged. He discovers that one of the spark plugs is faulty, replaces it, and starts the engine. Now, the question is, which is more important for the car to start: the engine or the spark plug? In a system, everything is equally important. Thus, systemic thinking takes everything into account. It considers all variables and elements of the system. Why is it important to consider all elements of the system? Because you may have a strategic idea you want to implement, but if you overlook many factors that constitute your resources, like "team understanding," the effectiveness of your strategy could suffer. Your team needs to understand that this strategy is beneficial; it preserves your reputation and credibility with customers and makes them feel valued. If you disregard team understanding and say, "Just do as I say," the outcome will be the same situation that many people struggle with.

4. Problem-Solving Skills

Strategic thinkers possess problem-solving skills. They think about issues before they arise and generate solutions. Problem-solving skills mean creating solutions. For example, you have an issue that is computational and logical in nature: why is the number of customers decreasing? Because we don't have professional customer service. Why don't we have professional customer service? Because we haven't conducted market research. We haven't engaged in conversations with our customers. Ask your customers about your services to resolve this issue. Analyze and break down the problem. Create a "problem breakdown" to address the issue. In strategic thinking, problem-solving is essential. If you ignore a "problem," it turns into a "challenge." If you disregard a challenge, it becomes a "predicament." If you leave a predicament unattended, it escalates into a "crisis." Ignore a crisis, and it turns into a "catastrophe." If you neglect a catastrophe, it becomes a "calamity." A minor toothache, if ignored, can lead to surgery and several weeks of recovery. A problem has logical and computational roots, not emotional ones. Therefore, strategic thinking is necessary for effective problem-solving.

5. Critical Thinking Skills

You should always maintain a scrutinizing and questioning attitude toward any thought or mental model. In simpler terms, dig deeper. What if it doesn't work? What are the alternatives? Napoleon didn't consider what others should do in his absence. He didn't ask himself, "What if I'm not here?" Because he lacked strategic thinking and didn't solve the issue, he faced a disaster.

6. Creative Thinking Skills

With creativity and innovation, find different solutions with multiple options, idea generation, and brainstorming. There are many things that have yet to be discovered. There's no need for something to be invented. Electricity was not invented; rather, the flow of electricity was discovered. The field of mechanics was discovered. The field of electronics was discovered. Magnetism was discovered. Fire was discovered. Therefore, what we need in creative thinking is discovery and the art of combining ideas, not invention.

7. Integrated Thinking Skills

If you want to have strategic thinking, utilize integrated thinking. Understand that data means raw information. When you categorize and filter data, it transforms into information. For example, if you have a database of phone numbers, you filter it to determine which numbers belong to managers, middle management, and employees. This filtering and categorization convert data into information.

There are two types of data:

hard data and **soft data.** Hard data is immutable. An example of hard data is statistical data. Information and research constitute hard data.

Soft data, on the other hand, consists of ideas, experiences, and comparisons. You compare one "market" to "another market" and find that you are not succeeding there. You might then consider comparing it to yet another market and discover you are stronger in that one. You produce a product and see that in comparison to your competitor's product, you lack strength in one area but are strong in another. These are soft data, which means they can be changed.

Strategic thinking is integrated thinking. What does integration mean? It means bringing together soft and hard data on paper to create results from the combination of statistics, ideas, and information. You have statistics showing that the population's median age is increasing. Iran is moving toward an aging population. What happens? This statistic cannot be changed. You brainstorm and say, "I will produce a product or service for the care of the elderly," which will continue to generate income for the next fifty years. You then develop a strategy based on this. You progress from the discovery phase to the creation phase and then to the improvement phase in strategic thinking. In this way, you can direct your decisions effectively. Consequently, you will have a vision of the results you want to achieve.

8.   Planning and Management Skills

Strategy is not just about solutions; it also includes implementations. After you analyze the data and understand the problem, along with identifying the solution, you need planning. Strong management skills are necessary to bring everything together and move forward. This is why strategic thinking is more important than planning; it shapes the strategic planning process.

9.   Experience-Based or Results-Oriented

Do you have experience-based or results-oriented strategic thinking? Many people who engage in strategic thinking fall neither into the trap of blind pragmatism nor idealism. Blind pragmatism means acting without thought. You might be hammering a nail into the wall with a hammer in your hand, but you are doing so with your eyes closed. Someone with experience-based strategic thinking does not engage in blind pragmatism or idealism. Idealism in strategy means seeking a detailed and optimized plan for every action. Blind pragmatism leads to nowhere, resulting in a "whatever will be, will be" attitude. The result of idealism is stagnation; to succeed in strategy, you must keep moving.

To gain strategic superiority, you must act powerfully.

Anyone embarking on an important journey first needs a map to find the correct path. What should they do next? They must move and take action. Movement and action require awareness. Acting without awareness is akin to self-destruction. A company's strategy is its pathway. Every day, you must check whether you are on the right path. Is your thinking correct? Delegate analytical tasks to one person, problem-solving to another, and creativity to yet another to create a fluid stream of strategic thinking.

▶ Strategic Action

Strategic action is the roadmap for implementing a strategy. In this roadmap, you determine which resources to allocate, how to guide individuals, and how to lead them. To ensure that the programs are executed, what structure have you put in place? The execution of a well-formulated strategy has the greatest impact on the success of an organization. It's not enough to think only about the strategy; its execution is equally important.

You have chosen what dish to cook, but you must also take action.

Challenges of Execution and Strategic Action

The challenges of execution and strategic action are as follows:

1. Incompatibility with Individual, Group, and Organizational Goals.
2. Irrelevance to Short-term and Long-term Resources.
3. Lack of Coordination among Skills, Resources, and Capabilities
4. Lack of Awareness and Self-Deception among Senior Managers
5. Managers' Focus on Maintaining the Status Quo
6. Past Achievements of the Organization
7. Precise Priority Setting

1. **Incompatibility with Individual, Group, and Organizational Goals.**
You cannot implement your strategy if it is incompatible with your individual, group, and organizational objectives. For example, you may want to set a market development strategy and decide to hold exhibitions in ten cities. You inform your employees that they should cancel their leaves starting tomorrow and tell their families that they will not be available for the last week of every month because they need to attend twelve exhibitions. So, what happens next? There should be a benefit for both you and them. Strategy encompasses resources, benefits, and positioning. Human resources, as one of your resources, must also derive benefits. Otherwise, there will be inconsistencies, leading to excuses and a lack of execution. When the strategy is incompatible with the individual and group objectives of the organization, numerous issues arise.

2. **Irrelevance to Short-term and Long-term Resources.**
It is crucial that the objectives are aligned with the resources. There must be coordination between the goals and resources. Sixty percent of companies fail to establish a connection between their strategy and their budgets. As a result, the strategy does not materialize because they cannot execute it.

3. **Lack of Coordination among Skills, Resources, and Capabilities**
One of the challenges of execution and strategic action is that the skills, resources, and capabilities of managers, employees, and the organization are not aligned with their objectives. A complete economic strategy involves coordination between what one has and what one desires. You must be prepared for what you want; your capacity must be ready. You need to be willing to accept that what you desire has a cost, and you must assess whether you can afford it. We often want many things, but if we are not prepared to attain them, we later wonder why it doesn't happen.

4. **Lack of Awareness and Self-Deception among Senior Managers**
Sometimes managers are unaware and deceive themselves. They believe

everything is excellent, thinking, "We wrote the strategic plan, and we printed it on a board for everyone to see." They may say that everything is fine. However, is everything really fine? Tasks are being carried out, but at what quality and with what outcomes? Are the resources consumed yielding the benefits necessary to position the company where it needs to be? Resources, benefits, and strategy are all interconnected.

5. **Managers' Focus on Maintaining the Status Quo**
Sometimes, managers are content with merely maintaining the status quo. When Shah Sultan Hussein Safavi was told during the Afghan invasion that "the Afghans have taken half of Iran," he replied, "That's not a problem; we govern over this half of the subjects." Later, they informed him, "Sir, they have taken all of Iran and are at the gates of Isfahan." He responded, "That's not a problem; we will rule over Isfahan." Finally, they said, "Sir, they have taken Isfahan and are at the palace gates." Shah Sultan Hussein remarked, "That's not a problem; we will manage this palace and harem." In the end, Mahmoud Afghan entered the magnificent palace, and Shah Sultan Hussein was killed in a horrific manner. Why? Because he only wanted to maintain the existing situation. If you merely aim to preserve what exists, you will lose everything. It is your duty to have a strategy and superiority over the business and market; strategic superiority is essential.

6. **Past Achievements of the Organization**
Another challenge is the past achievements of the organization. The organization may have been successful in the past and believes it is still successful, which can lead to complacency. This mindset prevents them from achieving the results they should or had previously attained.

7. **Precise Priority Setting**
The most crucial action is to determine precise priorities. Precise priority setting means identifying what the priorities are and how they should be executed. What are your priorities? You need to write them down because clarity is essential for action. It is great if you have done something well today, but if another task was supposed to be accom-

plished today and it was not part of the plan, then that task was not a priority.

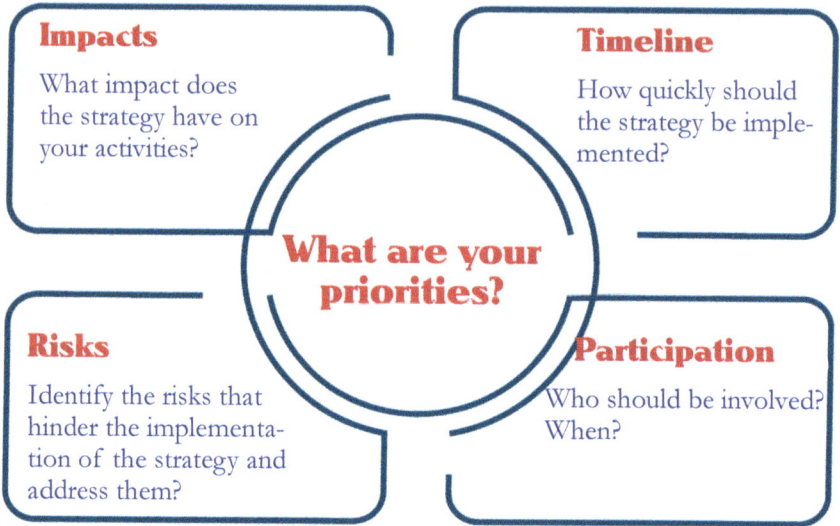

Impacts	Timeline
What impact does the strategy have on your activities?	How quickly should the strategy be implemented?

What are your priorities?

Risks	Participation
Identify the risks that hinder the implementation of the strategy and address them?	Who should be involved? When?

Features of Priorities:

- **Timeline**

How quickly should the strategy be implemented? Until when should it proceed?

- **Impacts**

What impact does the strategy have on your activities? The impacts of prioritization should be clearly defined. The effect of one task can be greater and more specific than that of another. Some important tasks may sometimes have a special priority, making them "the most important among the important." When certain tasks are completed, they can influence subsequent tasks and facilitate the completion of other tasks as well.

● Participation

Who should be involved, and when? Who is expected to participate as a priority in this strategy? What portion of human resources will be allocated as assets to achieve this strategic position? Resources, benefits, and positioning are central to the strategy.

● Risks

Identify and address the risks that hinder strategy implementation. Are there specific risks and issues that stand in the way of execution? Recognizing and mitigating these risks is essential, especially those that past experiences have shown to be significant obstacles. Knowing where previous attempts have stalled is crucial to prevent repeating the same mistakes. Why is taking action important? Because you're in a competitive environment, and to secure a competitive advantage, a superior strategy is required. You want a strategic position that, when a customer chooses between you and others, they see you as the superior choice, the leader, the expert. Competition is either ongoing or directed toward the future. For present competition, use strategy for competitive positioning, and for future competition, use strategy to guide the organization. The organization should aim to become resource-rich, benefit-driven, and well-positioned. More effectively, the direction should be toward achieving a respected market position.

Your primary position is what you seek to achieve with your resources. You aim to compete with active players in your industry. So, identify your position, align your strategy toward it, and decide where you want to compete. Vertical domains are usually areas where you share a market but offer different services. For example, an accounting firm and an advertising agency may have distinct services but share a market by serving companies and entrepreneurs. This competition reflects the present.

What about competition for the future? It asks where you want to go, your vision, your mission statement, and your performance objectives.

Current Competition

Strategy as Positioning
_____

Where do we currently operate?

Product market scope

Geographic scope

Vertical scope

How do we compete?

What are our competitive foundations?

Where do we want to go?
Vision:
What exactly do we want to achieve?
Mission statement:
Goals and performance:
How will we reach our goals?
Define the required resources for growth, acquisition, and ownership.
_____
Strategy as Direction

Future Competition

A company without a vision, mission statement, or clear performance goals is unlikely to survive. It cannot generate the revenue necessary for growth and development; it only manages to cover its costs and pay its employees. Revenue is essential not only for survival but also for financial freedom, enabling investment in research, new equipment, and specialized consultants.

In present competition, you must consider how to compete and define your competitive advantages. In future competition, the question becomes, "How do I secure these advantages?" You need clear development guidelines and prioritized investments in costs, capital, and research and development. Your growth might be organic, through mergers and acquisitions, or by collaborating with companies that share your market but offer different services, like the partnerships seen between Sony and

Ericsson or Konica and Minolta. Many companies merge to strengthen their market position, including acquiring competitors that could potentially capture market share.

▶ Strategic Products

A strategic product is essential. I previously mentioned that a strategic asset must be valuable, rare, and, most importantly, difficult to imitate. While competitors might replicate your product, they can't replicate your unique identity, values, or customer relationships. A strategic product should embody the following characteristics:

- Designed for a specific target market
- Distinctive and unique
- Solves a particular problem
- Offers services and easy access
- Incorporates product development knowledge
- Avoids the "product syndrome," where attachment to a product blinds the company to market changes.

A strategic product is designed with a clear target market in mind. The more specific the target market, the more unique the product. This level of focus often means the competition will be tougher. Strategic products have a well-defined purpose, to solve a problem, meet a need, or address a demand. They provide options, services, and accessibility. Product development involves responding to new customer needs and demands, adding options, improving services, and enhancing functionality.

More importantly, a strategic product is one that has not fallen into the misleading, insignificant, and limiting trap of "product syndrome." This happens when a company becomes so obsessed with its product or service that it fails to notice changes and opportunities around it. A strategic product gives you a strong market position. For example, in a restaurant, Shishlik (a Persian-style grilled lamb ribs dish) is the most popular meal, and people go there specifically to have it. Similarly, a knowledge-based engineering company may develop a specialized service or product that only they have the expertise to use. Why is a strategic product important? Every product follows a natural growth cycle, known as the Product Life Cycle (PLC). This cycle includes introduction, growth, maturity, saturation, and decline. Customer needs and market demands change over time, so businesses must renew and improve their products to stay competitive.

A strategic product secures a unique position in the market. Consider iPhone, it holds a distinct strategic position in the market, as does Mercedes-Benz with its carefully designed products that meet market demands. When these products reach saturation, innovation occurs to generate new opportunities.

▶ Key Points for Strategic Superiority

1. Ability to Understand the Significance of Events

In the market and economic environment, it is essential to understand the importance of events. Accept that with constant change, your strategies must remain flexible. Agility is necessary to adapt your strategies so you can seize unique opportunities and positions. Opportunities exist within specific positions; they represent potential benefits that you must transform into actual profits using your resources. Therefore, you need to recognize and understand these positions without bias. Use strategic thinking to work without prejudice and identify cognitive and intuitive errors. The Art of Thinking Clearly introduces 99 cognitive biases. For instance, understanding social loafing can prevent unnecessary hiring and resource waste.

2. Ability to Make and Understand Decisions and Actions

Another critical aspect of strategic superiority is the ability to make and understand decisions and actions. This means being able to make decisions, possessing decision-making power, and fully comprehending those decisions. You must also engage in action-oriented behavior and understand its importance. Think big, but act small. Is the organization you've built capable of implementing your vision and applying it to grow? Or does the organization itself need further refinement? In business mastery, everything is interconnected.

3. Alignment with Organizational Capacity

For a strategy to be effective and superior, it must align with your organization's capacity. It should be compatible with your organizational culture and structure. Avoid setting overly ambitious strategies based on illusions or perfectionism that your organization cannot realistically implement. As the saying goes, "Birds of a feather flock together." Do not attempt to battle hawks, eagles, and falcons if you are a pigeon. You must prepare for growth, agility, value creation, teamwork, and leveraging within your organization.

4. A Good Warrior or a Good Strategist?

Are you producing good warriors or good strategists? It is essential to cultivate strategists rather than warriors. Being a strategist requires both learning and mastery; both elements are necessary for your strategies to achieve superiority. In your organization, you should be both a good teacher to instruct in strategy and have employees who are ready to learn. Your staff should be capable of advancing their strategic thinking and actions and strengthening your strategic products.

5. Chicken or Egg?

Which came first, the chicken or the egg? This question remains unanswered, but I believe the chicken came first. When God sent Adam and Eve, He created a chicken alongside them with a mechanism that allowed it to produce eggs. As Jack Welch[1] says in Winning:

Strategy follows people. That is, you must first be a strategist for strategy to follow. Thus, if the right person is chosen, they will also create the right strategy. This individual could be a manager, employee, or stakeholder. Therefore, you must first establish this business approach. Strategy does not pre-exist; a strategist must create it. Strategy is what we do to advance and grow our business.

1-A former executive of General Electric (GE)

6. Brand Equity

Your brand's unique value can be a strategic advantage. If your customers genuinely like your brand, you possess a strong source of competitive advantage. Essentially, you have strategic superiority because you've created loyalty, making you popular with customers and giving you market power.

7. Technology Share

Another key point is the role of technology. By incorporating technology, you can gain strategic advantages. Staying up-to-date, improving speed, accuracy, and efficiency through technology can bring significant changes. Henry Ford used technology to surpass all global car manufacturers, establishing himself as a market icon. In the production economy, manufacturers were the primary players. Over time, technology was integrated into production, elevating these companies' positions. Eventually, the market became saturated, and manufacturers could no longer grow and compete; they then focused on customer service, excelling in the market. After that, market competition shifted to information, and the "information economy" era began. Now, we are in the "attention economy," where technology often replaces human skills and creates power for us.

8. Renewing Differentiation

The next element of strategic superiority is renewing differentiation. Branding is built on differentiation. Essentially, people buy what sets you apart from others, whether it is price, speed, accuracy, durability, functionality, ease of use, or a sense of superiority. Whatever it is, revisit and refine it. Work on your pricing and delivery speed. For example, McDonald's aims to reduce its food preparation time by six seconds, allowing it to serve customers faster. Saving six seconds means saving one minute for every ten customers served, enabling McDonald's to serve more people with the same resources. Why? Because they have gained a competitive advantage in preparation and production strategy by renewing their differentiation. As the saying goes, "Take account of yourself before you are held to account." Before you are judged in the market by quick-deciding customers, assess what has become outdated and renew your differentiators.

9. Crossing the Bridge

Strategy is like a bridge. Moving from goals to plans requires strategy. Strategy implementation bridges the gap between a great strategy and excellent performance. So, you must strengthen the "action" component as much as possible.

10. Sales Chain

Your sales chain can be a strategic advantage. A well-structured distribution and accessibility chain is also a strategic advantage. If you can manage customer demand effectively, you have a strategic edge.

11. What Has Changed?

In striving for strategic superiority, as you aim to surpass competitors, you should always ask, "What has changed?" Continuously collect updated customer information and use it to improve your products and services. This will help in building a strategic product. Form a focus group by gathering 5 to 7 customers in your office or a café to discuss their concerns. Talking to current or potential customers, who might also be competitors' customers, strengthens your strategic advantage. This way, you gain insights into what's happening sooner than your competitors, allowing you to review resources, benefits, and positions earlier.

12. Competitive Review

Conduct a competitive review to discover new approaches and identify the strengths of your competitors. I call this "Identifying Untapped Needs." These are needs that remain unaddressed. When reviewing competitors, you can see where they excel and where they are still lacking. By addressing these gaps, you may inadvertently gain a competitive advantage. Your primary concern should be identifying what your audience currently lacks that no one has yet provided and creating exactly that.

13. Discovering Competencies

Most importantly, when implementing a strategy, identify the competencies of yourself, your competitors, and your organization. Answer the following four questions right now, writing down whatever comes to mind. Give these questions to your employees and ask them to respond. Additionally, ask five to ten of your customers to answer these questions:

- What are four of your strongest strengths?
- What are the four fundamental wants and needs of your customers?
- Who are the four competitors performing better than you? (If fewer, write down those.)
- What do your competitors do better than you?

By using this approach, you can compare your competencies with those of your competitors and understand, from your customers' perspective, what makes you competent and superior. Ask your customers and find out their interests. Where are the benefits? They lie within your position. Use your resources to achieve those benefits and reach that position.

14. Obedience Takes Time

It's essential to recognize that making your organization and market obedient to your strategy is a time-consuming process. Achieving peak performance or excellence takes time. According to Harvard Business Review research, building the capabilities required to execute a strategy is time-intensive. Small organizations typically take around 18 months, while large organizations may take about three years to reach optimal performance.

15. Evaluation and Reinforcement

Your strategy evaluation approach should resemble the growth of a tree, not an electric kettle. In other words, you need to plant a seed, nurture it, and eventually harvest it, rather than just plugging in a kettle and letting it boil by itself. The results differ significantly. The strategic product, actions, and thinking all depend on that final outcome, which ultimately improves the result. In a given position, based on the resources we've invested, we create better benefits. Don't waste your energy on the wrong pursuits. Don't allocate resources toward achieving a position that brings no benefits. Strategy should be driven by evidence, not intuition. Don't make impulsive decisions out of fear of a competitor's actions. **Fear should not dictate your decisions; rather, it should drive your actions.** Manage fear to identify where you may have fallen short.

Discovering Competencies

Building the capabilities required to execute a strategy is a time-consuming process. Small organizations should plan for up to 18 months to reach their peak performance. For a large multinational company, it may take up to three years to reach this point. Your evaluation approach should be long-term and forward-looking.

Customer Needs and Desires	Strengths and Capabilities

Competition

What Competitors Do Better	Top Competitors

Designing a Strategic Product

Strategic Product aligns with Strategic Positioning in the Market.

Target Market Profile

What characteristics does the target market of this product have? (Age, geographic location, gender, cultural and social level)

....
....
....
....
....
....
....
....
....

What concern does your strategic product address, and how does it help the audience?

....
....
....
....
....
....
....
....
....
....
....
....
....

Access Method

What process must be followed to purchase the strategic product or service?

....
....
....
....
....
....
....
....
....

Product Options

What additional features and advantages does this product have compared to other services and products?

....
....
....
....
....
....
....
....
....
....

▶ **Write Your Five Key Takeaways from This Chapter:**

1..

2..

3..

4..

5..

▶ **Three Steps I Will Immediately Start:**

1..

2..

3..

▶ **One Golden Lesson to Share with Others:**

....

....

....

Download all the tables and exercises of this chapter from the following website.

https://hosseintaheri.ir/bmg/

Branding

Chapter 5:

Branding

Everyone desires the brand.

After reading this chapter, you will gain mastery over:

- The Three Key Elements in Business Mastery Branding
- How to Create the Brand's Purpose and Philosophy
- Brand Value, Promise, and Positioning
- Brand Identity, Personality, and Story

In the economy of entrepreneurship and value, the "brand" is the most valuable asset. According to brand science, whenever marketing experts create a new name, logo, or symbol for a product, they are in the process of building a brand. However, many managers believe that a brand is built over time and with popularity and credibility in the market. No, that's not the case. You are creating a brand from the very moment you start, even if you are unaware of it or do not believe in it. Established brands dominate the market, influence customer decisions, and this influence must be designed from the beginning.

Theodore Levitt, a professor at Harvard University, believes: "In the new era, competition is not about what companies manufacture in their factories; it is about what they add to the product after it leaves the factory. This includes packaging, services, advertising, support, offering financial facilities for purchase, facilitating the distribution process, inventory management, product maintenance, and other values delivered to the final customer."

Branding is what separates and differentiates your business from competitors. Brand identity is about giving character to your business.

The brand is essentially others' perception of your business, and branding is the activity you undertake to build and shape that perception.

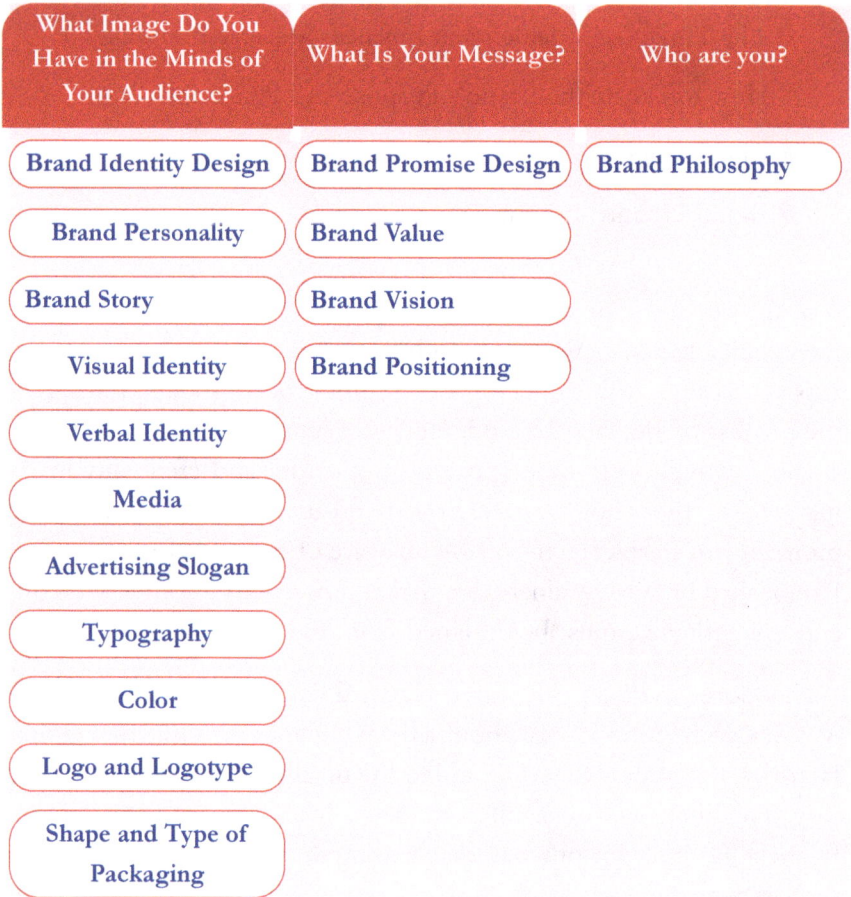

What Image Do You Have in the Minds of Your Audience?	What Is Your Message?	Who are you?
Brand Identity Design	Brand Promise Design	Brand Philosophy
Brand Personality	Brand Value	
Brand Story	Brand Vision	
Visual Identity	Brand Positioning	
Verbal Identity		
Media		
Advertising Slogan		
Typography		
Color		
Logo and Logotype		
Shape and Type of Packaging		

The three main elements in Business Mastery branding.

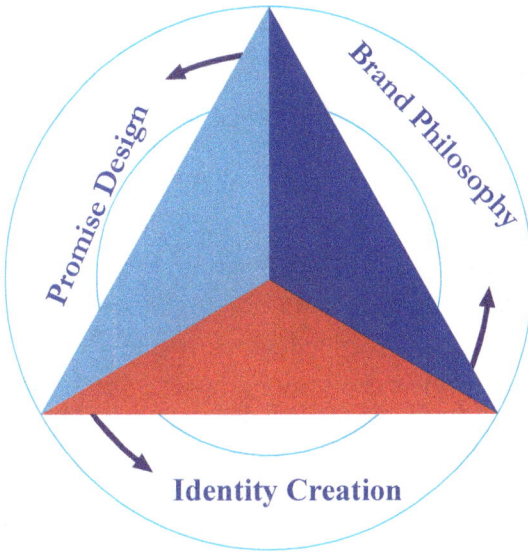

▶ Brand Philosophy

The brand philosophy defines the ethical codes and principles of the organization and aims to answer the question, "Why does your business exist?" This question is crucial because your ideology, value and ethical charter, operational methods, and the essence of your business are made clear and displayed for the organization, the market, and your customers.

In the simplest terms, Say the purpose for which this company was established:

....

....

....

....

....

The brand philosophy is the factor that differentiates your organization from others; it is not merely an introduction or an advertising slogan. If you find yourself challenged by the question "What is the purpose of your brand?" and struggle to provide a clear answer, your customers will likely face the same difficulty in understanding your brand's philosophy. This lack of clarity may cause them not to connect with your brand and eventually leave it.

If the brand philosophy is unclear and customers cannot grasp it, becoming a recognized brand becomes challenging. Your brand's philosophy acts like a lighthouse. When our team members think about their work, they reflect on the brand's philosophy, how to design services based on it to achieve integrated and sustainable growth. Growth is a holistic process for the organization; the organization must grow in all aspects. The brand philosophy is the essence of your business. Senior management and all members of the organization should define the brand philosophy based on the inherent nature of the business.

The brand's purpose is a foundational mindset that, in alignment with the organization's values and goals, helps you respond to changes and make decisions consistent with your vision. Your decisions should be inspiring and prioritize core values, guiding the actions of your team. If you are a business leader, ask your employees if they understand the purpose behind the work they do. Why does your company exist? Why do they get up every morning and come to work? Understanding the purpose of their work makes it easier for both you and those who work with you. The brand philosophy is the link between your brand and your employees.

Simon Sinek, in his book Start with Why, says: "The purpose of your organization is your brand's philosophy, presented through a model called the 'Golden Circle.' With this model, you can clarify the purpose of your brand. The model consists of three concentric circles: the outer circle is 'What,' the middle circle is 'How,' and the inner circle is 'Why.'"

What: The products and services you offer to customers.

How: The factors that differentiate you from competitors.

Why: Your purpose or philosophy of existence.

Sinek says: "People don't buy what you do; they buy why you do it. Your goal is not to do business with everyone who needs what you have; it's to do business with those who believe what you believe."

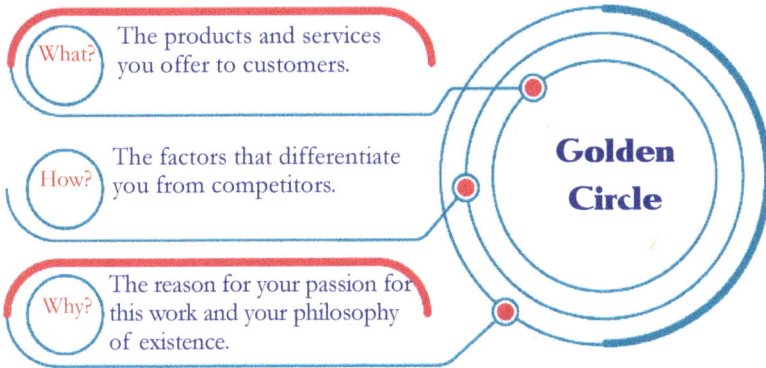

You have a product or service that answers this "why." So, the brand philosophy is the "why" of the company, determining how you should do your work based on this "why." Is it just to make money? To avoid being idle? Simply to keep a company going? Or is it truly needed? If it is genuinely needed, who needs it? Start your sentence with "why" to find your brand's philosophy. Now, as you think about it, you realize that the more you reflect on it, the more insights come to mind. This is a feature of business mastery, as the brand philosophy reveals the true value of the business. This "why" of the brand is what customers are willing to pay for.

The brand philosophy is related to your activity and guides your customers to discover more about you. McDonald's explains its brand philosophy in the simplest terms: "Food, People, Enjoyment." The brand philosophy enables you to discuss your products, advertising, location, and sales methods with customers. It helps create a unified and cohesive image for the audience, as you display the brand philosophy in your words, actions, and advertisements. The brand philosophy shows up in every interaction with your customers, and over time, they understand and perceive it.

▶ How to Create a Brand Philosophy

• Finding the "Why" Behind What You Do:

If you can make your audience clearly understand your "why," potential customers quickly become advocates who share your values and beliefs.

• How You Execute Your Work:

After defining your purpose, think about how you will achieve it. Your approach should be distinct from your competitors to establish your position in the market.

• What You Do for Your Customers:

All business activities aim to solve problems and meet customer needs. You must know which of your customers' needs your products or services fulfill.

• Edit and Refine:

Recognize that customer wants and needs are constantly changing, and it is essential to adapt your products and services accordingly.

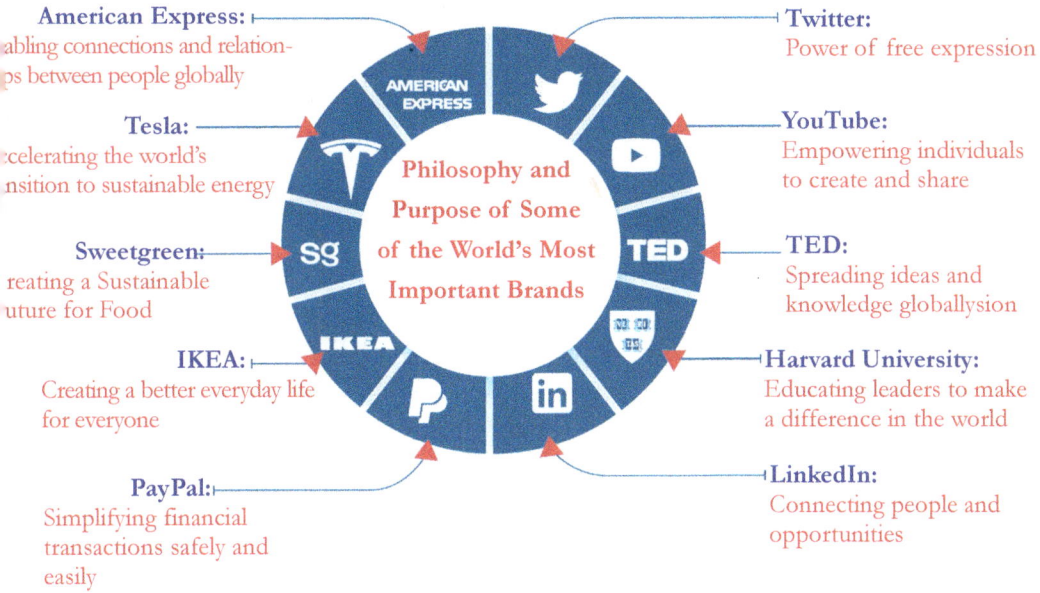

Philosophy and Purpose of Some of the World's Most Important Brands

American Express: Enabling connections and relationships between people globally

Tesla: Accelerating the world's transition to sustainable energy

Sweetgreen: Creating a Sustainable Future for Food

IKEA: Creating a better everyday life for everyone

PayPal: Simplifying financial transactions safely and easily

Twitter: Power of free expression

YouTube: Empowering individuals to create and share

TED: Spreading ideas and knowledge globallysion

Harvard University: Educating leaders to make a difference in the world

LinkedIn: Connecting people and opportunities

▶ Brand Vision

Behind every successful brand, there is a passionate person who inspires others to see the future differently. When you start a business, you must first define its fundamental principles so that, along the way, you know which opportunities to pursue and have a benchmark to evaluate your performance. For this reason, you need a brand vision.

The vision statement is designed to inspire employees, attract investors, and engage customers' imaginations. This statement outlines a picture of your business and the impact you want it to have on the world. There are key differences between the brand philosophy and the vision statement.

Vision	Brand Philosophy
What long-term growth do you aim to achieve?	**What do you do?**
What impact do you want to make on the world?	**What do you do?**
What ideal goals do you have for the future?	**Why do you do it?**

Your vision statement should reflect the personality of your organization. It doesn't matter how unique a statement is in terms of size, shape, or structure, a good vision statement must have the following characteristics:

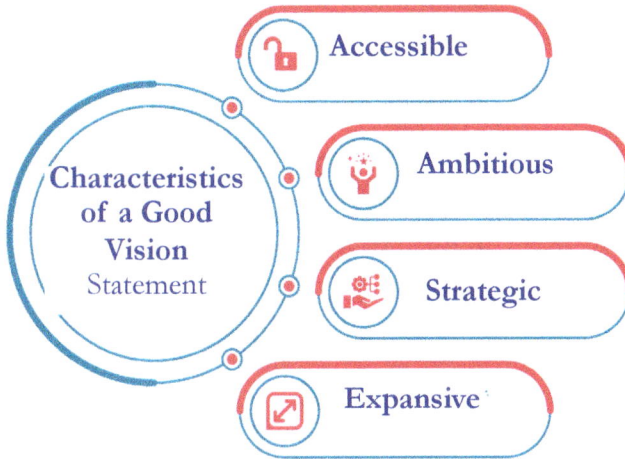

▶ Checklist for Writing a Brand Vision Statement

The brand vision reflects and supports the business strategy, energizes and inspires employees and partners, and sparks a wave of ideas for marketing programs.

• Identify Stakeholders

The vision statement should represent the views and values of the entire company. Therefore, when drafting it, incorporate input from various parts of the organization, such as shareholders, the board of directors, employees, and others.

Employees

....
....
....

Investors

....
....
....

Board Members

....
....
....

Partners

....
....
....

Shareholders

....
....
....

Customer Segments

....
....
....

List of Keywords Related to Different Sections

Keywords are words that, when heard, direct the mind toward a specific topic. You should at least gather keywords related to the following areas:

Your Products or Services

....

....

Your Mission and Values

....

....

....

Your Company's Goals and Initiatives

....

....

....

Your Company's Long-Term Strategic Plan

....

....

....

Attributes that Describe Your Company, Products, Services, Teams, Community, and Ideal Future

....

....

....

Attributes that Describe How Your Company Operates ....

....

....

Impactful Questions

What is the main goal of our organization?

....

....

....

What is the core mission of our company?

....

....

....

What are our company's strengths?

....

....

....

What are our company's values?

....

....

....

Why does what we create matter?

....

....

....

How do we want to make a difference as a company?

....

....

....

What are our most ambitious goals?

....

....

....

....

What impact do we want our company to have on the world?

....

....

....

....

If our company succeeded in everything it set out to do, what difference would it make in the world?

....

....

....

....

▶ Brand Value

Brand values are what your company believes in and stands by. These values are the principles that guide your business decisions and are inherent to your brand. Your brand values can help you create more meaningful relationships with your customers. In today's fast-paced world, you have only a few seconds to make an impact on your audience, so you need to know what you want to say and how to convey it. According to research, 64% of consumers stated that having shared values with a brand is their primary reason for choosing it.

When selecting your brand values, you should consider two points:

1. **Ensure that you choose values that are currently valid for you, not those you hope to achieve in the future.** These principles should reflect who you truly are. Your aspirations do not lend credibility to your brand. What quality do you genuinely offer now? If you select values that do not truly align with you, customers will feel deceived. For a moment, imagine choosing "quality" as one of your brand values, but your packaging seems unprofessional. Customers have specific expectations from a quality product, and it is essential that your business acts in accordance with this value. Always remain credible and trustworthy.

2. **Unique values are more memorable and meaningful.** Traditional values can also be chosen, but they must align with the organization's approach to ensure they are properly understood. Below is a list of **brand values** that you can use.

Accessible	Responsible	Precise	Adventurous
Transparent	Caring	Comfortable	Committed
Customer-Centric	Explorer	Diverse	Dreamer
Enjoyable	Fun	Passionate	Authentic
Discovery	Fairness	Faith	Family
Genius	Grateful	Guiding	Happiness
Kindness	Love	Leadership	Vitality
Sustainability	Playfulness	Positivity	Potential
Sharing	Service	Simplicity	Purity
Gratefulness	Wealth	Unity	Beauty
Compassion	Authenticity	Awareness	Mastery

Ease of Use	Stability	Confidence	Empathy
Environmental Care	Effectiveness	Elegance	Excellence
Flexibility	Equality	Ethics	Friendship
Humor	Focus	Freedom	Intelligence
Loyalty	Independence	Inspiration	Optimism
Quality	Motivation	Authenticity	Attention
Speed	Well-being	Prudence	Supportive
Courage	Creativity	Sustainability	Warmth
Being Present	Surprise	Welcoming	Expertise
Empowerment	Calmness	Excitement	Growth
Safety	Curiosity	Understanding	Joy
Talent	Energy	Sincerity	Peace
Reflection	Satisfaction	Patience	Truth

When you have chosen your brand values, make sure to use them in your communications with your customers. If you select values that genuinely represent your brand, your customers will be more drawn to it (remember that they likely chose your business because your values align with theirs). Promoting these values deepens their connection with you. When your brand values are authentic and unique, you can easily distinguish yourself and establish a strong relationship with your audience.

▶ Brand Promise

A brand is a promise, a commitment. If your customers are willing to spend money on you, what costs are you incurring for them? The brand promise is the frontline in the battle against competitors. In the brand promise, you define and specify the commitment your brand has towards its audience community. This promise is a duty you have towards your audience, based on your brand's philosophy.

"We were created to ...."

What you write in the blank is your brand promise. The brand promise should be simple and understandable. It should be enduring, meaning it should not be forgotten in ten years what commitment or promise you made to your audience. It should be exciting and, most importantly, believable. If you have a brand promise, your salespeople will not easily give empty promises during sales meetings.

We present the ... [brand philosophy] ..., ... [brand promise] ... with ... [products and services] ..., to fulfill this brand promise for ... [target market] ... and create ... [the benefits of collaborating with you] ....

Now let's complete the above statements and add the brand philosophy as well. The Walmart chain store states its brand philosophy as:

> "We exist to help people save money." What is its promise? It says: "Save your money and improve your life." Therefore, its services are designed in such a way that customers feel comfortable while shopping. You need to work on the brand promise and brand philosophy so thoroughly that it accurately reflects the commitment you want to convey to your audience in every aspect of your business.

In how you create your business, in human resources, finances, costs, and the equipment you provide, there should be traces of your brand promise.

The brand promise must be ingrained in the organization so that every time the audience interacts with the brand, this commitment is reiterated and recalled.

Advertisements and marketing messages are supposed to promote the brand promise. The brand promise should be convincing, unique, memorable, and clear. Nowadays, savvy customers can discern which brands have a genuine promise and which are merely trying to attract attention.

▶ Brand Positioning

Brand positioning means finding a suitable position in the minds of a specific group of customers within a market segment so that they view this product or service in a favorable and positive way. The goal of this is to maximize the potential benefits for the organization. In brand positioning, you must find your unique space that resonates with your audience.

Brand positioning allows you to differentiate yourself from competitors. This differentiation helps your business increase brand awareness and justify pricing. Not all brand positioning strategies are the same or have the same objectives.

▶ Brand Positioning Evaluation

Characteristics	Your Opinion	Managers' Opinion	Employees' Opinion	Customers' Opinion
	Excellent ☐ Good ☐ Average ☐	Excellent ☐ Good ☐ Average ☐	Excellent ☐ Good ☐ Average ☐	Excellent ☐ Good ☐ Average ☐

Name three of the most important charactcristics of your best-selling products or services:

....
....
....
....
....
....
....

For which characteristic of your products or services have you invested the most time and cost?

....
....
....
....
....
....
....

▶ **Brand Positioning Evaluation**

Characteristics	Your Opinion	Managers' Opinion	Employees' Opinion	Customers' Opinion
	Excellent ☐	Excellent ☐	Excellent ☐	Excellent ☐
	Good ☐	Good ☐	Good ☐	Good ☐
	Average ☐	Average ☐	Average ☐	Average ☐

What value do customers seek when purchasing your product?

....

....

....

....

....

....

....

....

What unique characteristics do your customers receive from your business that they cannot find elsewhere?

....

....

....

....

....

....

....

The brand positioning document serves as a roadmap that guides us on the path to success. This document encompasses all elements of a brand, from its name and slogan to its strategy, and shows us where we currently stand, what shortcomings we have, and where we need to go. You must provide reasons for individuals to choose you; otherwise, they will not distinguish between you and your competitors.

The most important questions you need to answer are:

What position do you offer to customers?

....

....

....

Why should they choose you?

....

....

....

What distinctive feature do you have for the audience to consider?

....

....

....

What method are you currently using to address their issues?

....

....

....

Are your benefits compelling enough for customers to abandon their previous product?

....

....

▶ **Brand Positioning Document**

What Needs to Be Done for Positioning	Description
Fundamental Differentiation	**Characteristics That Differentiate Our Brand from Others:** ....
Understanding Competitors	**Those Who Hold a High Position in Our Product Category and Have Taken Our Market Share:** ....
Finding Development and Advancement Resources	**Which Competitors Can We Take Market Share From? (Even in Other Product Categories)** ....
Identifying Target Customers	**Who Do We Want to Sell To?** ....

What Needs to Be Done for Positioning	Description
Identify Physical Benefits	In which areas are we strong (product efficiency), and in which areas are competitors weak? ....
Identify Emotional Benefits	What feeling does it convey to the consumer, and what experience does it create for them? ....
Explain the Reasons for Purchase	How do you strengthen and support your advantages? ....
Creating a Personality for the Brand	Designing a Human-like Personality for the Brand ....

What Needs to Be Done for Positioning	Description
Pricing Strategy	**On what basis are pricing and discounts determined according to positioning?** ....
Financial Goals, Required Budget	**Has the brand reached profitability?** ....
Market Share for This Year	**Awareness, Incentivizing, and Reminder** ....
Advertising Goals	**Product Trial, Repeat Purchase, Offering** ....

What Needs to Be Done for Positioning	Description
Sales Promotion Goals	**Various Methods and Channels**

Brand Story · Brand Personality · Visual Identity · Communication Style · Product and Service · Literature · Brand Feelings

Brand Identity

▶ Brand Name

Choosing a brand name is the first step on a long and challenging journey of branding; however, branding is more than just a name. Your business evolves, your customers change, but the name remains the same. The brand name is the most enduring element of a business. Customers recognize your business based on your brand name. Some brands use Persian words in their names, while others use foreign words. Some business owners also use their names for branding. Some have opted for abbreviations, while others have preferred not to use this method. Several brands have incorporated words related to their business, while others have chosen general names that do not have a direct connection to their field of activity. When selecting a trade name or brand name, do not limit yourself to a single pattern. There are many diverse styles available. However, many of us get fixated on a specific approach and overlook other methods and options.

What characteristics should a brand name have?

- It should be short and appealing;
- It should be easy to pronounce and write;
- It should be unique and specific to the brand;
- It should have international usability;
- It should be registrable;
- It should be visually appealing and legible.

DescriptiveNames
Names that describe our activity:
- WordCrafters
- Pizza Hut

Acronyms

Using acronyms together to create a pronounceable and acceptable word.

- IBM,
- BMW,
- KFC

Associative

Based on linking a feature with the organization's services. The type of brand naming allows for brand expansion in the future as well.

- Future Shop
- Starbucks.
- Uber (superior)

Unrelated

Names that do not relate to what they produce or offer. These names have independent meanings; however, this type of naming leaves you open for producing a wide range of products, but finding a connection to the brand in this method can be time-consuming.

- Apple
- Amazon
- Tesla

Invented

Names that have no specific meaning and are created by the brand owner themselves. Examples of invented names include:
- Kodak
- Sony
- VZOUX

Name or Surname of the Founder

Naming based on the name or surname of the brand's founder. This is more common in family businesses.

- "Dell" from Michael Dell in the laptop and computer industry

- "20th Century Fox" from William Fox
- Gucci – Named after Guccio Gucci, the brand's founder.
- Ferrari – Named after Enzo Ferrari, founder of the luxury car brand

▶ Evaluating Different Options for Choosing a Brand Name

Do not focus solely on one method. Consider all aspects of naming and incorporate more ideas to increase your chances of arriving at the best option.

• Be Cautious of Similar Meanings

If you intend to export or engage in commerce, pay attention to the meanings of names in other cultures and languages. Some words may have negative meanings in the literature and culture of other countries.

• Be Aware of Similar Brands

Ideally, your brand should be completely unique, and no one should have used it before. However, this doesn't always happen in practice, and you may find that the name you have in mind has also been used in another industry. For instance, there is both Mahan Airlines and Mahan Institute of Higher Education.

- To start a business, it is essential to ensure that your chosen brand name is unique within your field of activity. You can take the following actions:
- Search for your desired brand name online. This will help you determine whether your chosen brand name is used by another person or business.
- Visit the Intellectual Property Center's website. This site allows you to verify whether your desired trademark is registered in Iran.
- Search for hashtags related to your desired brand name on so-

cial media. This will help you see if your desired brand name is being used in the virtual space.

Our suggestion is that even if you are satisfied with choosing a brand name that has been used in other industries, at least ensure that it is not infamous in its own industry.

● Conduct a Radio Test

The radio test, sometimes referred to as a "phone test," is a simple test to gauge the appropriateness of a brand name. It is recommended to verbally (in person or by phone or any other audio method) tell your desired brand name to several people and ask them to write it down. Ideally, many of your audience should be able to spell the brand name correctly. If a large number misspell it, you may need to reconsider the brand name. Jeff Bezos initially considered another name for Amazon (Cadabra), but his lawyer warned him that this word could be misheard as "cadaver," and Bezos dropped that name.

● Check the Associations

You can tell a few people who are not familiar with your product or service the name you have in mind for the brand and ask what adjectives or features come to their minds. You don't need them to say exactly what you have in mind; rather, you should ensure that the name you have chosen for your brand does not conflict with the identity you intend to create.

● Ensure Domain and Social Media IDs are Available

All websites that register domains also have the ability to check the availability of domains. Make sure you can secure a domain for your brand. Conduct a bit of research regarding social media as well. Even if you can't create an account exactly under your desired brand name, make sure there are related and similar names available that you can use.

● Read the First Page of Google Results Link by Link

Search for your brand on Google and carefully review the first page.

Here, do not just look for records of similar brands; also consider a crucial question: Does this brand have the potential to reach the first page of Google with consistent and strategic efforts in SEO? If there are powerful and prominent competitors in the top ranks of the search results, it may be better to think of another name.

● How Much Potential Does Your Chosen Name Have for Future Expansion?

It is difficult to predict exactly what you will do three, five, or ten years from now. Many businesses have completely changed their paths over time. Nevertheless, think about what activities you might pursue in five or ten years and what other products or services you might offer. Does the brand you choose today have the capacity to encompass a broader range of products and services?

● Conduct Surveys from Your Brand Audience if Possible

If you have a media platform or access to your audience base or can allocate a small budget for research, present a few final options for review and evaluation by others. You might be able to create several identical product samples, only differing in brand name, and present them to the public to see which one they choose. Alternatively, you could design a landing page and direct people to it, making decisions about the brand's suitability based on visitor reactions. Even a simple oral survey is better than relying solely on your judgment.

▶ Brand Archetype

Brand archetypes can give your brand a fresh meaning, as they show the patterns you use to conduct your business. Carl Gustav Jung believed that we tend to engage in predetermined behaviors. In fact, archetypes are images and forms that have entered the human subconscious through the repeated experiences of ancient ancestors. Archetypes can present your brand's mission in a way that is familiar and easily recognizable to everyone. Anyone can describe you in hundreds of different ways, but you are the one who can direct others' thinking in the way you want and ensure that they see you as you wish. Before taking any action, you must understand what mindset people have about you.

Here, we describe twelve archetypes for you. One of them is your primary archetype. You can examine which archetype aligns with the behavior of those around you. I suggest you create a list of three to five words that you would like people to use to describe your brand. Then, write a list of three to five words that you do not want to be described by.

Do you want to take a quick self-awareness test? Text ten people who are close enough but not too familiar with you and ask them to describe you. Then see if their words match your list.

1. Caregiver / Supporter / Guardian

Description and Characteristics	Caregivers are individuals well-known for their commitment to helping others. They dedicate themselves to their actions and place great importance on personal relationships.
Archetypes	▶ Caring Parent ▶ Doctor and Nurse ▶ Supporter and Defense Attorney ▶ Nurturer
Examples	▶ Mother Teresa ▶ Pampers ▶ Volvo

2. Hero

Description and Characteristics	Where there is a will, there is a way. These individuals seek ways to demonstrate their heroism in chaotic situations. They have strong beliefs and stand firm on them. Such individuals are courageous, prideful, confident, motivated, assured, and determined.
Archetypes	▶ Pioneer ▶ Coach ▶ Bold
Examples	▶ Nelson Mandela ▶ Anousheh Ansari (the first Iranian woman in space) ▶ FedEx ▶ Nike

3. Creator / Innovator

Description and Characteristics	This archetype is often seen in entrepreneurs, writers, and artists. They dream and find a way to turn that dream into reality. These individuals seek to create something of themselves that will remain in a physical and visual form. Such a person is inclined to create a lasting product or experience that realizes their vision. They are innovators who do not accept compromise and are often the first to understand a concept, pushing the boundaries of creativity and design.
Archetypes	▶ Artistic ▶ Creative ▶ Inventor ▶ Idealistic
Examples	▶ Leonardo da Vinci ▶ Mahmoud Farshchian ▶ Steve Jobs ▶ Masoud Sarami ▶ Walt Disney

4. Explorer / Researcher

Description and Characteristics	They seek discovery and independence and are curious about everything. They are not afraid to take risks and feel invigorated and energized by pushing boundaries. They are optimistic and believe that anything is possible.
Archetypes	▶ Lone Wolf ▶ Explorer ▶ Pioneer
Examples	▶ Marco Polo ▶ Christopher Columbus ▶ Richard Branson ▶ Red Bull ▶ Jeep

5. Jester

| Description and Characteristics | The jester embody joy and find pleasure in the present moment. They have significant insights to share and thrive on breaking rules, drawing joy from entertainment, playfulness, and reflection. This archetype is influenced by religious, traditional, and social perspectives, resulting in a character that represents humor and amusement. If your primary audience consists of young people, consider incorporating the clown archetype alongside the rebellious character to engage them effectively. |

Archetypes

- ▶ Comedian
- ▶ Witty

Examples

- ▶ Charlie Chaplin
- ▶ Pepsi
- ▶ Fanta

6. Lover

Description and Characteristics	Love is one of the most important concepts in life. This archetype is associated with closeness to people, situations, and activities that we cherish. It is commonly seen in Hollywood films. Many luxury and cosmetic brands are also drawn to this archetype due to their inherent nature. For a lover, physical and emotional intimacy, as well as pleasure, are prioritized. Consequently, enhancing attractiveness is of great significance to them.
Archetypes	▶ Harmonizer ▶ Connector and Companion
Examples	▶ Chanel ▶ Victoria's Secret ▶ Dior ▶ Alfa Romeo

7. Outlaw

Description and Characteristics	An individualist who rebels and breaks the rules, these people go against the flow. If your target audience mainly consists of the younger generation, the rule-breaker archetype can be highly effective in your branding efforts. This archetype embodies a spirit of rebellion, opposing restrictive norms and conventions.
Archetypes	▶ Problem Solver ▶ Challenge and Competition Lover ▶ Tradition Breaker ▶ Pioneer
Examples	▶ Harley-Davidson ▶ Uber ▶ PayPal

8. Innocent

Description and Characteristics	Often depicted as a child, this character embodies a moral essence with good intentions, resembling an innocent child. This persona steers clear of evil and deceit, upholding ethics at their highest standard. Some business owners use this archetype, at least temporarily, to shape their brand image.
Archetypes	▶ Optimist ▶ Innocent ▶ Encourager
Examples	▶ Coca-Cola ▶ McDonald's ▶ Nestlé

9. Ruler

Description and Characteristics	The Ruler controls the conditions and brings order to chaos. These individuals aim to organize everything. If you choose this archetype for your brand, you should focus on instilling a sense of power and authority in your target audience. Accountants, managers, and senior financial staff often embody this archetype. Margaret Thatcher, the former Prime Minister of the United Kingdom, is a prime example of this archetype.
Archetypes	▶ Peacemaker ▶ Guide ▶ Powerful
Examples	▶ Benz ▶ Rolls Royce ▶ Rolex

10. Everyman

Description and Characteristics	These individuals are satisfied with who they are and want to connect with others. In the business world, managers who do not take themselves too seriously often use this archetype. They derive joy from watching football and interact with people who break social boundaries. Successful individuals in the sales field fall into this category. Such people do not intend to change you or your habits; rather, they choose to stay with you along the way.
Archetypes	▶ Realist ▶ Democrat ▶ Friend and Companion
Examples	▶ IKEA ▶ GAP ▶ eBay

11. Sage

Description and Characteristics	They help others gain a better understanding of their world. Plato is a prime example of this archetype. They convey the message that through study, you can achieve greater comprehension and insight. Some companies, like McKinsey, exemplify this archetype by hiring educated individuals and training them. If you align certain brands in educational, news, and media sectors with this archetype, you will understand their mission entirely.
Archetypes	▶ Coach ▶ Expert ▶ Researcher
Examples	▶ Ted ▶ Google ▶ The New York Times

12. Magician

Description and Characteristics	Come with me, and I'll introduce you to a world full of excitement and mystery. A magician never reveals their secrets and will astonish you with colorful and enigmatic tricks. Creating the impossible and turning dreams into reality is not out of reach with the magician brand personality. Brands that embody the magician archetype tend to embrace dreaming, charisma, imagination, and idealism. The magician pays attention to meaningful and unexpected events.
Archetypes	▶ Dreamer ▶ Healer ▶ Catalyst for Change
Examples	▶ Harry Potter ▶ Plastic Surgeons ▶ Sony ▶ MAC Cosmetics ▶ Walt Disney

The more our brand leans toward one of these archetypes, the more we favor that archetype. People, consciously or unconsciously, want to understand what a brand represents. If a brand consistently demonstrates the values and beliefs of a specific archetype, people feel that they know the brand and can trust it. Stability and reliability in representing an archetype are crucial for building that sense of familiarity and trust.

▶ Visual Identity

Visual identity means that a brand has an image in the minds of its audience. This image may include the logo, packaging, color, and more. When names like Takmakaron, Ahmad Tea, or Nike come to mind, what colors or images do you associate with them? This is the essence of visual identity.

Visual identity consists of various elements. It is akin to a person preparing for a wedding; we need to see what personality and style they have, and how they communicate. This visual identity of your organization reflects its style and model of presentation. Every business requires a distinct and memorable personality that can linger in the audience's mind. For this, a set of tools is needed to evoke a specific image of the brand in the minds of the audience. The power of an image is worth a thousand words. It is this mental imagery that allows your organization to establish a place in the minds of your audience.

The visual identity of a company includes several tools, the first being the logo. A logo is a symbol of the entire identity, encompassing the company emblem, logotype, or insignia. When you see the logo, it reminds you of that company.

Items such as packaging, letterheads, business cards, brochures, catalogs, guides, and also websites and applications are all tools of visual identity. These tools convey the brand's values to the audience using visual elements such as color, font, and design style. The shape, design, and packaging of products contribute to their visual identity. Some companies also include uniforms in their visual identity. The interior decoration and exterior appearance of your workplace are also part of your visual identity. For instance, the uniform appearance of Bank Mellat across all branches is part of that bank's visual identity. The organizational color or font you use also defines the visual identity.

Aim for consistency in the color schemes and fonts you use across your entire system to make a stronger impression on others. Visual identity serves as the display or showcase of your work, aiming to create a cohesive image that reflects the organization. If we liken the brand to a house, visual identity represents its decor. Whenever you notice that others are copying you, it indicates that you have succeeded.

Your brand needs a clear image to be etched in the minds of your audience. To create this image, all visual elements must be designed to communicate effectively with the audience. This includes:

- Designing logos and symbols
- Choosing colors
- Designing mascots
- Selecting brand fonts
- Creating brand patterns
- Choosing the brand voice
- Designing clothing
- Designing environmental and store elements
- Designing product and service packaging
- Designing forms and checklists
- Designing vehicle bodies
- Designing stationery
- Designing email signatures
- Designing social media layouts
- Designing Instagram highlights
- Designing flyers
- Designing favicons for websites
- Designing internal software and website banners
- Designing flags
- Designing badges
- Designing entrance signs
- Designing directional signs
- Designing employee IDs
- Designing promotional gifts
- Designing motion logos

● Logo

A logo is a unique graphic symbol that represents a company, product, or service. It serves as an identifier for the organization and helps customers remember and connect with your company.

Characteristics of a Good Logo:

- Simplicity
- Distinctiveness
- Immediate impact on the audience's mind

● Typography

Typography is a type of logo where the brand name is designed with a specific font. According to Steve Jobs: "Simple can be harder than complex." Designing a creative logo requires attention to detail. If you prefer typography logos, you will have several leading options. Some brands, such as Coca-Cola, create their own custom font **(Typeface)**, which is not only time-consuming but also requires a professional designer. You need to select a font that conveys the essence of your brand.

Feature	Dependency
Sensitivity to font and color schemes	Relates to the type and style of logotype design
Influence of details, meanings of symbols	Directly connected to creating visual identity
Skill in influencing audience emotions	Ability to create a sense of familiarity and immediate connection

● Alphabet Logos

These logos consist of a single letter. Often, businesses that use the first letter of their brand name for the logo also have another version that includes their full business name. Utilizing just one letter in a logo makes it practical for mobile applications, favicons, and profile pictures on social networks. Alphabet logos, which utilize letters, can effectively imprint themselves in the audience's mind. This type of logo visually represents the brand name using letters, along with attractive color schemes and designs.

Feature	Dependency
Includes only one letter	Suitable for brands with long names
Small and recognizable	Simple and undetailed design
High scalability	Strong potential for memorability

● Monogram or Abbreviated Logos

Monograms are a type of logo formed from the initial letters of a business's name. Most brands with a monogram logo are referred to by their abbreviated versions. For example, IBM or NASA are instances of brands that have become commonly known by their acronyms. Typically, we refer to the "National Aeronautics and Space Administration" as "NASA." Monogram logos also utilize fonts. The font used in these logos should convey the brand's identity. This font can either be chosen from existing options or custom-designed.

Feature	Dependency
Simple and elegant	High credibility and longevity
Scalability	Represents brand values
Conveys a sense of familiarity	Instant recognition by the audience

● Symbols and Iconic Logos

Logos can include symbols or images that distinctly represent the brand or activity. Typically, logos in this style depict an object from the real world. For example, the Apple logo features a simple symbol. Symbols can be used skillfully to convey the brand's values or messages; for instance, the Twitter logo represents hope and freedom.

Finding the right image or symbol for your logo can be a significant challenge for your business, especially if you are a new or emerging brand. Over time, there is a likelihood of growth, change, and the introduction of new products and services. It takes time for customers to recognize your logo and establish a connection between the logo and your brand in their minds. You can even incorporate your brand name into the logo.

The logo should be a lasting symbol that undergoes minimal changes over time and should align with the brand's name and values.

Feature	Dependency
Display of an object from the real world	Time-consuming to link the logo with the brand in the mind
Variety in design	High impact
Showcasing the brand's values or message	Creates a clear and memorable image

● Abstract Logo

Abstract logos are also image-based but, unlike images that depict a real object, these logos are more symbolic. For example, an image of a lion symbolizes the strength of the brand. Since abstract logos do not depict a recognizable and specific object, they have the ability to create a unique design. It is essential to clearly understand what message you intend to convey. Because the names of some brands may not be understandable in different languages, using an abstract logo is recommended for brands that aim to operate on an international level.

Feature	Dependency
Image-based	Symbolic, suitable for global brands
Unique	Differentiation among competitors
Simple and geometric reflection of values	Applicable in well-known brands

● **Mascot Logos**

Mascots are a type of logo designed around a character, such as the cow logo of "Mihan Milk". This character serves as a representative and ambassador for the brand, reflecting its identity. Mascot logos can be fictional characters or real individuals, and they establish a strong connection with customers because people naturally relate better to humans and personalities than to objects.

First, assess whether the nature of your business is suitable for this type of logo. Examples of successful mascot logos in the Iranian market include Cheetos and Chuckles.

Feature	Dependency
Illustrated characters as brand ambassadors	Creates a fun, friendly, and engaging atmosphere
Friendly and attractive	Suitable for families and children
Cartoonish and cheerful	Strong symbol in the minds of the audience

● **Combined Logos**

This style of logo is very popular due to the diversity among business-es. Companies create various versions of their logo and use them for different purposes. An interesting point is that all versions should have a clear and cohesive visual language. For example, the Lacoste brand uses a combined logo on its website, but on most of its products, only the green crocodile image is visible. For companies that are not yet well-known, combined logos are a good starting point and help create awareness and recognition for the brand. Over time, you will have the flexibility to use only the textual or visual part of your logo while still ensuring that your audience recognizes your brand.

Feature	Dependency
Contains both image and text	Better brand message delivery (especially if you have multiple message).
Effectiveness in communication	Help with brand recognition
Flexibility in usage	Quick connection to the brand

● **Dynamic Logos**

One type of logo is dynamic logos, which operate outside of the norm and can take on various shapes. This may seem strange, as the general rule of logo design is stability and uniformity. However, dynamic logos can be applied everywhere. These styles of logos require a framework that appears in every version of the logo. For example, when we open the Google website, we see its familiar typography, which represents symbols of historical figures, celebrations, or holidays based on the occasion. Nonetheless, we always recognize that this is the Google logo. In fact, the brand is so well-known that the logo is identifiable in any shape or form. This logo is not only relevant and up-to-date but also reinforces the brand's message.

Feature	Dependency
Out of the ordinary	Brands with strong influence
Based on a core framework but flexible	Reinforcing the brand message
Creativity generator	Conveying the brand's stories and values

▶ The Impact of Color in Branding

Color plays a crucial role in evoking emotions among audiences, which is why it is more memorable and distinctive. However, selecting a color that aligns with the organization's goals and values is a significant consideration that designers must pay attention to. A company targeting young audiences should use vibrant and lively colors. It is essential to consider the audience's demographics, including gender, social class, age, and culture, when making decisions about color.

Important Questions for Choosing a Brand Color

- Does this color have a positive meaning in the target market?
- Does this color remind people of competitors' products?
- Does this color have meaning in foreign markets?
- Is this color durable?
- What background colors can be used?
- Does this color show well after printing?
- What meaning has been assigned to this color?

What follows are the colors that are most frequently used in brands:

Color	Positive Traits	Negative Traits	Suitable	Unsuitable
White	▶ Purity and innocence ▶ Freshness and novelty ▶ Cleanliness ▶ Clarity ▶ Simplicity ▶ Perfection ▶ Honor ▶ Virtue	▶ Sterilization ▶ Coldness ▶ Isolation and loneliness ▶ Unfriendliness ▶ Emptiness ▶ Being inexperienced ▶ Being untrained	▶ Hospital and healthcare clinics ▶ Weddings and marriage celebrations ▶ Dairy products ▶ Automobiles ▶ Clothing ▶ Charities	▶ Hot food industry ▶ Agriculture ▶ Finance ▶ Energy
Black	▶ Power ▶ Security ▶ Credibility ▶ Elegance ▶ Durability ▶ Ceremony ▶ Opulence	▶ Oppression ▶ Darkness ▶ Terror ▶ Evil ▶ Mourning ▶ Fear and Threat	▶ Clubs ▶ Very Luxury Brands ▶ Technology ▶ Apparel ▶ Vehicles	▶ Food ▶ Healthcare ▶ Finance ▶ Energy

Color	Positive Traits	Negative Traits	Suitable	Unsuitable
Red	Passion and enthusiasm and love; Increase in appetite; Power; Fearlessness; Excitement; High energy; Warmth; Fire; Confidence; Attention	Decreased focus; Analysis; Anger; Danger; Warning; Defiance; Pain; War	Food industry; Sports; Recreation; Transportation; Automotive	Airplane; Clothing; Financial; Energy-related industries; Medical and healthcare
Blue "It has the most popularity among the people of the world."	Masculine color; Calming; Mature; Clarity; Communication; Stability and trust; Loyalty; Logic; Innocence	Loss of Appetite; Poisoning; Being rotten; Coldness; Insensitivity; Unkindness; Discomfort	Diets aimed at weight loss; Banks; Yoga clubs; Protective brands; Medical; Healthcare; Technology; Consulting; Energy; Financial; Communications	Clothing; Food industry

Color	Positive Traits	Negative Traits	Suitable	Unsuitable
Green	It does not strain the eyes It is better seen in the dark Evocative of nature Balance Security Reassurance Health Happiness Hope Freshness Prosperity Reduces blood pressure and heart rate Good luck Growth Wealth Relief Restoration Well-being Stability	Laziness Stagnation Envy Sluggishness and numbness Lack of energy Illness (surgical experiences)	Waiting rooms Financial organizations Medical centers Food industries Agriculture Environment Medicine and health Education Religious affairs Technology Energy Household appliances	Airplanes Clothing Vehicles

Color	Positive Traits	Negative Traits	Suitable	Unsuitable
Yellow	▶ Increase in metabolism ▶ Self-esteem generator ▶ It is more ▶ eye-catching than other colors ▶ Stimulating ▶ Atten ▶ tion-grab-bing ▶ Warmth ▶ Happiness ▶ Creativity ▶ Wisdom ▶ Cost-effec-tiveness ▶ Extraversion ▶ Optimism ▶ Financial capability	▶ Causing babies to cry ▶ Being irrational ▶ Fear ▶ Caution ▶ Anxiety ▶ Hopeless-ness ▶ Anger ▶ Danger	▶ Food industries ▶ Energy ▶ Household appliances ▶ Sports ▶ Transporta-tion	▶ Airplane ▶ Clothing ▶ Finance

Color	Positive Traits	Negative Traits	Suitable	Unsuitable
Brown It is More favored by men than women.	▶ Serious ▶ Strong ▶ Reliable ▶ Earthy color ▶ Earthiness ▶ Support ▶ Warmth ▶ Old	▶ Conservatism ▶ Feeling of confusion ▶ Regret ▶ Lack of humor ▶ Heaviness ▶ Lack of charm and seduction ▶ Sadness ▶ Dirtiness ▶ Violence ▶ Old	▶ Food industries ▶ Agriculture ▶ Carpentry ▶ Legal affairs	▶ Clothing ▶ Transportation ▶ Fashion and beauty ▶ Entertainment
Gray	▶ Professional ▶ Neutral ▶ Efficiency ▶ Formality ▶ Classic ▶ Serious ▶ Mysterious ▶ Mature		▶ Large legal firms ▶ Children's clothing retail websites	

Color	Positive Traits	Negative Traits	Suitable	Unsuitable
Lavender	▶ Complexity within planning ▶ Logic ▶ Insight and cleverness ▶ Compassion and kindness ▶ Self-respect ▶ Satisfaction ▶ Change and transformation ▶ Acceptance ▶ New ideas ▶ Passion and enthusiasm ▶ Creativity ▶ Innovation ▶ Balance	▶ Shocking ▶ Cruel ▶ Opposition and non-conformity ▶ Carelessness and audacity ▶ Irritability ▶ Irregularity ▶ Transience		
Purple	▶ Royalty ▶ Wealth ▶ Luxury ▶ Seduction ▶ Complexity ▶ Creativity ▶ Imagination ▶ Charm ▶ Spirituality ▶ Magic ▶ Mystery	▶ Introversion ▶ Degradation and corruption ▶ Suppression ▶ Inferiority complex ▶ Excessiveness ▶ Moodiness (Sudden mood changes)	▶ Luxury and modern professions ▶ Medical and healthcare ▶ Technology ▶ Finance ▶ Psychology ▶ Humanitarian	▶ Agriculture ▶ Energy

Color	Positive Traits	Negative Traits	Suitable	Unsuitable
Orange	▶ Cheerfulness ▶ Motivation ▶ Movement ▶ Inspirational ▶ Excitement ▶ Enthusiasm ▶ Energizing ▶ Joyful ▶ Conveying a sense of value ▶ Conveying a sense of comfort ▶ Warmth, shelter, and food ▶ Courage ▶ Self-confidence ▶ Innovation ▶ Playfulness ▶ Friendship	▶ Deprivation ▶ Hopelessness ▶ Immaturity	▶ Advertising for Children ▶ Creative and Artistic Fashion Brands ▶ Technology ▶ Healthcare and Medical ▶ Food Industry ▶ Sports ▶ Recreation ▶ Transportation	▶ Airplanes ▶ Clothing ▶ Energy ▶ Finance
Pink	▶ Femininity and Youth ▶ Innocence ▶ Fun ▶ Being Girly ▶ Modern ▶ Happiness ▶ Sweetness ▶ Elegance ▶ Love ▶ Calmness	▶ Ironical	▶ Cakes and pastries ▶ Women's brands ▶ Luxury and modern businesses ▶ Fashion and beauty ▶ Cosmetic and personal care products	▶ Airplanes ▶ Vehicles ▶ Finance

▶ Brand Color Formula

Plan to choose three colors:

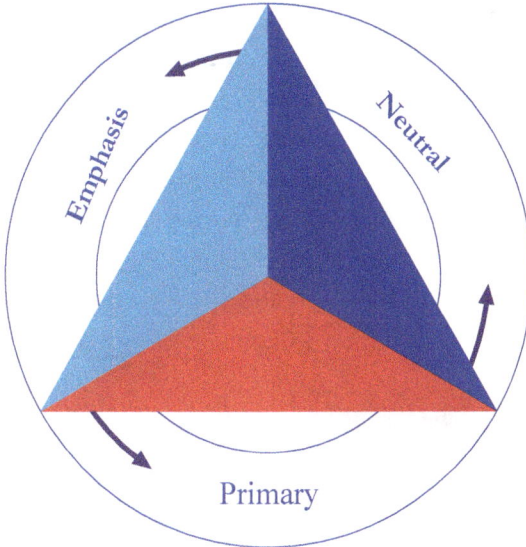

Your primary color should not only reflect the most important characteristic of your brand's personality, but it should also be appealing to your target audience. Your accent color will be the one you use the most after your primary color. This is slightly more complex than selecting the primary color, as there are more restrictions involved. In addition to aligning with the brand's personality, your accent color should visually complement the primary color.

Neutral colors are typically used as background colors to avoid drawing attention. These colors are usually gray, beige, white, or off-white. Black can also be an option, but it should be used carefully, as it can dominate the other colors.

Brand Visual Identity Checklist

Environmental Graphics

- [ ] Logo
- [ ] Font
- [ ] Letterhead
- [ ] Notepad
- [ ] Signature
- [ ] Business Card
- [ ] Signboard

Marketing and Advertising Tool

- [ ] Banner and print advertisement design
- [ ] Poster design
- [ ] Newspaper
- [ ] Web graphic template design
- [ ] Photos related to brand strategy
- [ ] Downloadable files
- [ ] Transport and management vehicles
- [ ] Packaging
- [ ] Label
- [ ] Carton

Website

- [ ] Brochure
- [ ] Catalog
- [ ] Price list
- [ ] Portfolio
- [ ] Name tag (Pin)

Internal and External Documents

- [ ] Email signature design
- [ ] Email newsletter design
- [ ] Facebook profile and cover
- [ ] LinkedIn profile and cover
- [ ] Instagram profile and cover
- [ ] Twitter profile and cover

Online Marketing

- [ ] Administrative forms
- [ ] Personnel forms
- [ ] ID card
- [ ] Social media

Organizational Id

- [ ] Direct signage
- [ ] Office entrance
- [ ] Building entrance

▶ Brand Verbal Identity

The way a brand communicates with its audience through the combination of three elements: language, text, and a defined tone, is referred to as the brand's Verbal Identity

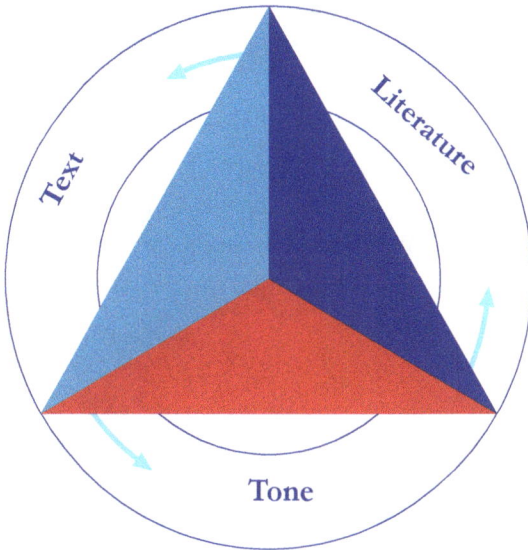

To introduce your brand, you must write a strong and comprehensive message that also addresses the questions and concerns of your customers. The tone is the way you engage with your audience, and it is made up of the words you choose and the rhythm of your speech. For example, the sentence "Mr. X has such a dignified personality" creates a different feeling compared to "Mr. X has such a heavy personality." This difference is due to the shift from the words "dignified" to "heavy." By changing words and the rhythm of your speech, you can create a distinct identity for your brand's verbal identity.

In defining your brand's tone, you determine whether it will be simple and friendly or formal and serious. This depends on your brand's core philosophy. For example, if your brand is aimed at children and teenagers, you cannot adopt a serious or formal tone. Are you speaking on behalf of an organization or a team? How logical or emotional is your language? In the messages you convey, do you rely on factual data and statistics, or do you speak of dreams and aspirations? In advertising messages, it's important to assess whether your language aligns with your brand's core values and promise. All the texts you create for your website, marketing tools, and advertising slogans should be designed with the target audience in mind, ensuring you communicate professionally. The words and sentences you use should reflect your brand's unique traits, which influence the personality, appearance, and behavior of your brand.

● Brand Voice

The voice of your brand is often remembered better than its visual identity, which tends to be weaker and more fragile. This is why you can easily remember songs you heard in your childhood or youth, even decades later. People can close their eyes, but they can't block out sounds. This is because sound is an involuntary and uncontrollable phenomenon, reaching the ear without prior permission and outside of one's control.

● Brand Packaging

Most brands focus solely on the product. Their emphasis is on designing and producing a product that proves its superiority in competition with others. However, packaging is often overlooked as part of the branding process. Product and goods packaging, regardless of the type, is very important. This is why the world's largest manufacturing companies collaborate with professional companies in the field of printing and packaging to ensure high product sales. Startups and newly established companies, aiming to enter the market, must compete with major brands. At the outset, these companies often do not have much capital for various forms of advertising, so the only effective method that does not incur extra costs is packaging. Of course, this doesn't mean that other marketing and branding strategies aren't important, but it's a method that can maintain the integrity of a brand's identity. Competitive branding in packaging products and services can be seen as an advantage. This can be done with both good intentions and business motives. In either case, corporate social responsibility can positively impact people's lives.

For instance, the packaging of Biotent gum uses Braille script. While this may seem like a simple touch, it positively influences consumer attitudes towards the brand. When customers see Biotent's packaging, they likely think that the brand cares about all its customers and is trying to pay attention to their differences, without neglecting their needs.

● Brand Messaging Design

The audience must receive a message from you to understand that they are your target and that you are capable of solving their problem and creating value for them.

● Designing a Slogan

According to research by Yankelovich, each person, on average, sees 5,000 brand names per day. This number has increased by 150% compared to thirty years ago. Think about advertising on social media, billboards, products and food items, radio ads, and more. So, how can you differentiate your brand? Slogans help people remember your brand. Advertising slogans are memorable phrases that convey positive emotions about a specific product while also highlighting its most important feature.

Exercise

Imagine you have been tasked with writing slogans for the following brands and their advertising campaigns. What creative slogans come to mind for you?

Brand	Your suggestion
Uber	
7up	
Cheetoz	
BMW	
HSBC	
Netflix	
Crest	
Puma	
Zara	
IKEA	

Add other brands and write your suggested slogans for them.

Brand	Your suggestion

This exercise will help you become more creative when choosing slogans for your advertising campaigns. This is because when you choose a slogan for another business or brand, your mind is more open and flexible. Below are examples of slogans used by these brands in their advertising campaigns:

▶ **Uber**
Current slogan: "On Our Way."
Previous slogan: "Get there."

▶ **7UP**
Current slogan: "Feels Good to Be You."
Classic slogan: "The Uncola."

▶ **Cheetoz**

Common tagline: "Dangerously Cheesy."

▶ **BMW**

Iconic slogan: "Sheer Driving Pleasure."

▶ **HSBC Bank**

Current slogan: "Opening up a world of opportunity."

▶ **Netflix**

Common tagline: "See What's Next."

▶ **Crest**

Current slogan: "Crest. Healthy, beautiful smiles for life."
Past slogans include: "Look, Ma, No Cavities!"

▶ **Puma**

Current slogan: "Forever Faster."

▶ **Zara**

Commonly associated message: "Love Your Curves."

▶ **IKEA**

Current slogan: "The Wonderful Everyday."

▶ Checklist for Designing an Advertising Slogan

For the convenience of designing slogans and taglines, you can use the serial table below. The difference between a tagline and a slogan is that a tagline reflects the identity of the brand and applies to all products, while a slogan reflects a specific event or campaign over the long term.

Slogan Content

Does it clearly convey your goal?

....
....
....
....
....

Does it express an emotional benefit for the audience?

....
....
....
....
....

Does it maintain its meaning across all cultures?

....
....
....
....
....

Is it Powerful enough to be used as a tagline for the long term?

....
....
....
....
....

Key Words for the Slogan

Write rhyming words that don't distort the meaning of the slogan (for rhythm in the slogan).

....

....

....

....

....

Write synonyms related to the key words of your slogan.

....

....

....

....

....

What extra words are in your slogan that don't create any image in the mind? Remove them.

....

....

....

....

....

What words can you use to create a real and positive feeling?

....

....

....

....

....

How to Understand the Slogan

What concepts can be extracted from your slogan?

....
....
....
....

Is the slogan more about you or about the benefits that the audience understand?'

....
....
....
....
....

Do they see this slogan as beneficial to them and society or to you and your organization?

....
....
....
....
....

How can you shift the perception of benefit from an individual perspective to a societal one?

....
....
....
....

▶ Brand Story

In addition to the brand promise, we also need a brand story. The brand story is so important that many organizations have dedicated a unit for it. The role of this unit is to identify the positive developments happening in the company today. The brand story can be the original story in which the brand's philosophy and promise are defined. It could also be success stories of customers, showing how the brand has improved their lives.

A story involves a concern or challenge that the main character faces. The character thinks about how to overcome the challenge, comes up with ideas and thoughts, takes actions based on those ideas, and eventually achieves a result. In other words, the character overcomes the challenge that emerged at the beginning of the story. We see this pattern in many novels and stories. The brand story is the story of its customers. Organizations are established to improve the lives of their customers. They want to improve the resources, time, money, and well-being of their customers. Brand stories are tools for connecting with customers and building emotional relationships with them.

The key to finding your brand story is to put yourself in the customer's shoes. Imagine that I, as a businessman, need a website design company to help me introduce myself better to my customers and provide a seamless purchasing experience. Now, put yourself in the customer's shoes and write three sentences like this: "As a ... I need ... to ...". For example, "As a father of a twelve-year-old daughter, I need a child and adolescent counseling service to have a better connection with my child." Or "As a trader, I need a professional consultancy group for export to Armenia to make better analyses and determine which product to offer in that market."

Have you ever looked at your business from this perspective? Business mastery opens your eyes to what you already have. When you put yourself in the customer's shoes, you will have a better feeling about your business, and your customers should have the same feeling.

To make your brand feel real and credible to your customers, what actions have you taken? Business growth depends more on the right mechanisms and strategies you put in place than on government policies. Writing customer stories in the branding process helps improve communication and relationships with your audience. Continuously improve and expand this story. The business process is about surviving and continuing. What works should be improved, and efforts should be made to help the business run more efficiently.

Think about how to improve just a little each day. Improve the way you **value** and **market**, make branding a little better, make your organization more agile, increase your competitive advantage, enhance your team-building, and improve the key elements of your business. What do car manufacturers do? They improve each part of the car. They make the chassis a little stronger, the engine a little better, and everything just a bit better each time. This is what growth is about. The brand philosophy, promise, and story should complement each other and complete one another. When you do this exercise, your brand's philosophy, promise, and story will improve. These ideas existed before, but by doing this exercise, their place in your business will become clearer. It's up to you to discover and use them.

Work on these aspects every day and review what you've read so far, as you'll have more focus and will make better discoveries in your quiet time. In your organization, think about your business. Creating a growth environment is possible when the business details are thought through. Why should we consider business details? Because when customers interact with us, they think about our system's details and say, "Wow! This organization has thought of everything!" The brand's philosophy, promise, and story can solve many issues. The values you create for your organization and the brand stories aim to offer a better definition of the organization to the audience. Many people love to hear stories, even if those stories are repetitive. When we were children, how many times did our grandparents tell us the same stories, yet we still loved to hear them? That's because stories have the power to create vivid imagery. When you tell a story, mental images form in the listener's mind. They unknowingly start to believe these images because their minds are convinced that what they visualized has actually happened.

Due to its high visual power, the story of Mommy Goat, although not real, is believable. This is why children are eager to hear it, because it creates an image in their minds. In business, you should do the same by creating a compelling image. Share the stories of your customers, stories that reflect their successful experiences, which have great credibility and make customers want to repeat their buying experience with you. Continued purchases mean loyalty. Loyalty is the fruit of a brand, meaning you've created loyal customers. The iPhone has done this in such a way that even before the new version arrives, many people line up to buy it. Creating a positive feeling in customers and transferring that feeling to others, through sharing and showcasing positive customer experiences as brand stories, has a huge impact on repeat purchases. In brand storytelling, engage directly with your audience and base your activities on that. The brand story should serve as a guiding force for thoughts and a proper introduction to your business.

In a brand story, you must answer five key questions. The first question is: Who are you? In other words, what is the brand's existence philosophy? Through your story, convey your brand's philosophy to your audience. In the brand story, you introduce your values, and if you tell this story well, people will share it with others, which in turn leads to word-of-mouth advertising. Those who have used your services or know your organization will become free brand ambassadors. What could be better than that?

Questions you must answer in the brand story:

Who are you? (What is your brand's existence philosophy?)

....

....

....

What exactly do you do?

....

....

....

How do you solve problems?

....

....

....

How do you create and maintain value?

....

....

....

How and in what way do you convey this value and service to your customers?

....

....

....

Stories have incredible power, and they can make your audience not only use your products and services but also live with them, becoming a part of their well-being.

▶ Types of Stories
The Personal Story of the Brand Owner

The founder's journey and the story of their brand, full of unique experiences, can serve as a guiding light for future generations if told well.

- The story of the beginning and the challenges faced at the start.
- Influential people in their life.
- Achievements.
- Failures.
- Critical and defining moments.

Empathetic Story

A story that, when others hear it, changes their perspective on the brand, making them want to share it with those around them. It's as if they want to feel empathy and connection with the brand.

- The things that didn't happen.
- The creativity.
- The fears.
- The continuation of the journey.

Price Justification Story with Brand Promise

If your customers have an issue with pricing, stories can be a solution.

- The brand promise.
- The money you save for the customer.

Example: "We know you can get this product at a lower price, but we won't let you suffer loss. If we were to produce it at a lower price, we'd have to reduce the quality of the raw materials, and you'd end up paying more in the long run." With this statement, you introduce your brand promise. You promise to deliver a product that won't require the customer to spend more later.

Story of the Value You Create

Introduce the value you create so that those who care about it will come to you. The value that only you create, and no one else has created before.

Story of Team Members

Tell the story of a committed and specialized team member whose performance has led to personal and organizational growth.

Story of Our Customers

This is the most important story you tell, as it reflects your achieved goals for your community. Their success is your achievement.

- The story of how they started working with you.
- The change it brought to their lives.
- The impact they've had on those around them.

However, creating and telling a brand story requires creativity in order to express it and illustrate it in the best way possible.

When we ask **Masoud Sarami (the founder of Salamat complex and Isfahan City Center)** about Salamat complex, here's how he tells its story:

"A massive project called Salamat complex Isfahan, instead of being built in the city center or on the heart of the city, I decided to build it on the outskirts of the city, in a place where no one would ever imagine. After constructing this project, the value of the surrounding area increased several times over. But the story doesn't end here. This place is set to become a hub for health tourism in the Middle East. Alongside the hospital, a hotel and a university have been built, so those working in the hospital can receive the necessary training and expertise, and the patients' companions won't have to worry about where to rest. You might not have seen the place up close, but now, you no longer just see it as a hospital. In fact, a new image has been created for you, and this shows the impact of stories on the minds and emotions of the audience."

▶ Story Design Template

With the template we've designed for you, you can create a unique story for your customers.

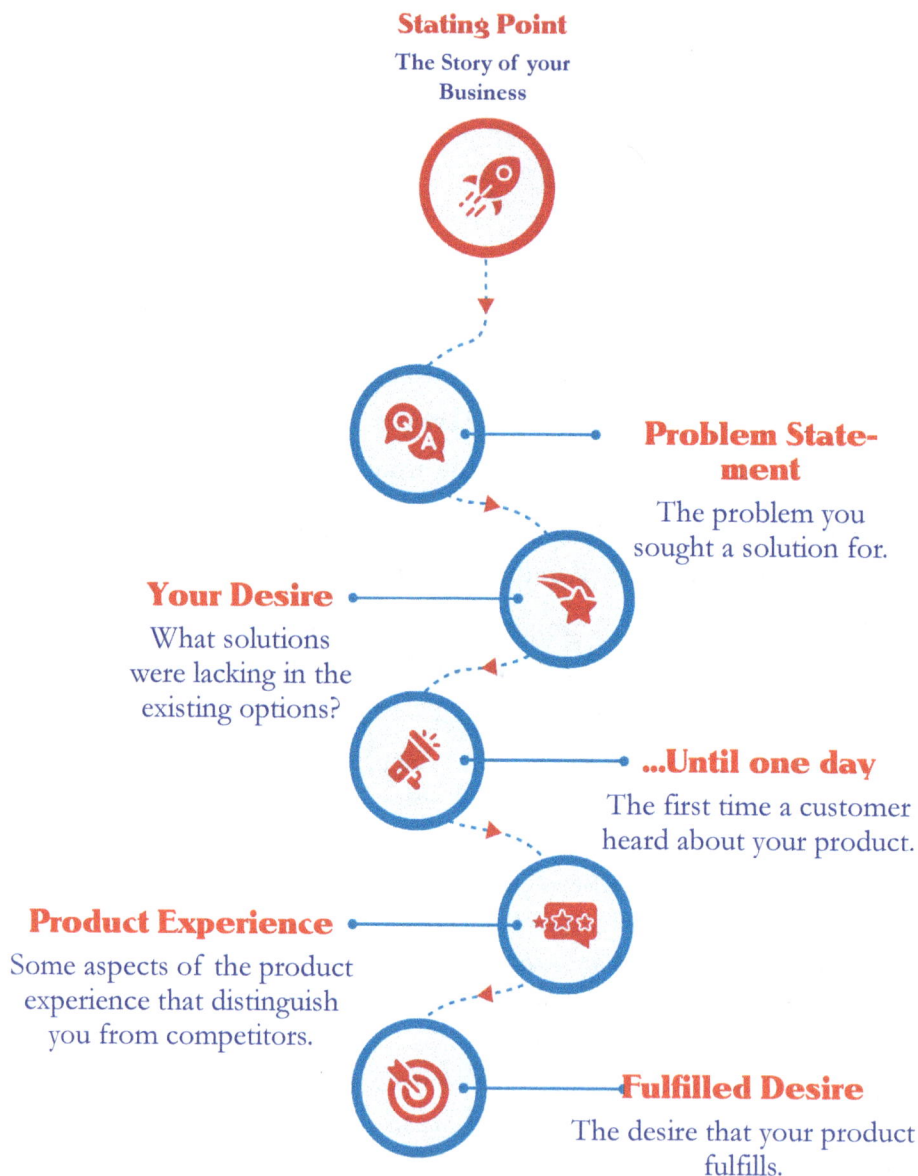

Stating Point

The Story of your Business

Problem State-ment

The problem you sought a solution for.

Your Desire

What solutions were lacking in the existing options?

...Until one day

The first time a customer heard about your product.

Product Experience

Some aspects of the product experience that distinguish you from competitors.

Fulfilled Desire

The desire that your product fulfills.

● Starting Point

Every brand goes through a journey full of ups and downs from the moment it is born. That's why behind every success, there is a story. People love hearing these stories. A business with a compelling story can capture attention. To complete this section, you need to answer the following questions:

When did you start your activities?

....

....

What was the economic and social situation in your city or country at that time?

....

....

....

Did you start alone, or were there people who accompanied you?

....

....

....

What was your economic and family situation at the time?

....

....

....

How many people did you start with, and what was the size of the space you used?

....

....

At the beginning, what was your area of expertise and skill?

....

....

● Problem Statement

A unified and continuous narrative of everything that happened to your brand and the new challenge that arose for its growth. Describe all the events, occurrences, bittersweet moments, achievements, and facts that lie behind your business. To complete this section, answer the following questions:

What problems did you face that needed to be solved?

....

....

....

....

How did your competitors deal with this problem?

....

....

....

....

....

What was your mindset at the start of your business?

....

....

....

....

....

● **The Wish You Had**

As your brand evolves, your knowledge and capabilities will undoubt-edly grow, and the product or service you offer to your audience may change completely. This can be a significant achievement and a symbol of your transformation and growth. To incorporate this section into your brand story, you need to answer the following questions:

How did you realize that the structure of your product or service needed to change?

....
....
....

Were you the first group to reach this achievement?

....
....
....

What abilities and expertise needed to be added to your team?

....
....
....

How much time was spent in fulfilling this wish?

....
....
....

Why did the market need this achievement of yours?

....
....
....

● Until one day...

In your market research, you have concluded that a change is needed, but you only become sure of the work you've done once the product or service reaches the customer and you can get real feedback from them. Before that, you are unsure if your desire is the same as your customers' desire. By answering the following questions, you can complete your story:

What was the first feedback from customers after the changes in the product and services?

....

....

....

How did the market react to these changes?

....

....

....

Has the demand for your product and services increased?

....

....

....

What tools and strategies have you used to introduce these changes to the market?

....

....

....

What achievements has this brought to your organization and even your country?

....

....

....

● **Product Experience**

When you receive positive feedback from the market and customers, it means that what you have done has satisfied them. This feedback provides an excellent opportunity for you to raise awareness among more people about what you have accomplished.

What features has the product been equipped with?

....

....

For which industries and businesses is it applicable?

....

....

If customization is possible, what are the conditions?

....

....

● **Fulfilled Wish**

If your product or service helps your customers reduce their troubles, then you have helped them achieve their desires. To express this, you need to remind your customers of their previous troubles and show how your product or service resolves these issues.

What troubles and costs has it reduced?

....

....

If there is a foreign example, how can it compete with it?

....

....

▶ Identifying your target audience

You are not meant to be known by everyone, as it serves no purpose. You need to be recognized among those who need you. You cannot please everyone, and at the point where someone thinks they know everything, they won't trust you. Choose a segment of the market and focus all your attention on serving that specific segment.

Who are your target audience?
Age, occupation, culture, social status, gender, education level.

What problems do they have?

....
....
....
....

What fears do they have?

....
....
....
....

Which social media platforms are they actively present on?

....
....
....

Who do they consult with?

....
....
....

Which role models do they follow?

....

....

....

What are their interests?

....

....

....

Not the entire society is your target audience. You are not supposed to offer your services to everyone. What specific image and characteristics do your main audience have? The most important questions you need to answer are:

The most important questions that need to be answered are:

Who should know about you?

....

....

....

....

What are the most important groups?

....

....

....

What strategies do you have to reach your goals?

....

....

....

Who can influence the people you are targeting?

....

....

....

Where can you find them?

....

....

....

....

Who are not your customers and why?

....

....

....

Brand Story Guide

Before writing your brand story, answer the following questions:

Who are we?	☐
What do we do?	☐
Why did we choose and continue this business?	☐
What is our history?	☐
What is the main feature of our business?	☐
What are our vision and goals?	☐
How did we reach our current position?	☐
What are the weaknesses and gaps in our business?	☐

Gathering Information from Customers

Who are your customers? What are the characteristics of your target audience? ☐

How do your customers find you? ☐

What benefits do you provide to your customers? ☐

What titles do they recognize you by? ☐

In their view, in which product or service are you a reference? ☐

Through which channels can you communicate with your customers? ☐

Monitoring Competitors and Being a Leader

What is your competitive advantage over your competitors? ☐

What are the benefits and values you can offer? ☐

What are your strengths? ☐

What is the difference between you and your competitors? ☐

How do your competitors tell their stories? ☐

Establishing a connection between the provided answers

Tell the story in a friendly and approachable tone, and present it simply. ☐

Narrate the story in a way that creates a mental image for the audience. ☐

Every story should have a strong beginning and ending. ☐

Write short and energetic paragraphs. ☐

Most importantly, do not forget that the hero of the story is the customer. ☐

Make sure the story mention your website and social media channels. ☐

▶ Communications

The communication methods through which your audience can get to know you better and you can stay connected with them.

How will they recognize you?

....

....

....

....

....

How will you be recognized by your audience?

....

....

....

....

....

How will you create a strong relationship with your audience?

....

....

....

....

How will you highlight your position?

....

....

....

....

....

Where do your audience typically go?

....

....

....

....

....

What is their pattern of social media use?

....

....

....

....

....

What activities do they engage in during their leisure time? Reasons to Believe

....

....

....

....

....

▶ What gives you credibility.

When your audience hears your offer, an internal dialogue occurs in them, deciding whether to accept your offer or not.

Why should the audience believe you?

....

....

....

....

....

....

....

What makes you trustworthy in the eyes of your audience?

....

....

....

....

....

....

What evidence do you have to gain their trust?

....

....

....

....

....

....

The 30 key elements of branding:

Brand Positioning, Promise, and Brand Pledge	Communication Channels with Audiences
"How do your audience think about you?"	Social media Article Billboard advertising Website Email marketing
What do you do?	**What image is formed of you in the minds of your audience?**
Product and Services Support Pricing Target Audience Customer Experience	Logo Brand Image Font Brand Color Brand Graphics Packaging Brand Scent
What is your mission?	**Who are you?**
Brand Value Brand Mission Brand Vision	Brand Name Brand Personality Brand Story

Branding Checklist

Essentials of Business

- [ ] Logo
- [ ] Brand Voice
- [ ] Email Signature
- [ ] Brochure / Catalog / Booklet
- [ ] Symbol
- [ ] Stationery, Business Cards, Letterhead
- [ ] Envelope, Folder
- [ ] Postcard
- [ ] Large Banners
- [ ] Posters
- [ ] Gift Cards
- [ ] Stickers

Essentials of Business

- [ ] Website
- [ ] Responsive Design
- [ ] Landing Page
- [ ] Web Management
- [ ] Web Development
- [ ] E-commerce
- [ ] Mobile Application
- [ ] Website Banners
- [ ] WordPress

Social Media

- [ ] Development Strategy
- [ ] Bio Description
- [ ] Social Media Designs
- [ ] Communication Management
- [ ] Online Advertising

Marketing

- [ ] Direct Mail
- [ ] Value Proposition
- [ ] Print Advertising
- [ ] E-newsletter
- [ ] Pricing Strategy
- [ ] Search Engine Optimization
- [ ] Click and Display Ads

Event Essentials

- [ ] Brand Execution Actions
- [ ] Outdoor Advertising
- [ ] Back Office
- [ ] Postcard
- [ ] Catalog / Brochure

Organization Identity

- [ ] Flag
- [ ] Personnel Forms
- [ ] Badge
- [ ] Internet Advertising
- [ ] Promotional Items

Brand Identity Checklist

In people's minds, a set of beliefs and perceptions about you, your company, products, or services has formed. These perceptions and beliefs shape your brand. It is possible that the image of your brand in the minds of customers differs from the image you want to create in their minds. Before starting the design process in your branding journey, answer these questions.

Customer Analysis

- What process does a customer go through to use your products or services? ☐
- Why should they buy from you? ☐
- What needs do they have that are still unmet? ☐
- What is the main characteristic of your audience? ☐
- When do they make purchases from you? ☐

Competitor Analysis

- What are the strengths and strategies of your competitors? ☐
- What are the weaknesses of your competitors? ☐
- What visual elements do your competitors use? ☐
- What is the reason for the popularity of your competitor? ☐

Brand Analysis

- What are the visual elements of your brand? ☐
- What is the essence of your brand? ☐
- What are the distinct values you offer to customers? ☐
- Does your brand offer a guarantee? ☐

Brand Communications Analysis

What is your brand's slogan? ☐

What is your brand's sound? ☐

What is your brand's corporate color? ☐

What is your brand's graphic symbol? ☐

What is your brand's personality? ☐

What is your brand's graphic design? ☐

What is your brand's story? ☐

What is your brand's experience? ☐

▶ **Write Your Five Key Takeaways from This Chapter:**

1. ....

2. ....

3. ....

4. ....

5. ....

▶ **Three Steps I Will Immediately Start:**

1. ....

....

2. ....

3. ....

▶ **One Golden Lesson to Share with Others:**

....

....

....

....

Download all the tables and exercises of this chapter from the following website.

https://hosseintaheri.ir/bmg/

Marketing

Chapter 6:

Marketing

Marketing means that your market finds you, not you finding the market.

📖 **After reading this chapter, you will gain mastery over:**

- The Concept of Marketing
- Four Key Principles of Business Dominance
- The Most Important Goal of Marketing
- Concepts of Needs, Wants, and Demands
- Seven Determinants of Marketing
- The CATT Funnel in Digital Marketing
- How Content Marketing Works

"Marketing" is one of those concepts that, when discussed, often leaves business owners and managers confused about its meaning. Many people confuse marketing with advertising. Perhaps this is because, in the past, marketing was synonymous with advertising, as companies and brands used mass advertising for their services and products, which led to higher revenue and sales. However, with the expansion of the digital space and the changing nature of the market, the needs and desires of customers also changed. This shift caused organizations and brands to seek a deeper understanding of modern marketing and move from mass marketing toward more focused and targeted marketing.

You might have heard the story of someone who had a key and wandered around the city looking for a matching lock. This story is a metaphor for many business owners and managers who, in the present day, are focused on market expansion and increasing their profit and revenue. Meanwhile, a smart marketer, or better yet, a master of marketing, must be able to identify the locks in the market (the problems, challenges, and "would-be-nice" situations) and create keys to open them (the solutions and answers).

▶ Should the Market Come to Us or Should We Go to the Market?

The concept of marketing goes beyond simply promoting a product or service. In today's world, every purchase, every visit, every advertisement, and every choice represent a pivotal moment in the marketing process. Marketing professionals, by analyzing and predicting these pivotal moments, can gain a deeper understanding of customer behavior and needs, ultimately leading to a better and more suitable purchasing experience for them. To better understand this concept, let's examine the definition of marketing from different perspectives.

▶ Definition of Marketing According to the American Marketing Association

Marketing is a set of activities and processes designed to create, deliver, and exchange offerings that have value for customers and society.

▶ Definition of Marketing According to Philip Kotler (Father of Modern Marketing)

Marketing is a managerial and social process through which individuals and groups obtain what they need and want through the creation and exchange of value. Kotler emphasizes the concept of value, which extends beyond just products or services. In short: "The process of satisfying needs through the production and exchange of value."

▶ Definition of Marketing According to Dr. Ahmad Roosta (Father of Marketing in Iran)

Marketing includes three main pillars:

- Market Knowledge: Understanding customers and their needs.
- Market Creation: Creating and obtaining market share (customer acquisition).
- Market Maintenance: Maintaining market share (customer retention).

Based on the definitions of marketing provided, we realize that the concept of "customer marketing" is vastly different from what is typically in the minds of managers and business owners today. Marketing is a true story that we tell to our target audience, who are eager to hear it. They should be able to find their own role in this story and discover the solutions to many of their problems and challenges through it, so that they can make a change in their lifestyle. This story, if told correctly and reaches the audience properly, will allow the market to find you, instead of you searching for the market.

In fact, we are living in an era of service. People are very smart and will fully understand that as an organization, our goal is not merely to increase income, pay off debts, or secure our own benefit. Our mission is to bring about change, create opportunities, and design proposals that allow us to serve our audience better. The goal is to provide value, offer solutions, and create real impact in the lives of our customers.

▶ Three-Sentence Promise

In marketing, there is a concept known as the "Three-Sentence Promise." I recommend that before studying this topic, review the following three key sentences in your mind, and then note them down in the table. Suggestion: Set aside the first three that come to your mind and record the following ones in the table.

My product is for those who believe that...

....

....

....

....

....

....

I will focus on individuals who want to...

....

....

....

....

....

I promise that using my product or service will help you...

....

....

....

....

....

▶ **The Importance of Marketing for Businesses**

Among the many business owners and producers I have interacted with over the years, there is a common belief: "My products or services are good enough that I don't need marketing. The market and customers will find my products and use them on their own." or the story of many business owners and managers who, in an effort to expand their market, mistakenly believe that the market will find them and buy from them without proper introduction or marketing. However, not presenting your product or service properly is equivalent to not being present in the market at all. Expecting customers to come without introducing your product or informing your audience is both an unrealistic and unreasonable expectation.

▶ **The Nearsighted Syndrome**

Another issue is "the nearsighted syndrome," where we become so enamored with our products and services that we fail to identify their flaws. As a result, we believe we are doing perfectly and, if the market is not responding well, we blame others, never ourselves. In such cases, we place the blame elsewhere, even though the issue lies within our own approach. As I always say, sitting behind a desk is not the best way to understand the market.

▶ **The Anton Syndrome**

In the early 19th century, Dr. Gabriel Anton suffered from a condition that caused headaches, dizziness, and fatigue. Over time, his condition worsened, and after a while, he lost his vision. The surprising part was that the patient did not realize that he was losing his sight. If someone asked him about something on the table, he would complain about the room being too dark or the lights being off, not realizing that his vision was deteriorating. This condition became known as the "Anton Syndrome" or "Denial of Blindness Syndrome." Many business owners and managers experience something similar, believing their products and services are so great that they do not need marketing or advertising. They fail to recognize the flaws in their business approach, which leads them to blame the market or others for their lack of sales, when the real issue lies in the approach to marketing itself.

If you don't conquer the market, the market will conquer you

The importance of marketing has increased more than ever in 2023, due to the rise of new technologies, changes in consumer behavior, and the growing competition. Companies now need strong marketing strategies to remain competitive. This is because consumers, more than ever, are aware of their choices. With the internet and social media, they have access to vast amounts of information about products and services. They can easily research companies, compare prices, features, and reviews. This means that businesses need a strong online presence and a clear value proposition to differentiate themselves from competitors. The level of competition is increasing in every industry, and organizations must continually innovate and grow, rather than simply surviving. Additionally, marketing in 2023 is data-driven. With the advent of artificial intelligence, machine learning, and big data, businesses can now collect and analyze vast amounts of information about their customers and target audiences. This allows them to create personalized and effective marketing campaigns tailored to their specific market.

Ultimately, we can say that marketing is critical in 2023 because it helps businesses adapt to changing trends and consumer preferences while staying aligned with ethical standards and social responsibility. Companies must show that they are committed to making a positive impact on society.

In conclusion, marketing in 2023 is crucial for businesses that want to succeed in a fast-evolving competitive environment. Whether for a small startup or a large corporation, having a strong marketing strategy can play a vital role in achieving success. By developing and implementing a solid marketing strategy, businesses can effectively reach their target audience, increase brand awareness, generate more leads, and ultimately drive higher sales and profitability. Therefore, we can confidently say that marketing is a lifesaver. If you don't conquer the market, the market will control you, causing fluctuations, inflation, and affecting your business's success.

▶ **The four principles of control in business:**

Your decisions in these four areas can determine your success or failure in controlling your business.

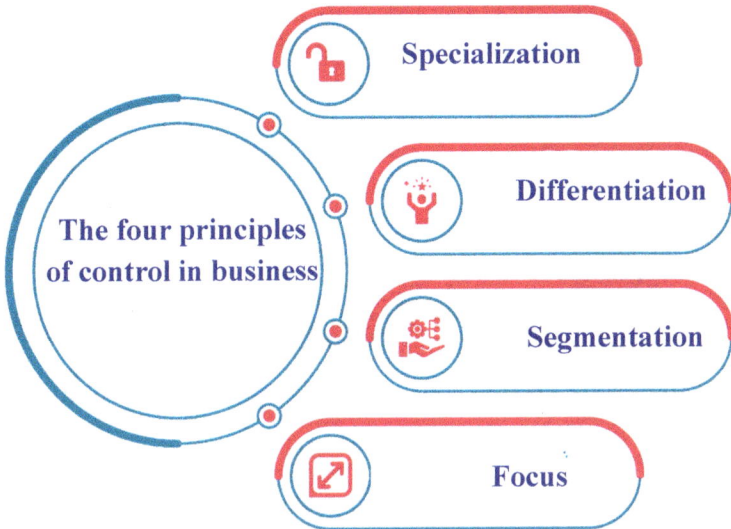

The four principles of control in business

- Specialization
- Differentiation
- Segmentation
- Focus

Specialization

What is your area of expertise?

....
....
....
....

If you were to start over today, what specialization would you choose?

....
....
....

Focus

Which customers should you focus your time, capital, and effort on?

....
....
....
....

What are the best ways to connect with your ideal customer?

....
....
....
....
....

Focus

What is the best media for reaching them?

....

....

....

....

....

Given the above, what are your top three products or services?

....

....

....

....

....

Which products, markets, or customers should you eliminate?

....

....

....

....

....

Which customers pay the most for the work you do in your area of expertise?

....

....

....

....

....

Differentiation

What is your competitive advantage?

....

....

....

....

....

What do you consider to be your superior quality?

....

....

....

....

....

What is your unique selling proposition? (What makes your product or service more desirable than the competition?)

....

....

....

....

....

Where can you be the best or where are you already the best?

....

....

....

....

....

Segmentation

Who are your appreciative customers?

....

....

....

....

What are their demographics? (The demographic table is provided below.)

....

....

....

....

....

What is their psychology and mindset? (The psychological and mindset table is provided below.)

....

....

....

....

....

How do you define your perfect customer?

....

....

....

....

....

Customers

Demographics

What is their age range?

....
....
....
....
....
....
....

What is their gender?

....
....
....
....
....
....
....

What is their average monthly income?

....
....
....
....
....
....

Demographics

What level of education do they have?

....
....
....
....
....

What industry are they employed in?

....
....
....
....
....

Where do they generally live?

....
....
....
....
....
....

What is their family situation?

....
....
....
....
....

Psychographics

What goals are they pursuing?

....
....
....
....

What are their desires, needs, and motivations?

....
....
....
....

What are their hopes, dreams, and aspirations?

....
....
....

What problems do they want solved?

....
....
....
....

A great marketing plan attracts a steady stream of qualified customers and, by emphasizing its unique selling proposition, positions your product as the first and best choice in the minds of the audience. Strategic thinking and planning help you achieve better results with lower costs. Based on your answers to the above questions, please answer the following:

Which action will you take immediately?

....

....

....

....

How will you measure the success of your action?

....

....

....

....

What timeline have you set to achieve success?

....

....

....

....

....

► Maximizing Communication

What never changes is the constant evolution of the market. There-fore, the only thing you need as a business owner in your role as a marketer is preparedness. Preparedness is about staying aware of your position in the market and how the market reacts to your product and performance. The most important goal of a marketing program is to maximize the following:

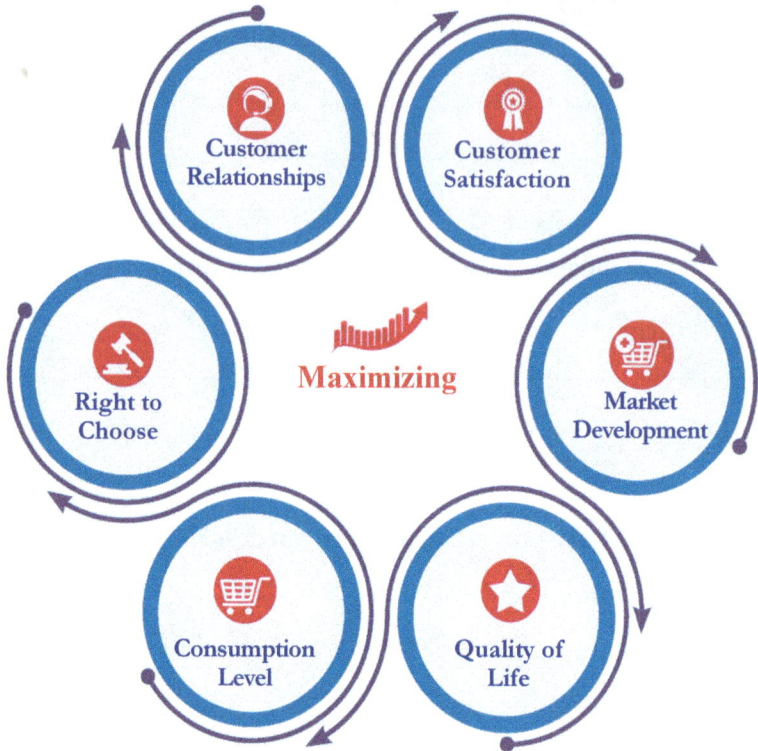

▶ Maximizing Consumption Level:

The goal is not to encourage excessive spending but to create a balance between production and consumption, ensuring consistent demand that matches your production capacity.

▶ Maximizing Customer Satisfaction:

It emphasizes understanding customer needs and addressing what might discourage them from making purchases. By anticipating these needs and taking proactive steps, businesses can ensure customer satisfaction.

▶ Maximizing Choice:

This refers to product development and offering diversity within your product range, which becomes a key differentiator in the market.

▶ Maximizing Quality of Life:

Businesses should aim to enhance customers' personal or professional lives by providing value in exchange for their resources (money, time, or energy). The idea is that the product or service should offer something that significantly improves their quality of life.

▶ Maximizing Market Development:

The process of market development focuses on understanding which values you aim to create for the market, ensuring that these values align with the financial situation and needs of your target audience. Businesses should always be engaged in market development to avoid stagnation and to continue growing and expanding. These principles encourage strategic planning in marketing to ensure that the business remains adaptable and continuously meets the evolving needs of customers while maintaining a competitive edge in the marketplace.

▶ Maximizing Customer Satisfaction:

A business's uniqueness is defined by its ability to keep customers. This is the shared trait of all those who are masters of their business. Customers should not even think about replacing the business or its products with something else, even if they have to pay more, invest more energy, or spend more time. This is the most valuable result of preserving and improving customer satisfaction for your business. **In fact, the power of a business lies in the strength of those who support it, whether they are stakeholders, partners, team members, or customers.**

Customers feel empowered when they are surprised. As a result, remember that this is only possible for customers who have been properly selected. Consider the customers you already have. Among them, you will find a few who are more passionate than others because they are your most powerful customers. Customer satisfaction is a two-way power that benefits both you and your business. However, if you focus only on one of these objectives, you will lose balance in this cycle.

Losing balance results when one goal is sacrificed for another. If you sacrifice one goal for another, you will achieve neither. A plan that only focuses on increasing sales and attracting more customers, without taking into account their needs and desires, is destined to fail. Contrary to popular belief, increasing sales is not the main goal of marketing; it is the result of successful marketing.

▶ What is Marketing About?

We want to explore how marketing takes shape. We know that customers have needs. If you serve customers only at the level of their needs, even if you add value, you haven't done marketing; you've only made a sale.

Imagine walking down the street and feeling thirsty. You buy water and after drinking it, your thirst is quenched. The need for water has been met, but did the person who sold you the water perform marketing? Did it increase your consumption or satisfaction? Did it create a deeper connection with you? Admit that working at the level of a customer's need is neither a differentiator nor requires marketing.

Many products and services simply meet needs, and without a unique competitive advantage, no growth will result. By focusing on customers' desires instead of just their needs, you can leverage marketing power to create growth. For example, you need to know the current time. You buy a watch, but the reason for purchasing it isn't just to know the time. You want others to notice it, to gain respect, to show you are wealthy and powerful. This watch is no longer just a tool to satisfy a basic need but a desire that reflects your status. Many times, customers have desires that they don't even recognize. This is because they lack awareness of the products or services that could satisfy these desires. Many times, customers themselves don't know what they want, and it is up to you to identify and convert their wants into demand.

This is why customer interaction and elevating communication are so critical in marketing. If demand does not take shape, there is no economy. Marketing is the game between supply and demand. Once demand exists, customers will begin spending money.

Once a person desires a home, for example, they start looking for one with specific characteristics, such as a pilot garage or proper access. This desire, which is not a basic need but a deeper want, is what marketing taps into. When you start looking for a house with these specific features, demand begins to form. This is where marketing plays a pivotal role in guiding the customer towards fulfillment.

Marketing shapes at the demand stage, where people take action. All your marketing efforts should focus on managing and assembling these demands to create better results. In business mastery, marketing directly correlates with the creation of results. If you haven't created the right results, it means you have either misidentified or failed to properly address the needs, desires, and demands of your customers. Creating results in marketing means that what you have planned has occurred and you've achieved the desired outcome. Sometimes customers have wants that are obvious to us but still surprise them. When these desires are fulfilled, they express admiration and say, "Wow, this is amazing, it's really you who has given direction to these demands."

By transforming needs into wants and guiding those wants towards demand, you will create value, demonstrate profitability, and show sincerity in your business. Thus, transform needs into desires and manage them effectively toward demand.

Once you create demand, you won't be overly concerned with competitors, as you are focusing on satisfying customer desires and meeting demands. While many companies may have small differences in their products, those with strong organizations that address the customer's wants and demands don't get involved in the usual competition.

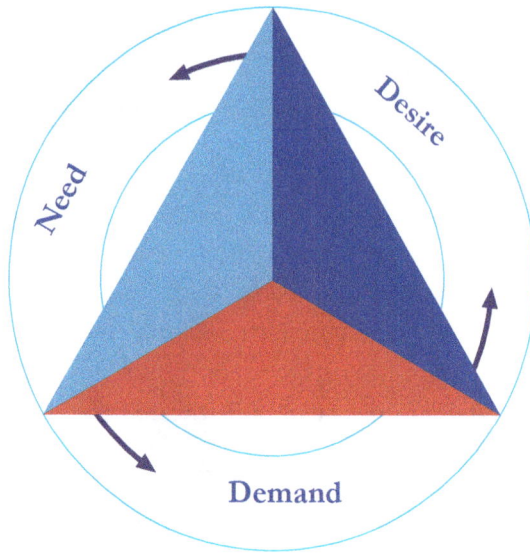

Why do I say demand is important?

Up to this point, we have understood that there is a need, a want, and a demand, and we need to differentiate between them. Based on demand management, marketing should be carried out because it is demand that leads to the creation of results.

Conversion marketing	Negative demand
Motivational Marketing	Lack of demand
Developmental Marketing (Revealing, developmental)	Hidden demand
Revival Marketing (Re-marketing, reactivation)	Unstable Demand
Simultaneous Marketing (Adjustment)	Irregular demand
Protective Marketing (Preservation)	Complete demand
Depleting Marketing (non-marketing, marketing to reduce demand)	Excessive demand
Counter Marketing	Unhealthy demand

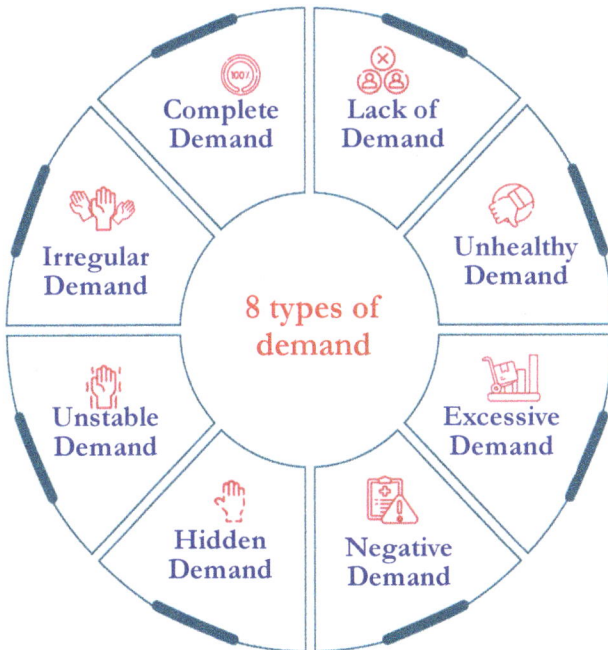

8 types of demand

Complete Demand
Lack of Demand
Unhealthy Demand
Excessive Demand
Negative Demand
Hidden Demand
Unstable Demand
Irregular Demand

Negative Demand

Description

Negative demand means that people are unwilling to buy or use your products or services, or if they are willing, they have developed a negative attitude due to your improper handling of the product. Sometimes, they are even willing to pay a penalty for not purchasing the product or service from you.

Solution

In the case of negative demand, conversion marketing comes into play. The idea is to reverse the demand, meaning converting negative demand into positive demand. Advertising campaigns, promotional offers, sales festivals, and rewards are ways to achieve this conversion.

Lack of demand

Description

Lack of demand means there is no demand, and people are indifferent to having a product or service. An example of this is life insurance, which people typically don't pay much attention to. In such situations, you need to stimulate other demands from customers that are on the periphery of your services or products.

Solution

In the absence of demand, motivational or stimulating marketing is helpful. In this approach, you provide people with additional value for purchasing your product to motivate them to buy from you. For example, offering something as a gift that complements your product or creating a difference in the delivery system so that the customer has no concerns in this regard.

Hidden demand

Description

Hidden demand is the potential desire of the consumer. When a service is truly needed by many people, but they are not aware of it.

Solution

Development marketing is an effective response to hidden demand. Development marketing is your effort to activate the thought sensors of individuals to help them realize their need. It's the moment when they say, "How interesting, it seems I really needed something like this."

This effort can be reflected in the honest recommendations from your salesperson or in your content creation programs.

Unstable Demand

Description

Unstable demand is a demand filled with doubt, and it occurs when, at the beginning of a marketing campaign, you experience good sales, but despite more advertising and production, you do not experience the same level of demand. It's as if the market has lost its elasticity for purchasing your product. As a result, you might even lose some of your customers.

Solution

This is where Reaffirmation Marketing comes in. Reaffirmation marketing is your effort to reclaim new markets, attract new customers, innovate in product and service production, explore new distribution methods, alter pricing policies, and even change advertising strategies.

Irregular demand

Description

In some seasons, supply and demand are not equal. For example, in the clothing industry, demand exceeds supply during the New Year or the start of school and university terms, while at other times, supply surpasses demand. Similarly, hotels face lower demand during exam periods.

Solution

Irregular Demand requires Simultaneous Marketing, or as it is sometimes called, Adjustive Marketing, which aims to align supply with demand. Although the best time for marketing is always crucial, there is no fixed amount that can be set for advertising expenses. During a sales downturn, advertising becomes ineffective because it's not close enough to the time when customers are likely to buy. For instance, during a trade show, the best advertising choice would be outdoor billboards near the exhibition. People tend to remember the last message they receive, and here you've synchronized supply with demand.

Complete demand

Description

This is the most desirable situation a business can face. When the level of supply and demand are balanced at a specific time, though this rarely happens.

Solution

In this case, Protective Marketing is needed. Make sure the customer strives to maintain complete demand. By responding to their desires and fulfilling their immediate preferences, you will counteract the threats posed by competitors.

Excessive demand

Description

Excessive demand occurs when demand exceeds supply, and it usually happens in difficult market conditions or during crises. Sometimes, due to crises, your supply cannot meet the volume of demand.

Solution

In this case, Decremental Marketing or Reducing Marketing is needed. Temporarily reduce your marketing efforts because the inability to meet customer demand can lead to their discouragement and dissatisfaction. You can even focus your marketing on other products that you have the capacity to supply.

Unhealthy demand

Description

Unhealthy demand is a demand that is not only unprofitable for us but also inefficient to supply.

Solution

In this case, counter-marketing is needed. This approach aims to counteract the marketing and sales of a product or service.

▶ Seven Determining Elements of Marketing

We know that marketing has seven effective elements.

When we talk about business, it means discovering each of these elements and understanding how well you have mastered them. Being number one doesn't happen by accident, but rather requires coordinating these seven elements. This means that when we talk about the product, you need to know exactly how it is defined and what benefits it provides. Should the benefit be for you or for your community? And to achieve that, what should be worked on? When we talk about price, we mean understanding which part is the cost and which part is the revenue. Which part of it will be returned?

Pricing is not just about choosing a number. In fact, prices represent the values that products create. Earlier, I discussed value in detail. How can the place or method of distribution of that service or product, along with the price we have set, be? How can promotional programs for market development, which is one of the key objectives of marketing, be designed? How can we enhance the quality of life for customers? What could be public programs and concrete evidence? What processes are defined along these paths?

All of these are the seven arms of marketing that help create balance between supply and demand. The coordination of these seven elements does not just improve sales, it makes it magical and increases it miraculously.

Product

The product name, brand reputation, product quality, shape, design and color, size and dimensions, delivery conditions, purchasing facilities, warranty, after-sales services.

Price

Level of price, discount rate, deductions, commissions, payment terms, price lists, flexibility, pricing policies.

Place

Determining the distribution location, accessibility to the location, distribution channels, distribution tools and methods, coverage of distribution, use of intermediaries, control of sales channels.

Promotion

Advertising, personal sales, sales promotion, public relations, selection of advertising media, sales policies, preparing advertising messages.

People

Staff training, checking their qualifications, involving employees, motivating employees, paying attention to their appearance, their conduct, customer behavior, customer contact.

Public Witnesses

Checking the environment, preparing it, color of the environment, noise level, provided amenities.

Process

Policies, degree of automation, workflow, activities, customer guidance, customer journey maps.

▶ Product:

A product is anything you sell that is intended to fulfill the needs and demands of your customers in a tangible way. It doesn't matter what your product or service is, you must determine its nature before selling and establish the method of its presentation to the customer. Developing a product or service that no one wants to buy will have no benefit for you. This is an important point that many businesses overlook. They first introduce a product and then try to find the customer and market for it.

Successful companies follow the concept of marketing. They first identify the customer's needs and then develop a product or service that matches the level of those needs. In fact, they don't look for customers for their products; they find the product for their customers.

Now, let's review some important points about the product:

- A product is not necessarily a tangible object. For example, insurance can also be a product.

- A product can be considered excellent if it creates value for the customer. The value that is in line with the customer's perspective. In fact, you must offer the customer what they want, not what we think they want.

- Receiving feedback from customers to improve the product or service is crucial.

Product

What are you selling? What benefits does it provide for you?

....
....
....
....
....
....

What does it eliminate, add, or maintain?

....
....
....
....
....
....
....

How does your business change or improve the life or work of your customer?

....
....
....
....
....

Product

Product Name: Naming the product is one of the key elements in marketing mastery. You cannot just choose any name for the product and expect it to penetrate the market and dominate it.

Brand Recognition: The product must have the ability to create brand recognition. Brand recognition means creating a strong perception in the market. For example, insurance products known as "life insurance" might create the perception that after death, someone will inherit the policyholder's wealth. In contrast, other cultures interpret it as a product that provides benefits during the policyholder's lifetime.

Product Quality: No one seeks out a low-quality product. Quality is not a distinction; it is a necessity. The main task of any business is to ensure product quality.

Shape, Design, Color, and Size: You may not believe it, but the design and appearance of a product can address many of your audience's concerns, fulfill their desires, and stimulate their emotions.

Delivery Conditions: Assuming you've ensured all the aspects mentioned above, how, when, and where the product reaches the customer is crucial. The delivery conditions of a product can be part of the product's value proposition.

Purchase Facilities: What facilities do you offer for purchasing? How attractive is it? The purchasing facilities are not just a help to your customers; when designed properly, they can be profitable for you too.

Warranty and Guarantee: The warranty is a significant part of your product's value and the credibility it shares with your customers. When you say your product is guaranteed, you offer your customer more security, even if you charge them more for it. The money the customer willingly spends is, in fact, the security they feel.

After-Sales Service: Woe to businesses that lack after-sales services. After-sales is where customer satisfaction is measured. Do you follow up with your customer after the sale? Do you ask them how your product has worked for them? Have you even inquired about their experience?

For every product, many businesses have a product manager. The role of the product manager is to think about all the factors mentioned and design necessary plans to ensure that the product maintains its expertise and dominance in the market.

Exercise

Based on the points mentioned above, complete the following table:

Product
Product Name:
Brand Recognition:
Product Quality:

Shape, Design, Color, and Size:

Delivery Conditions:

Purchase Facilities:

Warranty and Guarantee:

After-Sales Service:

....

....

....

....

What Changes Can You Make to Your Products or Services to Make Them More Attractive?

▶ Price:

In marketing, a product is worth as much as the customer is willing to pay for it.

- The price of your products or services reflects your position among your competitors. If your customers are from the high-income class, you should not offer your products at a cheap price.

- The higher the price of your products or services, the higher the customer's expectations for quality or value.

- Current customers are more price-sensitive compared to new customers. Therefore, if you increase the price, you must offer corresponding value to the customers.

Price

What is the price of your product?

How do you receive it?

How does the customer pay?

Is there a better way to pay or receive payment?

Price

Price Level: What is the basis for defining your price level? Based on need, want, or demand? In many cases, if you are unable to create the right demand for your audience, you harm your price level. Price at a product level that only addresses a need, with no competitive advantage, is always low and cannot rise unless it aligns with the desires and demands of the audience, creating value for them.

Offers: Offers should encourage purchasing and prompt action. Offers can be in the form of reducing the customer's payment for early purchases, sales festivals, or providing an additional product or service without charging for it when purchasing the product.

Discounts: You may sometimes need to adjust your price. So, consider offering a specific discount. It's better not to simply reduce the price but to offer a unique feature or benefit to the customer. For example, if you are a hotel owner and don't intend to discount your rooms, you could change the check-out time.

Commissions: Commissions added to the price often jeopardize our relationship. After the purchase, if you tell the customer they need to pay n% for shipping or services, and the customer adds 9% tax, this calculation reduces their satisfaction. Try to calculate all these elements in your pricing while preserving and enhancing the value of what you provide.

Payment Terms: Sometimes, even though you know exactly how much to charge the customer, you can create a comparative effect using the supplementary pricing theory.

Price List: A base price is chosen for the product, and based on the price list, the customer can detect price changes based on the features they select.

Pricing Flexibility: The customer may have no issue with the price, but they might face issues with payment terms. As we mentioned earlier, you can offer more flexible pricing using offers and discounts.

In situations where price increases for civil products or services, or those with fixed prices, are not possible, the focus of marketing shifts to order volume, ancillary services, complementary products, and brand building.

Exercise

Based on the above points, complete the following table:

Price
Price Level:
....
....
....
Offers:
....
....
....
Discount Rate:
....
....
....
Commissions:
....
....
....

Payment Terms:

....

....

....

Price List:

....

....

....

Flexibility:

....

....

....

Pricing Strategy:

....

....

....

▶ Place of Distribution:

According to the marketing concept, your product must be available to customers at the right place, at the right time, and in the right quantity. Simply put, you should sell your product where there is demand or potential demand for it. For example, opening an air conditioner store in the North Pole makes no sense! Likewise, selling coats and warm clothes in Ahvaz during the summer is also illogical.

The place of distribution also refers to the method of delivering the product. Therefore, your display, whether it's the store window, website design, or product packaging, must be eye-catching.

Place

Where do you sell your products or services?

....

....

....

....

Where else can you sell your products or services?

....

....

....

....

How can you change or improve your sales locations?

....

....

....

....

Place

Determining Distribution Locations

You have a great product at a reasonable price, but if it's not on the shelf (physical store shelf or virtual shelf on a website), it doesn't make any difference from being at zero. Determining and ensuring distribution locations plays a significant role in improving the quality of your marketing.

Access to the Location

If access to the distribution location is difficult for customers, it means that the marketing strategy is unsuccessful and insufficient (whether it's geographical access or virtual access on a website or app).

Channels of Distribution

The distribution channels for your product, their performance quality, and how these channels behave are critical aspects that should not be overlooked because they are essential in marketing.

Distribution Tools and Equipment

The tools and equipment you use for product or service distribution should not be chosen carelessly. Believe it or not, "differentiation" comes from the difference in performance in these areas.

Distribution Coverage

The coverage or the scope of distribution describes the extent to which a product is available in the market. Have you defined the coverage level you're aiming for?

Use of Intermediaries

Intermediaries in distribution are anyone or anything that plays a role in the distribution process and delivering the product to the target market. Company representatives, wholesalers, and retailers are part of this group. Intermediaries can either increase or reduce the steps in this process.

Control of Sales Channels

By controlling the output, you can manage the input. Sales channel control allows you to distribute products on time, in the required quantity, and appropriately.

Exercise

Based on the above points, complete the following table:

Price
Determining Distribution Locations:
Access to the Location:
Channels of Distribution
Distribution Tools and Equipment

Distribution Coverage

Use of Intermediaries

Control of Sales Channels

Are your products and services correctly priced for the current market? How can you adjust your pricing to make it more competitive?

▶ **Promotion:**

The principle of promotion in marketing refers to communicating a company's capabilities and products to customers. This principle includes branding, advertising, organizational identity, expanding social networks, participating in exhibitions, and special offers.

In fact, the promotion principle ensures that your advertising is engaging, conveys a consistent message, attracts customers, and most importantly, highlights your product's competitive advantages.

Some key points about promotion:

- A good promotion is not one-sided; it should establish a connection with customers both in-person and online.

- A good advertisement should showcase not only the features but also the benefits of a product for the customer.

- Your website plays a significant role in the marketing concept, especially in the promotion principle. The initial impression a customer has can greatly influence their decision to buy from you. Therefore, always ensure that your website is up to date and visually appealing.

- Use new channels for advertising. Today's world offers many advertising options for business owners.

- Text ads should be able to grab the attention of customers as quickly as possible. They should be legible and clear so that customers can quickly understand why they should buy your products.

Promotion

Advertising

Any activity that encourages your customers to stay and make repeat purchases.

Personal Selling

Although it is an old method, personal selling remains highly important. One-on-one interactions between salespeople and customers are an effective strategy for many organizations to promote their products. In personal selling, your salespeople should talk about the differences, distinctions, and values you offer.

Sales Promotion

This method focuses on increasing sales in the short term by offering special proposals or reducing purchasing costs.

Public Relations (PR)

Public relations activities focus on customers' needs, wants, and demands, without attempting to directly sell a product. The goal is simply to assist the customer in becoming more aware of their needs and how your product can meet them. In PR, you should focus on discussing the value your product or service adds to the life of your audience. You select the appropriate media channels for this purpose.

Choosing Advertising Media

Choosing the right advertising media helps you decide how and through which media to share your content and story. Depending on where your target audience spends most of their time, you can choose which platforms to be more active on.

Sales Policy

Sales policy refers to the conditions under which your product is sold and the offers or reasons provided to encourage customers to buy.

Creating Advertising Messages

What is the subject of your advertisement? What is your central message? Are you one of those companies that don't take enough time to craft their advertising content? The best message in advertising is one that showcases your brand's values, personality, and mission.

Exercise

Based on the above points, complete the following table:

Promotion
Advertising
....
....
....
....
....
Personal Selling
....
....
....
....
....
Sales Promotion
....
....
....
....
....
Public Relations (PR)
....
....
....
....
....

Choosing Advertising Media

Sales Policy

Creating Advertising Messages

How can you optimize the marketing or sales of your products or services?

People

"People" refers to everyone involved in the marketing and sales of a business, those who influence the quantity of a product's sales. An effective marketing strategy will only produce desirable results if it is carried out by the right individuals. This principle is one of the marketing secrets: you need to know who is best suited to perform a specific task and in what situation.

People
Who are the key people inside and outside your business?
....
....
....
....
....
Which individuals determine the amount of your sales?
....
....
....
....
....

People

Training Employees	To train your employees, you should have special programs. Today, employee training is considered a part of marketing.
Assessing Employee Competence	Employees who work with you and grow alongside you, learning new skills, should have their competence assessed regularly, not to check if they can continue working with the organization, but to determine whether they are ready to take on more responsibilities, improve their skills, and adapt better. What tools do they need? How should they be equipped?
Involving Employees	Engage employees in key activities within the organization to give them a sense of superiority, expertise, and usefulness. Let them view your organization as their own and care about its success.
Encouraging Employees	Encouragement and rewards are not only financial. Encouraging employees should go beyond simply thanking them; it should mean that their efforts, thoughts, and time spent are recognized. Let your team know that you see their hard work.

Attention to Employee Appearance	Pay attention to their appearance and attire. Appearance directs their behavior.
Employee Interaction	Have you thought about how employees interact with customers? Have you discussed it with them? Do you have guidelines for how they should approach customers? A professional team knows how to behave and interact with clients.
Customer Interaction	Customer behavior involves how employees present products, announce prices, and communicate the benefits and advantages of collaborating with your company.
Contacting Customers	Customer contact isn't limited to phone calls. Any type of communication between your employees and customers should be considered. Think about the quality of these interactions, how they can uncover customer needs, create desires, and prompt demand, ultimately playing a key role in your marketing process.

Exercise

Based on the above points, complete the following table:

People
Training Employees
....
....
....
....
Assessing Employee Competence
....
....
....
....
Involving Employees
....
....
....
....
Encouraging Employees
....
....
....
....

Attention to Employee Appearance

....
....
....
....

Employee Interaction

....
....
....
....

Customer Interaction

....
....
....
....

Contacting Customers

....
....
....
....

▶ Public Witnesses:

How do your product, your people, the environment you operate in, the facilitating processes, sounds, and colors appear to the audience? In the 7P model, less attention is given to public evidence, yet it carries notable insights.

Public Witnesses

Environmental Analysis

What characteristics does the environment and location where you provide your services have? What kind of impression does the environment leave on the audience? Does the design of the decor reflect its importance? Does this environment have the ability to distinguish your business in the minds of customers, such that they feel your business is more complete than others?

Preparing the Environment

Prepare the environment where you provide your service from different aspects. Measure any shortcomings within a specific time frame and take action to improve them. Even assess the strengths and ask yourself: in a world where change happens at every moment, are these still considered strengths?

Color of the Environment

Many businesses do not pay proper attention to the colors and lighting of their environment. The lighting of a space can subconsciously makes the audience feel secure or insecure. Lights and colors have the power to either deter the customer from making a decision or, on the contrary, persuade them to act and purchase.

Noise Level

What sounds can be heard in your environment? If you're in a noisy environment, what measures do you take to control and reduce the noise? What sounds can you play to make individuals enjoy listening and make better decisions?

Facilitating Provided Services

How do you streamline the process? Is this facilitation limited to the process of providing your services, or does it extend to commitment and attention as well? How can you create a positive perception of speed, precision, and care for the audience?

You don't always need to do big things to make a difference. After a conference, don't think that major changes or differentiation always require significant actions. For example, cars would exit the parking lot quickly and easily because the organizer had already paid for the parking fees. Just imagine if this had not been done , the delay in letting 300 cars leave the parking lot would have overshadowed the positive impact of the event. This simple action showed respect for the value of the audience's time and left them with a pleasant feeling.

Exercise

Based on the above points, complete the following table:

Public Witnesses
Environmental Analysis
Preparing the Environment
Color of the Environment
Noise Level
Facilitating Provided Services

▶ Process:

The process includes how your business operates, how services are provided, how products are packaged, how customers move through your sales funnel, payment, shipping, delivery, etc. Essentially, the process describes a set of actions or fundamental elements involved in delivering products or services to customers.

Process
Processes How do you define organizational processes? To get to the CEO's office or the sales room, what steps must someone take that could be effective in your marketing?
Automation Does the automation you use speed up your processes and the performance of your organization, or does it create obstacles instead?
Flow   **of**   **operations** Is the flow of operations in your organization a smooth, ongoing process, or is it a hierarchy that delays things more than it facilitates them? Are the financial, marketing, reception, and other processes working in an organized manner?
Marketing   **activities** How are marketing activities defined? Do you use templates, or do you design them based on the factors we discussed?
Customer   **guidance** How do you guide the customer along the desired path?
Contact with customers Do you design roles for the journey that customers take to reach you? How do the touchpoints along this journey accompany the customer? The customer journey map is the story of their interaction with your brand, from the first encounter to deeper interactions. Along this journey, they often ask themselves, "Does what I see align with what this business promised?" By analyzing the last five to ten customer purchases, you can identify behavioral patterns and common questions they have.

Process

Policies

....
....
....
....
....

Automation

....
....
....
....
....

Flow of operations

....
....
....
....

Marketing activities

....
....
....
....

Customer guidance

....

....

....

....

Contact with customers

....

....

....

....

▶ The 7 Key Elements of Marketing Execution

To successfully execute marketing strategies, it's essential to plan, implement, and evaluate actions. For example, evaluate whether registering a personal ID for entering your website or software enhances customer engagement or harms it. After assessments, you will realize that some activities were effective, and others were not. Learning is a continuous process, meaning investing time and money into improving knowledge and skills for you, your organization, and your industry. During this learning process, you might ask, "What have I been doing until now?"

Stay in a constant state of learning, even at the cost of disrupting your business. Let innovations be born within you and your business.

Once you learn, return to execution. Plan, implement, and evaluate, and never stop learning. Let the cycle continue. As the cycle continues, its speed increases, and consequently, your growth accelerates. Be mindful that your job isn't about reinventing the wheel, it's about making it turn faster. If you stop the cycle, your industry stops, and so does your competitiveness, leaving the playing field open for your rivals.

Marketing Concept

Marketing focuses on critical actions such as identifying target customers, understanding their needs, and analyzing factors influencing their purchasing decisions. Additionally, marketing is about persuading customers to buy from you rather than your competitors. All these activities require a coordinated, thoughtful, accurate, and realistic strategy.

Creating a marketing strategy begins with closely examining both primary and secondary markets. Companies look at the social, political, economic, cultural, and technological trends in the market and assess their position in these trends. They also determine the resources required to affect or influence those trends. In the next phase, the strategy is set with a clear objective and budget. With a well-defined goal, alternative methods to the current situation and ways to reach them are clarified.

In general, planning a successful marketing strategy is closely linked to the overall business planning process because they are interrelated and must be approved by the management. Marketing is, after all, a team effort that requires coordination among various skills, perspectives, and people within the organization.

▶ CATT Funnel in Digital Marketing

Create wealth! Want to know why digital marketing works so well for some businesses and fails for others? Let me tell you. The CATT Funnel is a powerful framework that helps you effectively attract and engage your target audience.

So, what exactly is the CATT Funnel, and how does it fit into marketing? CATT stands for:

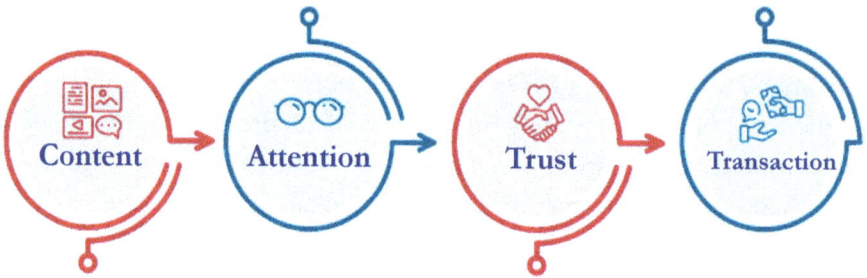

Let's explore the principles of the CATT Funnel and its role in marketing.

Content

To build a strong brand, you must understand the pulse of your customer and their interests. Therefore, provide your customers with a wealth of information about your products or services. In fact, you should display all your abilities through content. If your content is of high quality, the audience will naturally enter the CATT funnel and convert into customers. Content marketing has gained significant importance in recent years, as "content is king." If your content is engaging and captures the audience's attention, it will lead to high engagement rates across all platforms.

Attention

If your content is attractive and able to capture the audience's attention, it will have high views and engagement rates across various platforms.

Trust

What exactly is trust? Imagine walking into a clean restaurant. You might think, "I trust this restaurant, and I'm willing to pay to eat here."

Creating trust is how your customers will follow you, and you are the one who defines their needs.

Transaction (Purchase)

After trust, customers are ready to purchase your products or services. Using the CATT funnel, you attract attention through content, gain the audience's trust, and eventually lead them to make a transaction. At the bottom of the CATT funnel lies wealth. It's a simple formula that can elevate your success.

▶ Content Marketing

Every message has its place. Imagine you are about to buy a mobile phone. One advertisement says, "This phone is the best!" Another content piece details the features, hardware, and software of the phone, and another uses product comparison techniques. Which one attracts you more? Statistics show that content that generates the most leads (prospects willing to buy) is the best type of content. So how do we know which technique to use for content creation, and where should we place each piece of content?

The phrase **"Content is king"** is widely known in marketing. Let's get familiar with the "king of marketing." **Content marketing** is the process of planning, creating, distributing, sharing, and publishing various types of content using various channels. In essence, what I want to say is that if content is king, then content marketing is the ruling force. According to Andrew Davis, "Content builds relationships. Relationships are built on trust, and trust is the precursor to revenue."

● Types of Content Marketing

Content used in marketing comes in various forms, such as images, infographics, podcasts, motion graphics, promotional teasers, written content, and more. There are also numerous channels for distributing this content. Therefore, you have many options regarding the type of content, where to publish it, and even when to publish it.

● Online Content Marketing

Content marketing can be either online or offline. Therefore, any marketing activities focused on content published in the digital space fall under the category of online content marketing. On the other hand, publishing business-related content in a local newspaper is outside this category. Typically, the term **online content marketing** has a broader meaning, distinguishing it from social media and blogging content.

In this context, all activities are related to your website's main pages, landing pages, etc. This form of content marketing helps you rank higher in search engines and, as a result, attract more audience to your brand.

● Blog Content Marketing

The first blog was created in 1994 by Justin Hall, and since then, blogging has become one of the most important tools for marketing. The right strategy for keywords helps both your SEO and guides you in creating engaging content for your audience. Blog content is usually between 1,000 to 4,000 words long, with an average of 1,500 to 2,500 words. Search engine robots use various factors like blog length, keywords, structure, etc., to rank blog pages.

Some important tips for creating effective blog content include:

- Write content for your audience, not for search engines.
- Optimize blog pages and content for loading speed.
- Use high-quality images in your blog posts.
- Use catchy headlines for text content.

● Social Media Content Marketing

The total number of social media users worldwide has exceeded 4.5 billion. While I consider a business website as the main office in the virtual world, I also acknowledge the power of social media in attracting an audience. Many large global brands have social media pages, and businesses should recognize the potential of social networks to drive engagement.

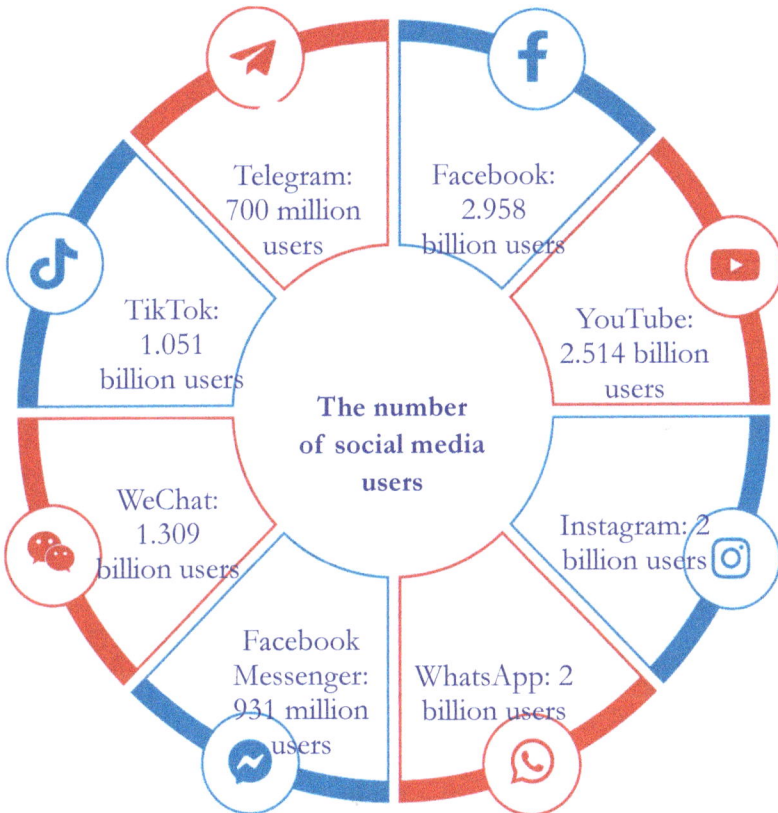

Telegram: 700 million users

Facebook: 2.958 billion users

TikTok: 1.051 billion users

YouTube: 2.514 billion users

The number of social media users

WeChat: 1.309 billion users

Instagram: 2 billion users

Facebook Messenger: 931 million users

WhatsApp: 2 billion users

It is interesting to know that many of the audience first get acquainted with your business through these networks. Then, they search for your website on Google or visit your site via a link. Lee Odden, one of the greats in the marketing world, believes that: **"Content is the engine that drives social media for your business."** Pay attention to the following when choosing the best social network for your business:

- Check where your target audience is most active;

- Check which platform is best suited for your business area;

- Check which platform your competitors have a strong presence on;

- Review the platform's capabilities for advertising on it;

- Review and calculate the costs of content publishing and marketing on the platform.

● **Content Marketing Using Infographics**

Infographics are a type of graphical visual display that convey different and sometimes complex information in the quickest and simplest way to the audience. Businesses use infographics to increase brand awareness, generate leads, and boost online sales. Search engines also consider the presence of infographics as a plus for a website. Infographics can convey information in the form of a visual story in several sections. They can sometimes include the key points of a topic, along with charts, photos, graphics, and statistical data.

● **Content Marketing Using Podcasts**

According to statistics, around 60 million people listen to podcasts through different platforms. Many people prefer podcasts and audio content over text content. Podcasts can be considered a digital evolution of radio broadcasting, consisting of producing one or more audio files. For example, you could explain the principles of your business or the process of producing your products in episodic podcasts to your audience. A successful example of using podcasts for marketing is the "Future" podcast series, published by the Microsoft brand. In this series, the company takes an extensive look at the world of technology, and in these podcasts, you get familiar with the latest technological advances in health, public sector, computers and mobile phones, software and hardware, process automation, data management, and more.

Some of the benefits of using podcasts are as follows:

- Listeners can listen to podcasts anywhere using their mobile phones and headphones;

- Listeners get more familiar with your brand after hearing several episodes;

- Podcasts provide a more tangible interaction with the brand;

- Podcasts can be published on websites, blogs, and some social media platforms and applications.

● Video Content Marketing

As one of the leading animation companies in the world, Wyzowl has reported that more than 73% of consumers prefer to learn about products through videos. Therefore, video content marketing is a type of content marketing strategy that uses the creation and publishing of different types of videos to increase leads (interested customers) and boost sales.

For example, marketers learn through this strategy how to create videos that are appropriate for the type of product or service and the business area, what type of video aligns best with the marketing campaign goals, and how they can measure the feedback from the videos.

Some benefits of this type of content marketing include:

- Using videos can increase site traffic by up to 76% (Wyzowl research);

- Video content, animations, and motion graphics can portray complex ideas or abstract concepts, which can be difficult to explain even in written content;

- The return on investment for advertising videos is very high;

- Videos have a significant impact on building trust, as what is seen sticks better in the mind.

Content Marketing with Paid Advertising

Sometimes marketers compare "Content Marketing" with "Paid Advertising" as two separate strategies and methods. However, there is a shared subset between these two strategies. Every advertisement needs appealing content, and "Content Marketing with Paid Advertising" has a professional selection. For example, in the Google Ads advertising method, you need compelling headlines (suitable for the type of Google Ads campaign), the best keywords, attractive images, or videos. On the other hand, if your landing pages do not have appropriate and compelling content, you will not see a satisfactory return on investment.

One important point about advertising text content is the use of words that have a strong impact on the audience. Some words attract the audience's attention, others create emotional connections, and some convey a sense of superiority about the brand, product, or service.

In the table below, we will review some of these words and phrases.

Pleasure	Heavenly	Prize	Free	Gift
Limited access	Special	Top, Best	first-class	Secret
Today	Final	Hurry	Last chance	Last moment
Countdown	New	Quality	Guarantee	Safe
Immediately	Valid	Tested	Unique	Uunparalleled

For "Content Marketing with Paid Advertising," there are various options, including:

- Paid advertising on YouTube;
- Google Ads advertising;
- Paid Instagram advertising;
- Retargeting advertising;
- Sponsored Gmail ads.

● **Content Marketing using Email:**

Writing and sending emails is still one of the effective methods in marketing. With email, you can introduce new products, provide necessary information about sales events to customers, or send them feedback forms. In modern marketing methods, bulk email sending is no longer used; instead, customers are segmented into different groups, and email content is produced accordingly.

Marketing Checklist

Timing

Date and time of sending .... ☐

Record in calendar .... ☐
(preferably in Google Calendar or email marketing service calendar)

Ensure no overlap with other emails .... ☐
(make sure no other emails are sent)

Sending Details

Subject line (personalized) .... ☐

Updated headers .... ☐

Footer .... ☐

Business address sent .... ☐

Unsubscribe links .... ☐

Social media icons .... ☐

Email content

Body content (readable with appropriate font) .... ☐

Images (related with ALT usage) ☐

Images (related for background headers) .... ☐

Call to Action (CTA) .... ☐

Personalized email content .... ☐

Dynamic content (up-to-date, specialized, and engaging) .... ☐

Sending List

Suppression (unsubscription /spamming) .... ☐

Exclusions (removing parts of the list) .... ☐

Data (subscribers within your target audience) .... ☐

Email Sending

Input control (sending sample to yourself) .... ☐

A/B testing method .... ☐

Sending schedule (send immediately, send in the future) .... ☐

Post-send analysis (how did it perform?) .... ☐

What is Content Marketing Strategy and How is it Done?

In today's competitive market, even providing products that are of interest to the brand's audience is not enough. This is because you need to be able to present products in the best way through various marketing methods, such as content marketing, and encourage the audience to make a purchase. Accordingly, content marketing is a planned and goal-oriented approach that focuses on creating valuable, relevant content, publishing it, and analyzing the results. According to HubSpot's research, around 70% of companies worldwide have a dedicated budget for content marketing and all of them are confident that this investment helps to boost their business. What Actions Should We Take to Start?

▶Set Goals

The four common goals in content marketing are:

- Increasing brand awareness
- Building customer loyalty
- Educating the audience
- Increasing engagement with customers

Combining these goals can drive sales growth.

▶Understand the Audience Persona

Understanding the audience persona means recognizing characteristics such as age, gender, geographical location, habits, lifestyle, and preferences of the customers. For example, the text you write for teenagers differs from the one you would write for middle-aged company managers.

▶ Note Down Ideas

Allocate time to note down all ideas and tips about content marketing for help from your colleagues, and then prioritize the ideas.

- Choose the Best Marketing Channels

- Decide where each piece of content should be presented and how.

- Create a Content Calendar

- The timing of content publication is very important. For instance, brand audiences on social media expect a new post every day

- Analyze Results

- Only by gathering and analyzing content marketing data can you evaluate the success of your efforts.

Remember in Content Marketing:

- Content marketing is a method for introducing your brand, products, and services.

- You can use different types of content to explain how to use your products.

- Content can highlight the differentiating factors of your product or service compared to others.

- Content marketing can turn the audience into a lead (interested audience).

- More leads result in higher sales.

- Creating effective communication with the audience through content increases customer loyalty.

- Content can showcase your brand's values.

Content Production Calendar Checklist:

A content production calendar is a tool used to develop content strategy and marketing. By using this tool, we can ensure that content does not repeat, is published on time, and that team members' roles are clarified. The content calendar helps create a clear picture of the one-year plan. The checklist below will guide you step-by-step in preparing your content calendar.

protocol and Structure		Protocol and Structure	
Identifying the Audience	☐	Selecting Content Title	☐
Choosing the Right Content	☐	Defining the Publication Date	☐
Purpose of the Content	☐	Considering an Appropriate CTA	☐
Selecting the Content Type	☐	Identifying the Content Author	☐
Defining Key Days	☐	Using Keywords in the Text	☐
Reviewing Standards and Resources	☐	Inserting Links in the Text	☐
Identifying Holidays or Special Occasions	☐		

Content Testing Before Publishing

Has Statistical Analysis been done for the content?	☐
Is the content SEO-friendly?	☐
Is the content shareable and promotable?	☐
Is the content suitable for the audience's preferences?	☐
Are marketing points observed in the content?	☐
Is the content displayed correctly on all devices (mobile and laptop)?	☐

Tools for Creating a Content Production Calendar

Excel	☐
Google Sheets	☐
Google Analytics	☐
Google Calendar	☐

▶ Content: The Main Way to Interact with the Audience in Business

The concept of content marketing dates back before the emergence of the internet, and many businesses used to introduce their brand or products in media outlets like newspapers and television. However, in today's digital world, content marketing has gained much more importance. This is because both small and large businesses with various budgets can now create content and publish it across multiple marketing channels. Familiarity with these channels and marketing tactics is extremely valuable.Content is crucial for increasing the effectiveness of this strategy. **In the economy of value creation and entrepreneurship, it forces you to think seriously about these aspects. Why? Because it bridges marketing and branding. This is where the product inside your business needs to be introduced.** What does this product do for the customer? What value does it offer? What problem does it solve for the customer? How does it improve the customer's quality of life? Through which channels should it be distributed? Before distribution, which channels should it be introduced through? What nature does it have? What kind of content will support it in the market? In reality, the product is contained within a circle called marketing.

What will this product become famous for? Let me express my point better with a question. When you say "Mercedes," what is Mercedes famous for? And how about "Lada"? Brand means the perception of the world about your business. Brand means the identity and value positioning of your business.

You might ask, what is meant by value positioning? As I mentioned earlier about needs, wants, and demand, the person who buys a Rolex watch is positioning wealth. The value that Rolex sells is not about showing time, but about showcasing wealth. It is about demonstrating belonging to a certain social class. This is the bridge between branding and marketing.

▶ **Branding In Business Mastery**

Branding plays an important role in marketing perspectives and in how the world perceives your company. How is your company recognized? What does the world understand about your company? What does your target market think of you? What do they say about your company? Is it worth it? Does it have a good reputation? Is it responsible? Does it have expensive products, but good distribution? You can see that the seven elements of marketing are part of branding.

The following diagram reflects this well:

Branding sits at the heart of commercial activities aimed at shaping your brand.

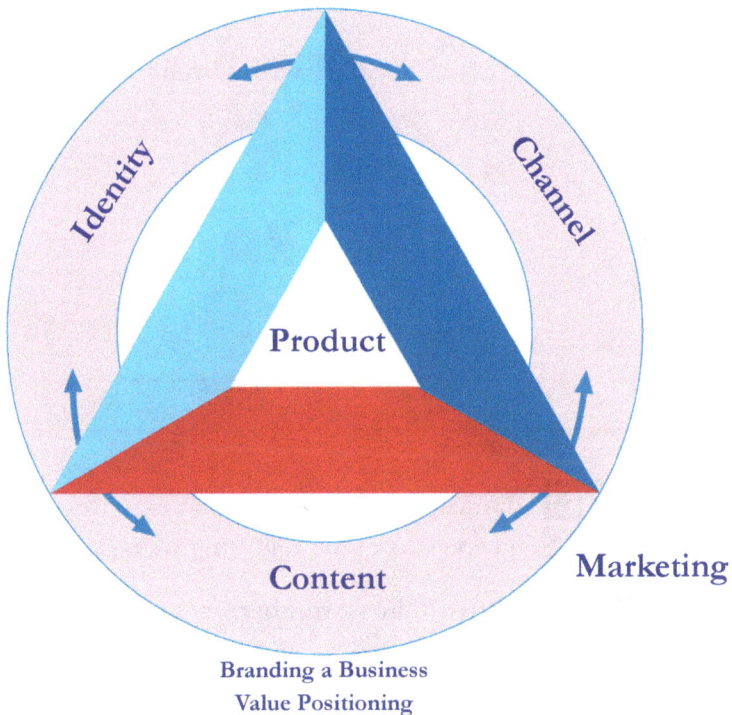

Branding a Business
Value Positioning

▶ **Write Your Five Key Takeaways from This Chapter:**

1. ....

2. ....

3. ....

4. ....

5. ....

▶ **Three Steps I Will Immediately Start:**

1. ....

2. ....

3. ....

▶ **One Golden Lesson to Share with Others:**

....

....

....

....

Download all the tables and exercises of this chapter from the following website.

https://hosseintaheri.ir/bmg/

Sales Creation

Chapter 7:

Sales

Sales Creation

Sales is not controlling the customer; it is controlling the customer's needs.

📖 **After reading this chapter, you will gain mastery over:**

- Customer identification and segmentation
- Principles, processes, and strategies of customer acquisition
- Customer journey
- Principles of customer care
- Attitude and skills of a proficient salesperson
- Characteristics of an effective sales system

Section One: The Customer

"Not all your customers are the same. I know that sales are exciting, but attracting everyone means spending all your time, energy, and resources on people who might not even have an interest in your product. Sales are not driven by excitement, but by enthusiasm. This is because *enthusiasm* leads to *confidence*, and confidence is the result of *focus*; focus on a desirable and reasonable target market.

• **Desirable target market:** A market that is interested and willing to pay for the benefit derived from your product.

• **Reasonable target market:** A market that you select based on your criteria and calculations so you can earn revenue from it."

```
┌─────────────────────────────────────────┐
│  Reasonable      Focus Area    Desirable │
│  Market                        Market    │
└─────────────────────────────────────────┘
```

▶ Not every paying customer is your customer

We all face many individuals while selling our goods and services who, in fact, are not our customers because:

- They are buyers, but they want more than what they are willing to pay.

- They are always complaining and prevent you from focusing on other customers.

- They do not appreciate the value of your product and only want to try purchasing from you once.

- After agreeing on the price, they still try to negotiate.

- They prioritize price over quality.

- Your product is not suitable for them.

Naturally, you cannot hold up a **"No Entry"** sign to prevent people who cannot be your customers from entering. However, you can design a scanning system to assess their behavior or purchase history.

▶ What are scanners?

1. Receiving a customer brief form before the transaction (accurate customer information)

Brief forms can be placed on your website or the product/service purchase page, or emailed immediately after the first customer contact for a purchase.

2. Conducting interviews to measure the suitability of a buyer's behavior with other key customers

Interview sessions between the salesperson and the buyer are one of the most effective ways to identify a customer. In addition to creating interaction, it reassures the interviewee that the organization values their money and time. Interviews begin with gathering information from the customer and continue with questions, conversations, and listening to their needs and concerns. What distinguishes these sessions is not just the output, but the impact they have on those who, even if they are not your customers, will talk about the importance you gave them everywhere.

3. Assessing the buyer's financial status and behavior

If your market is accessible, you can explicitly or implicitly ask other members of your business community about how they interact and the financial status of your buyers. Keep in mind that in such cases, do not rely solely on the answers from one organization to make a final decision.

4. Tracking the customer's journey, from the first contact to the last interaction

To attract and retain your ideal customers, you must fully understand their journey. How did they get to know you? What actions have they taken? By answering these questions, you can understand their needs and desires and determine whether they are the customers you're looking for.

▶Who is the "main customer"?

Up to this point, to answer this question clearly, we have defined who is not a customer. In its true sense, a customer is an individual, group, or organization that buys a product or service from a business and usually intends to use it to fulfill a need or desire, even if they are not the direct consumer of that product or service.

We complete the above definition with a slight difference and call the customer the "main customer." Your main customer is someone who:

- They understand the value of your product and are willing to pay for it without hesitation;

- They have the potential to become a loyal customer;

- They always follow news and information about you;

- Using your product or service has become a part of their life-style;

- They are good critics and their feedback helps improve your product or service.

These customers form a group with similar behavioral patterns and, based on the criteria and key performance indicators defined in your "post-sales system," they are distinguished from others and ultimately considered your main customers.

▶ Customer Prospecting

In 1986, Alain Prost, the French Formula 1 champion, participated in the German Grand Prix without completely filling his car's fuel tank. During the semifinal stage, his car ran out of fuel, and despite being ahead of his competitors, he did not reach the finish line. Even when his car stopped, he refused to accept defeat and tried to push it to the finish line, though in reality, the finish line was too far away, and Prost could only watch as other cars passed him.

If you are a racing champion and drive the best car, but don't fill its tank, you won't win. Fuel is what keeps a cycle moving. What I mean is simple: customer prospecting is filling the fuel of your sales funnel, keeping your sales cycle in motion. Every sales activity depends on your ability to keep this funnel filled with opportunities, leads, and potential customers. What you need to focus on is being aware of the inventory in your funnel and continuously refilling it. You might ask, "How?" Don't worry, I'll tell you.

▶Who is chasing whom?

This is your economic launch pad. Customer prospecting is a cornerstone of any healthy sales process. Every qualified customer, upon entering your unique sales cycle, enters your sales funnel and undergoes the process of moving through the funnel and transforming into your main customer. This journey is defined by the level of engagement during the touchpoints you create. All the targeted activities you perform in this process, from generating leads to converting an individual into a main customer, are referred to as "customer prospecting."

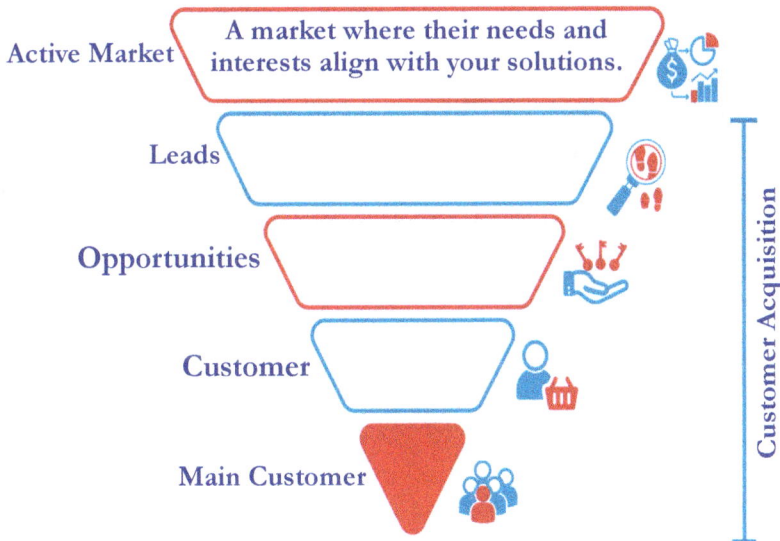

Through customer acquisition, you ensure that you are engaging with an audience that is open to your value proposition. This step is often the most challenging and time-consuming part of the sales process, and it frequently gets delayed, just like any other important task. This may be because it isn't as thrilling as closing a deal.

Before anything else, you first learn business in the market. The language of business is mathematics and simple arithmetic. This means that in this process, the more leads you generate, the greater your chances of making a sale because each lead represents an opportunity. However, it doesn't always result in an immediate sale. You may generate multiple sales over time from the same opportunity as you nurture it into becoming a loyal customer. Here, "economic launch pad" truly becomes meaningful.

▶ Why does sales play a role in customer acquisition?

The playing field has shifted. Buyers now take the sales process into their own hands and, before reaching out to you, they are already searching for their purchase. In this environment, as a seller, you cannot avoid customer acquisition and claim that generating leads is solely marketing's responsibility. It turns out, things aren't as bleak as they seem. The people you're looking for are actually already looking for you. Customer acquisition requires patience, perseverance, and diligent research, and if done correctly, it can not only create an exciting experience but also enhance your sales skills.

How to Acquire Customers?

Step1: Designing Opportunity Profiles

Where should we begin? With such a broad spectrum of individuals, organizations, and industries each with unique characteristics, this is the most important question to ask at the starting point.

Exercise:

Write down the names of your five best customers	Write down the names of your five worst customers

Which customers bring you the most profit?	Which customers bring you the least profit?

Now, for each of the four above groups, create a profile:

Customer Behavioral Profile	Organizational Behavioral Profile
What characteristics do they have?	**How did you get in touch with them?**
How did they appear in the first encounter?	**How did you appear in the first encounter?**
What questions did they ask?	**What questions did you ask them?**

Customer Behavioral Profile	Organizational Behavioral Profile
What answers did they provide?	**What answers did you provide to their questions?**
What are their payment habits like?	**How do you determine payment terms?**
What concerns do they have?	**What solutions do you offer them?**

Customer Behavioral Profile

What do they emphasize the most?

....
....
....
....
....
....

How is their buying behavior?

....
....
....
....
....
....

What influences their decision-making?

....
....
....
....
....
....

Organizational Behavioral Profile

What do you assure them about?

....
....
....
....
....
....

How do you present your product to them?

....
....
....
....
....

How successful were you in connecting with the decision-makers?

....
....
....
....
....

All the people who want to buy from us and whose information we have are our customers. This is the most basic and superficial sales approach, which we have previously discussed. By doing the exercise above, you will come to the conclusion that, in the best-case scenario, at least half of your potential customers are not suitable for what you want to sell to them.

Now, you must ask yourself which profiles are worth investing in and allocating resources to (considering time, content, product information, communication, and campaign design)? How much should you strengthen your relationship with them? After answering this question, see which other companies that are not yet your customers match your ideal customer profile and could be considered opportunities. This technique, called 'Account-Based Marketing,' makes your marketing and sales team more coordinated.

Step 2: Developing a Commercial Route (Locating Opportunities)

Go back to the starting point of the journey. Where did you meet your best customers? Where are the most profitable customers found?"

● **Social Media:**

Using social media such as Instagram, Facebook, Twitter, YouTube, and LinkedIn, you can engage with your target audience. LinkedIn, often neglected by business owners, allows you to connect and interact with individuals and leaders in your field. Twitter, on the other hand, serves as a platform to share your opinions and decisions with your audience. The more effectively you present your ideas and products, the more people you will attract.

● **Website**:

A professional website is a powerful marketing tool. It can help introduce your brand and provide product information, attracting more potential customers to your business.

● Retargeting Ads:

Do not forget the audiences who have visited your website at least once. With retargeting ads, you can remind and introduce your products and services to them, encouraging them to return to your sales funnel.

● Trade Events:

Networking is a valuable source of opportunity. Trade shows allow you to connect with individuals who share similar goals or interests. At these events, you can start conversations about mutual experiences, interests, and concerns. The more you share with others, the more likely you will continue to build relationships in the future.

Trade shows are excellent for "introducing" products and services to a targeted community. Focus on the presentation style and the way your business interacts with others, as this reflects your company's values and helps create valuable business relationships.

● Step 3: Prioritize Your Contact List

All your contact information should be well-organized. Potential clients should be categorized, and you should ensure that the contact process happens at a specific time. Phone calls can have a significant impact on moving individuals through your sales funnel. Remember, these calls are not just about sales; they are about prospecting.

Key Questions to Keep in Mind During Calls:

- What are they looking for?

- What is occupying their mind?

- Do they have a solution in mind?

- Do they have enough information?

- Is there personalized information you can send them?

Step 4: Send Personalized Emails

Never think that prospecting via email is ineffective. It remains one of the most popular communication channels. What will influence your audience in emails is:

- Show them that you have valuable knowledge, information, and experience about their field.

- Ensure your email content meets their needs.

- Know what to say and when to send it.

Sending emails is a powerful way to reach and maintain your target customers. Emails and newsletters allow you to keep your audience informed about what you offer and your plans ahead.

Email sending guide on the website www.hosseintaheri.ir

Step 5: Happy Customers

No salesperson performs better than a happy customer. This customer passes on their happiness to the people they know. Many business owners find it easier to connect and make a purchase from salespeople introduced through their friends.

A customer is happy with their purchase when they have a pleasant experience. A pleasant experience results in that customer recommending you to others, sharing the positive feelings they had with you. You can also invite your customers to a special event and, by offering an extra invitation, ask them to bring one of their friends along. Just make sure that these events are not for sales but for customer acquisition and creating a pleasant experience.

Step 6: Be a Reference

To make your customers happy, you must be a reference. People ask references who provide them with useful and effective solutions. Being a part of the community is what distinguishes you in your field of work.

Step 7- Follow-Up

The outcome of your business is not achieved by just one action. Timely follow-ups make you appear trustworthy and committed. Sending various emails, offering useful information, and making effective calls all increase your chances of making a sale while building relationships.

Follow-ups can involve tasks such as scheduling the next contact, sending product details, providing guidance on product usage instructions, or simply sending a thank-you message through text, video, photo, or audio. Follow-up is considered valuable by customers and maximizes the return on your time.

▶ Customer Journey

No one suddenly decides to buy your products and services. Every customer's buying path, from "awareness" to "loyalty," is a complete journey that you can manage, control, and navigate. The customer journey includes all interactions that a customer has with a brand or business. From the moment the customer becomes aware of their need, they begin to consider and evaluate new products and services until they make a purchase decision.

▶ Are We a Good Travel Companion?

The customer is the most important asset of any business. Organizations that focus on the customer gain more profit than their competitors. When we talk about the customer journey, we want to delve into the details of the path the customer has traveled with us, from the first encounter until now. The primary reason for focusing on this topic is the effort to earn a title: "A Good Travel Companion."

▶ Customer Journey Map

We need roles that map the customer's interaction path and allow us to observe our products and behaviors from a different perspective so that we can analyze customer behaviors, identify our weaknesses, and offer appropriate solutions. The customer journey map helps you discover the factors that contribute to creating a satisfying customer experience in five stages. After understanding this journey, you can better plan for delivering your products and services.

	Awareness	Attention	Decision	Services	Loyalty
User Action	• Advertising and Campaign Review • Inquiry from Friends and Colleagues	• Competitor Analysis • Advantage Evaluation • Response to Purchase Reasons	• Purchase and Product Receipt	• Searching for Product Use and Function • Product • Product Usage	• Building a Positive Relationship with the Product • Sharing Purchase Experience • Repeat Purchases
Touch-points	**Digital:** • Online Advertising • Mass Email • Digital Billboard **Physical:** • Public Relations • Radio • Television	**Digital:** • Blog Landing Page • Other Person's Website **Physical:** • Packaging	**Digital:** • Website **Physical:** • Store Environment • Call Center • Salesperson; Cashier Behavior	**Digital:** • Online Chat • Product Delivery System **Physical** • Telephone • Product Delivery System	**Digital:** • Email Newsletter • Content Posting on Social Networks **Physical:** • Bulletin • Exhibition • Seminar

User Experience

Weaknesses

• Message Complexity
• Confusing Landing Pag
• Cluttered Catalog

• Unsupported deliveries Lack of Product Guide

Solutions

• Improving Landing Pages
• Segregating Advertisements
• Creating Help Links
• Product Categorization

• Designing a Delivery System According to Customer Preferences
• Creating Post-Purchase Guide Content

1. Pre-Purchase Stage
●Awareness

At this stage, the customer is aware of your services, but they are not yet engaged. What you need to do at this stage is encourage them to research whether they should buy from you or not. You can display answers to their questions (What is this product? What benefits does it offer? Who is it suitable for?) at the touchpoints you create in this stage.

Note: At this stage, you have customers who are aware of your product. Now, you need to turn their awareness into evaluation by prompting them to assess the pros and cons of using the product. Your competitive advantages should be placed in the customer's path here.

2. Purchase Stage
●Purchase Decision

At this stage, the customer becomes involved by purchasing your product. The touchpoints at this stage should be designed and arranged meticulously to avoid the customer changing their mind.

3. Post-Purchase Stage
●Services

At this stage, the customer begins using your product. Their experience here is not just shaped by using the product, but also by the accompanying product guide, product support, explanations about its uses, and many other services that make your brand stand out. This can provide them with a more pleasant experience.

●Loyalty

Any factor that convinces the customer that price is not the deciding factor in purchasing your product, and creates satisfaction and a desire to recommend you to others, builds loyalty.

▶Customer Journey Map

The customer journey is not a linear and predictable path. Depending on various factors, a customer can move from one phase to another. They may engage with some touchpoints and miss others. **The customer journey map allows you to understand any potential engagement or disengagement of the customer with your product or organization.** This way, you can provide them with better experiences. This map not only covers the period related to the purchase but also includes the stages before and after the purchase. In this way, you go beyond just meeting the customer's needs and can identify the best ways to communicate with and support your customer throughout their journey.

Note that this map is completed by gathering information from the customer through surveys, interviews, forms, and with the help of your team.

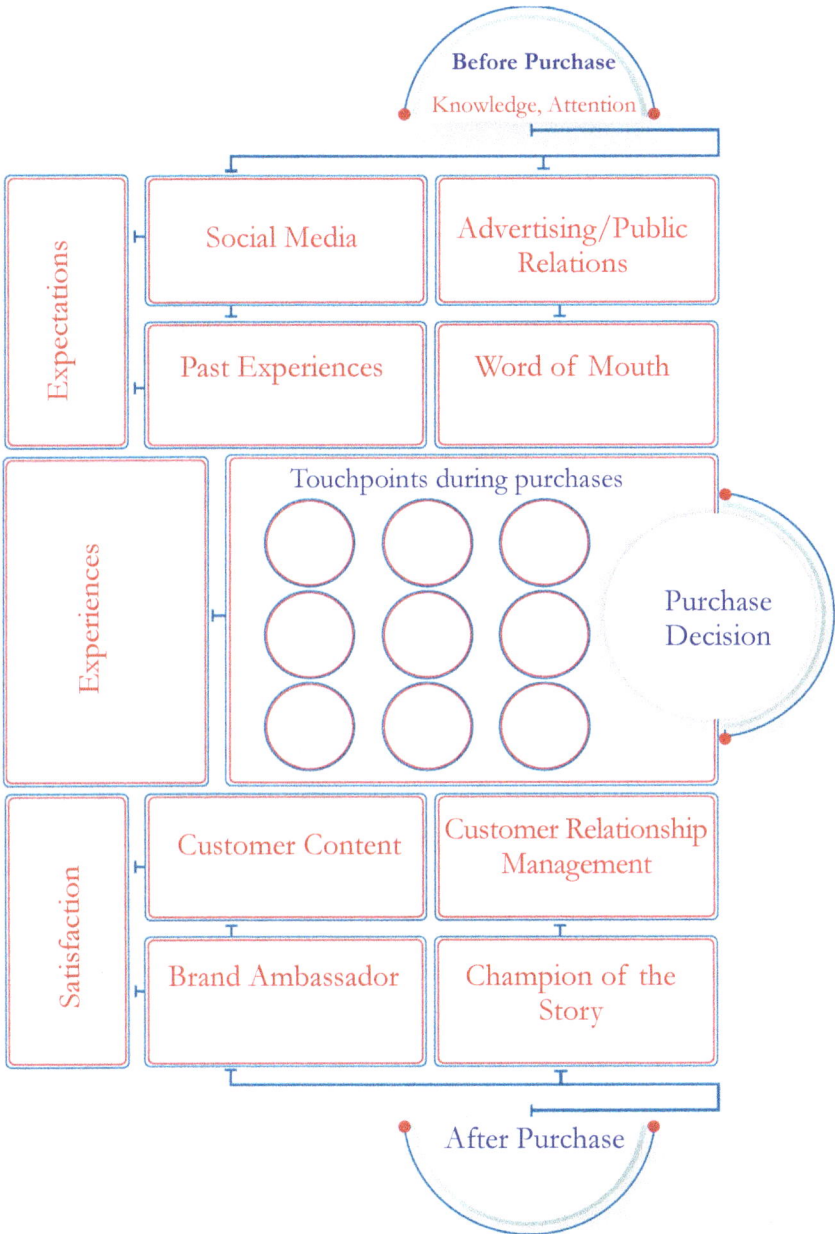

Before Purchase

Knowledge, Attention

Expectations

Social Media

Advertising/Public Relations

Past Experiences

Word of Mouth

Experiences

Touchpoints during purchases

Purchase Decision

Satisfaction

Customer Content

Customer Relationship Management

Brand Ambassador

Champion of the Story

After Purchase

▶ **Before Purchase**

• Advertising and Public Relations:

How do you present your values and services to your audience? Which advertisements have engaged your target audience and created awareness about your product?

• Social Media:

What kind of information do your social media platforms provide about your product to the audience? Which content on which platform has influenced their decision-making process?

• Word of Mouth:

Have they heard anything about your product from family, friends, or colleagues? What was their opinion about the experience of buying from you? What solutions do you have to address negative feedback and ideas to nurture positive ones?

• Past Experiences:

What experiences do your audience have with similar service providers and their products? How have your best competitors created such experiences?

• Touchpoints During Purchase:

From the moment a customer enters your store (physical or website), this phase begins. There are several touchpoints that can influence whether or not the customer makes a purchase. List your existing touchpoints here and rate each one from one (least influential) to five (most influential) based on its ability to affect the customer's decision. Then, assess which touchpoints need to be nurtured and which need improvement. (Example: store environment, salesperson behavior, cashier behavior, optimized user experience landing page, easy access to products).

• Customer Relationship Management:

Have you maintained communication with your customer after the purchase? Have you followed up on how they are using the product?

• Supportive Content:

Have you sent any post-purchase guides to your customer? (This guide can be an e-catalog or a short video that includes recommendations for using your product or service).

• Champion of the Story:

What aspects of using your product make the customer feel like a winner? What makes them share their success story with family, friends, and colleagues and recommend you to them?

• Brand Ambassador:

Which individuals are willing to defend your organization and product anywhere and recommend it to others without hesitation? Does your recommendation hold any value for them?

• Expectations:

What expectations did customers have before purchasing your products or services?

• Experiences:

From the moment they interacted with your organization to the purchase, how would they rate their experience from one (least satisfactory) to five (most satisfactory)? What experiences have stayed in their minds?

• Satisfaction:

Has fulfilling your commitments met their expectations and earned their satisfaction, or is there a big gap between your promises and what you've delivered? Reviewing the customer journey allows you to determine where your customers engage with your business and have an experience. This way, you can design a journey that creates an unforgettable and enjoyable experience for your customers.

▶ Customer Retention:

Customer retention is the result of care.

It's enough to show your customers that you "care" about them, their needs, emotions, and, of course, their pockets. Caring leads to two pleasant outcomes:

- The customer, once they are yours, will be more inclined to make more purchases from you.
- The industry in which you operate will no longer tolerate ineffective and weak products and services.

If we want to analyze the word **"CARE,"** we can think of it as a combination of four elements that form the core of a customer-centric business:

C: Creativity

Creativity is the first prominent feature of caring organizations. They spice up their services, communications, and support programs with creativity to engrave themselves in the customer's mind.

A: Appreciation

Appreciating the customer's choice in both words and actions is essential for every customer-centric organization.

R: Responsibility

Responsibility is the foundation for building trust and long-term business relationships.

E: Effectiveness

Ultimately, effectiveness is what we do to ensure longevity. In the continuation of this section, we will explore ideas, principles, and strategies that can nurture these four elements, leading to customer retention and, in other words, increasing customer lifetime and value.

Before anything else, go to a quiet and private place and honestly answer these seventeen important questions.

Questions	Almost Always	Some-times	Almost Never
1- I learn my customers' names so that I can have better conversations with them.			
2- In my conversations, I offer appropriate recommendations for each individual.			
3- I do tasks under the title "going beyond the job" at specific intervals.			
4- Every week, I personally follow up on the issues of a few customers randomly.			
5- I have designed a response system and team for the questions and concerns of my customers.			
6- I design alternative options so that my customers can analyze and make the right decisions.			
7- I understand the benefits that my product creates and I try to inform my customers about them.			
8- If a customer truly needs me, I will dedicate some of my personal time (lunch break, after work hours, or rest time) to assist them.			
9- I design my business interactions with customers in a way that makes it feel like they are my friend.			

10 - I design programs that are also related to the customer's surrounding world (family or job), and when I talk to them, I ask about them.

11 - While thanking the customer for choosing us, I also show this gratitude through action.

12 - When my organization makes a mistake, I honestly apologize to the customer and work to correct it.

13- If my organization cannot solve the customer's problem, I refer them to another source (even if it's a competitor).

14 - Even when my customers are not present, I do what is beneficial for them, not what is faster or easier for me.

15- I ask clear questions from the customer to make sure I fully understand their situation.

16 - If I make a promise to a customer, I fulfill it as soon as possible.

17 - I try to add something creative in most of my interactions with customers that leaves my personal signature and makes them smile.

First, congratulate yourself for the ones you marked as **"Always"**. Think about what you can do to nurture them. Write down your ideas next to each one.

Next, review the questions you marked as **"Sometimes"**. Discuss them with your organization's managers and team. What can you do to improve on these? Write your thoughts next to each one.

Now, look at the questions you marked as **"Never"**. For each of them, write down a solution so your mind acknowledges it, and then ask your team and organization to implement it.

Finally, look at these seventeen questions again. If you were a customer yourself, would you expect the salesperson to behave in this way toward you? Is there anything else you would like to add to these questions?

Additionally, below is the customer loyalty framework from Hossein Taheri's website for you.

Rewards	Scenarios (Conditions)

Sections	Goals

Channels	Data

Processes	Integration

Rewards

Different sections can be motivated by various types of rewards.

▶ **How do we currently encourage customers to make a purchase?**

....

....

▶ **How do we reward loyal customers now?**

....

....

▶ **How do we want to reward customers in the loyalty program?**

....

....

We try to link sections, conditions, and rewards together. This is why these sections are placed together in the loyalty canvas.

Conditions (Scenarios)

To define scenarios, we ask questions like:

▶ **Which purchasing behaviors do we improve through the customer loyalty program?**

....

....

▶ **What type of conditions should be created in the loyalty program?**

....

....

Clear and specific conditions relate to customer behaviors. These behaviors are beneficial, and we want them to be repeated more often.

Sections

This section outlines the different types of stakeholders and how we can segment our customers. In this section, we ask the following questions:

▶ How are customers currently segmented?

....
....
....

▶ What are the three most important segments?

....
....
....

▶ What are the shopping habits of specific segments?

....
....
....
....

Goals

In this section, we need to validate the challenges of our business by answering the following question:

▶ After introducing a loyalty program, what outcome do we expect?

....
....
....
....

Channels

This section shows how the loyalty solution will be presented and offered to potential users. We ask the following questions:

▶ How are customers encouraged to join the loyalty program?

....

....

▶ How is a loyalty program advertised online?

....

....

▶ How is a loyalty program advertised offline?

....

....

....

Data

In the data section, we aim to define the type of data resources we currently have and what kind of data we need to start collecting to implement our ideal loyalty program. The questions are:

▶ What type of customer data do we currently have?

....

....

▶ Where is the data collected from?

....

....

▶ What data should we collect?

....

....

....

Processes

In this section, we ask:

▶ **When have we collected customer information?**

....
....
....

▶ **What processes need to be followed to collect customer data?**

....
....
....

▶ **What processes need to be done to stimulate a loyalty program?**

....
....
....

Integration

To finalize the definition of loyalty solutions, we must identify our integration needs. In fact, we need to examine which internal and external tools are essential to implement the designed loyalty solution. In this section, we ask:

▶ **Which systems should the loyalty program be integrated with?**

....
....
....
....
....

▶ **Human-Centered Business Model**

In every business transaction, you experience two levels of interaction: the **business level** and the **human level**.

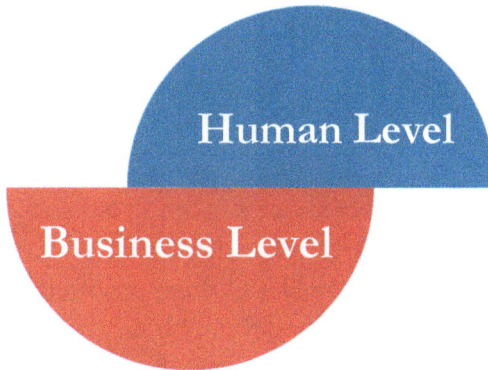

Human Level

Business Level

Today, differentiation no longer comes from "focusing on the business level" but rather from influencing your activities at the **human level**. In fact, people are eager to be recognized as humans. Understanding what people want and designing things that satisfy them and take care of them is the most important way to achieve your business goals. So, what we need is a **human-centered business model,** and this requires awareness of the human needs of customers. Implementing this model creates valuable experiences for customers and brings profits for us as well.

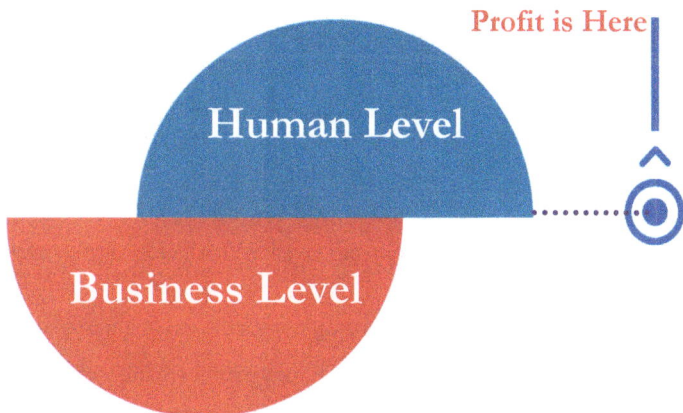

Profit is Here

Human Level

Business Level

▶ The Principle of Surprise

Do something extraordinary and attention-grabbing. Surprise is an action on our part to create a sense of **"excitement"** in the customer's mind. When we are taking care of a valuable individual, we strive to improve what they experience with us. Surprise is one of the amazing ways to care for and retain customers. We can only create it when we think and ultimately act beyond their expectations and our own commitments.

To design surprises, have discussions with your team and hold brainstorming sessions. Start with the most unrelated ideas and encourage your team members to be bold and direct in offering their opinions. Below, we've provided ideas for different businesses. You can use them as inspiration, enhance them, and apply them to your business.

Business	Ideas
Nuts Shop	Give a toothbrush as a gift with every packet of nuts.
Café & Restaurant	Instead of a "Welcome" or "Greeting" meal design a small food item with interesting packaging to say goodbye.
Flower Shop	Collect the birthdates or special occasions of customers' family members spouses or friends and remind the customer of the occasion on that day (via SMS email or postcard).
Educational Institution	Take photos of students at different moments (at the front of the class during breaks during talks with professors or during leisure time) and post them on the announcement board.
Gynecologist	Put ultrasound photos and the first baby photo in a small album and give it to the family as the baby's first album.
Bank	After completing a customer's transaction give them a card with the bank's logo that says "I'm happy I could take care of your task today."

Dentist	Send a gift card the day after the patient's visit with the message " To buy yogurt; it helps improve your gum pain and inflammation."
Clothing Store	Gift a scented essence with every piece of clothing.
Interior Design	Gift a set of accessories that match the designed environment.
Cake & Pastry Shop	Collect customers' addresses and special dates then send them a cupcake with a candle on their special day. Alternatively for a customer's family birthday send them the recipe for making a homemade cake.
Gym	After the first session send the individual a message saying "If you experience muscle soreness try these three exercises at home."
Publishing House	Place a fancy pencil or highlighter with the message "Read with me" inside every book's packaging.
Car Wash	Place an air freshener in the car after the first visit.
Auto Repair Shop	Produce and send content titled "Things You Can Fix Yourself" in video or text format.

▶ **Compensation Principle**

Every business makes mistakes, and this is something everyone accepts. In fact, what often discourages your customer from making a deal or buying again is not a mistake or error, but the lack of acceptance of that mistake by you. Any part of your organization that makes a mistake must acknowledge it and take steps to make amends. Adhering to the principle of compensation can make your customer even more loyal than before, as they understand that in dealings with you, if anything goes wrong, they won't need to worry.

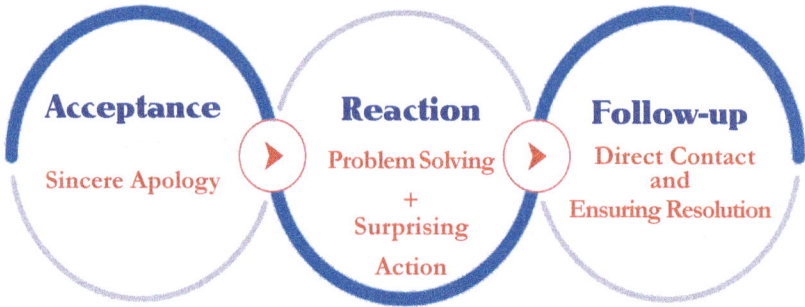

Acceptance	Reaction	Follow-up
Sincere Apology	Problem Solving + Surprising Action	Direct Contact and Ensuring Resolution

The principle of compensation has three steps:

● **Acceptance:**

Acknowledge the mistake and apologize. Tell the customer, "You are right." By doing this, you show that you are not standing against them, and there is no need to fight with you.

● **Reaction:**

Don't stop at just accepting the mistake. Act immediately. To make up for the error, do something for the customer and surprise them.

● **Follow-up:**

After some time, reconnect with the customer to ensure that their issue has been resolved and that they are satisfied with your solution.

Exercise: Write down the names of five customers who have stopped working with you in the past three months. What were the reasons for their departure? How did you respond? What can you do to bring them back?

Customer Name	Problem/Issue	Your Response	Solution to Provide for Re-engagement

Based on your proposed strategies, take immediate action to bring two of these customers back to your list.

Final Strategies for Customer Care

1. Design a Customer Communication Calendar: Don't let the customer feel that you only contact them when you want to sell something. Create a calendar for customer communication, with specific days dedicated to particular topics. For example, set aside one day specifically for gathering feedback. These calls can create opportunities for sales.

2. Create a Customer Education Program: Educate your customers on how to use the product. These trainings can be published on social media, but it's better if they are personalized for each customer. The surprising impact of this technique is when the customer realizes that they are learning something from you.

3. Send Company and Product Newsletters to Customers: Do this regularly. Design and schedule an email newsletter so that every time a customer opens their email, they see your name and are reminded of you. You can also create a bulletin about your activities and send it to your customers monthly.

4. Design Actions to Strengthen the Moment of Choice: For the first contact or first visit of the customer, have actions in place. Know exactly what you want to say and how you can strengthen their moment of choice. Even if they don't buy from you, make sure you remain memorable in their mind.

5. Design Environmental Advertising for Customer Care: Environmental advertising for customer care is a creative way to turn the interior of your organization into a pleasant and inspiring environment. By using this method, you can constantly remind your employees and customers of key customer care messages.

▶ **How to Measure Customer Retention Rate:**

The customer retention rate is measured over a specific period of time with the following formula:

$$X=(\frac{E-N}{S})\times100$$

- **S:** Number of customers at the start of a specific period
- **E:** Number of customers at the end of this period
- **N:** Number of new customers added during the period
- **X**: Customer retention rate

Section 2: Salesperson

▶ **Preparation and Attitude**

When you don't sell, you're still selling.
This rule ensures that the customer doesn't think your goal is simply to sell them your product. The salesperson is responsible for creating popularity for a brand. By nurturing the salesperson's attitude, you empower your sales. Because your attitude as a salesperson is far more important than the skills you have.

▶ **What is Attitude?**

Attitude is your way of thinking and feeling about a specific issue. Your speech and behavior stem from your mindset. The way customers perceive you is also shaped by your attitude and way of thinking.

The correct attitude in sales is not about being overly optimistic, but rather about having a mindset that constantly seeks out new opportunities, thinks about how to get better results from them, and takes immediate action. In fact, instead of focusing on just selling, think about designing the path that will lead the customer to decide to buy from you. Because in the science of marketing and sales, there are two types of ownership:

legal ownership (when something belongs to someone) and intellectual ownership (when a customer decides to buy and believes the product belongs to them). Therefore, the decision to purchase is equivalent to the purchase itself.

▶ The Question as an Effective Lever in Developing Attitude

Questions shape the mind. In any situation you are in and for any outcome you want to create, ask yourself questions. Your question keeps you focused and drives you to seek an answer. For example, ask yourself:

Why should they buy from me?

....

....

....

What can I do so that my customers don't reject my offer?

....

....

....

How can I increase my profit margin instead of focusing on sales volume?

....

....

....

What makes me stand out to my customers?

....

....

....

How can I connect with my customers and build an effective network?

....
....
....
....

How can I provide them with high-quality content about my brand?

....
....
....
....

How can I recognize the signals that indicate a customer is ready to buy?

....
....
....
....

Why is the number of my customers declining?

....
....
....
....

What unique service can I offer with my product to encourage customers to buy from me?

....
....
....
....

What is causing some of my orders to be canceled?

....

....

....

....

What phrases, messages, and content will make customers decide to buy from me?

....

....

....

....

What abilities do we possess?

....

....

....

....

We are meant to improve. In what area? In influencing others. Being effective comes from being equipped. We must ask questions to listen more and to improve our ability to establish effective relationships. We must always think broadly, understand who and when to react, and know what challenges we face and how we can solve them. A combination of these skills transforms us into professional salespeople, ensuring our success in sales.

▶ We are all salespeople

This is something we all know. What we might not know is how to determine our own worth as a salesperson. Have you ever asked yourself what value you bring when *you* sell a product or service? We are talking about a *salesperson* whose credibility and abilities are impactful. First, sell yourself to yourself.

The Abilities of a Professional Salesperson

The development and mastery of the abilities of a professional salesperson involves fifteen key sales skills that prepare you to master them and succeed. These skills form the foundation for becoming an effective and impactful salesperson.

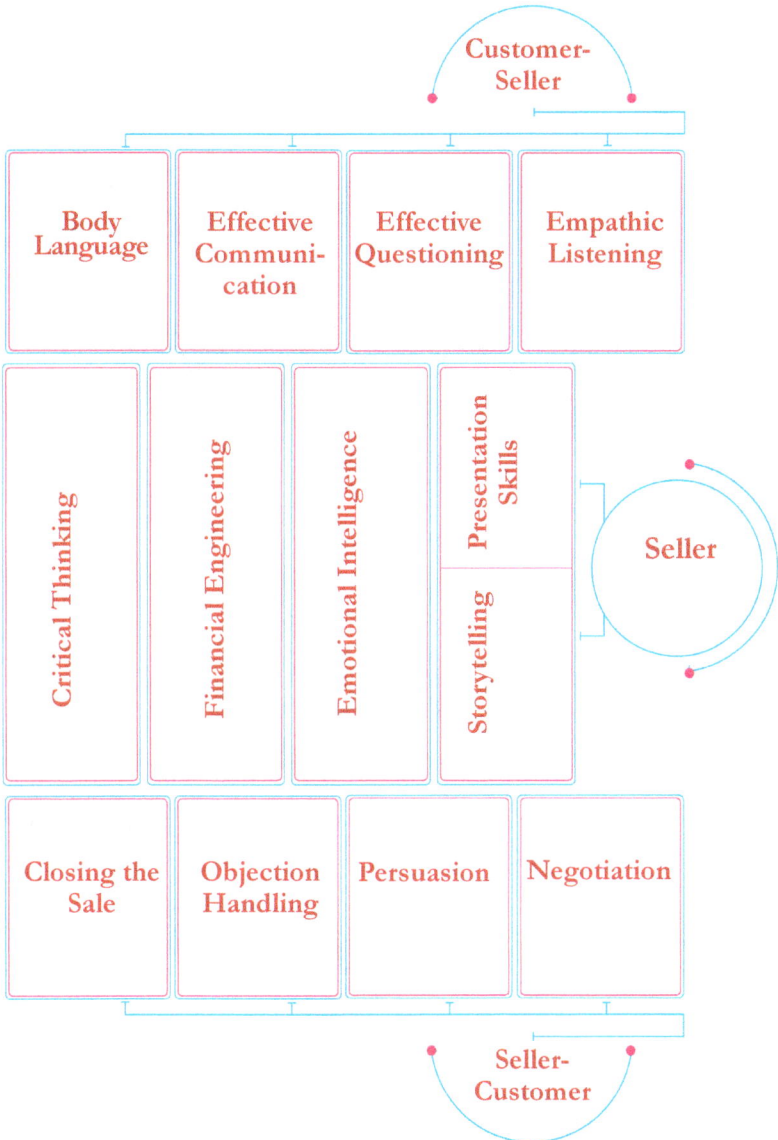

Customer-Seller

Body Language	Effective Communication	Effective Questioning	Empathic Listening

Critical Thinking	Financial Engineering	Emotional Intelligence	Presentation Skills
			Storytelling

Seller

Closing the Sale	Objection Handling	Persuasion	Negotiation

Seller-Customer

▶ Effective Listening

We have never been taught the art of listening.

In school, we were taught to write neatly and pronounce words correctly. However, no one taught us how to listen properly. They only taught us how to write and speak, but never the importance of listening. If no one has told you this before, I will: You must live by listening. Manage your organization through listening. Understand your market by listening. Listen, and provide solutions.

Your ears are your most important sales tool.

Listening carefully is essential in effective sales. The goal of listening in the sales process is to reach an agreement on what the problem is and offer a solution. According to Scharmer, listening can be classified into four levels:

1. Downloading

Listening to the ambient sounds without focus.

2. Debate Listening

Listening to respond. Most of us get stuck at this level.

3. Empathic Listening EMP

Listening to put ourselves in another's shoes and see things from their perspective.

4. Generative Listening

Listening without any intention of selling or doing anything else. At this level of listening, we don't decide anything in advance. As a result, through mutual understanding, new insights or ideas will emerge. We do not judge or postpone the issue. How do we reach this level? It's not an easy task.

We usually instinctively protect our own viewpoint, opinion, and insight. Thus, reaching this level requires practice and repetition.

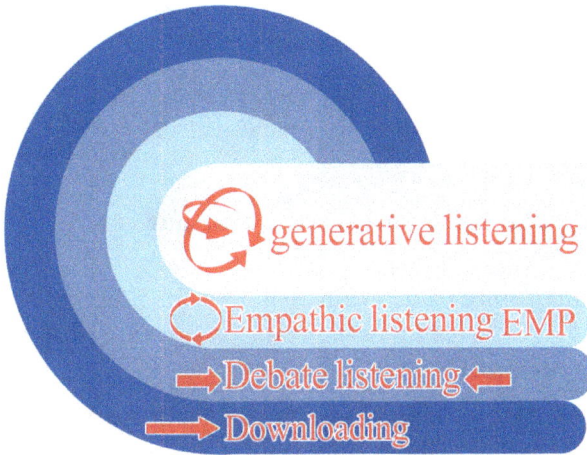

Three Key Principles for Enhancing Generative Listening:

1. Continuous Listening

We have all experienced endless talking without taking a pause. Try it once, listen without creating breaks in the conversation. Practice this so much that it becomes one of your remarkable habits.

2. Listen While Looking

Your customer might look around or stand up and walk around the room. When they see that your attention is still focused on them, they realize they are being listened to.

3. Eliminate Distractions

Remove anything that distracts you from listening attentively. Now, to complete this section of the model, answer the following questions:

- What factors interrupt your focus while the other person is speaking, preventing you from fully understanding their message?

- What things in your environment divert your attention from the conversation?

▶ Asking Questions:

Your Key Factor for Success

Questions are your saviors. Every question answered takes you one step forward in the sales process. Therefore, what you ask is extremely important.

Canvas for Crafting Quality Questions

Asking high-quality questions compels your audience to compare. The fruit of every comparison is a memory that remains in the individual's mind. The question-creation canvas helps you become aware of the situation you are in, enabling you to position yourself and your client in a beneficial and profitable context.

Guiding Questions	Encouraging Questions

Exploratory Questions

Final Questions	Multiple Choice Questions

Follow-up Questions

Encouraging Questions

Questions that are difficult to answer in less than a sentence and encourage the audience to engage in a conversation:

▶**Can you explain to me about...?**

▶**Can you explain how...?**

▶**What is your opinion about...?**

▶**What does this describe?**

Can you add something?

Guiding Questions

Questions that help bring the focus back to the subject if the audience deviates or stops talking. These questions often include "when," "where," "who," "how," and focus on benefits, not features (i.e., what the product or service offers the customer).

▶**When did you observe these changes?**

▶ **What do you gain from this product?**

▶ **How does the service ... help you?**

▶ **Who uses this service?**

▶ **What does this remind you of?**

▶ **How did this problem arise?**

▶ **Why do you think this happens?**

Can you add something?

Exploratory Questions

Questions that help you understand what the customers are looking for in your products and services. The answers to these questions give you more details.

> ▶ **What time frame are you considering? When you say "best time," Can you give an example?**
>
> ....
>
> ....
>
> ▶ **When Yousaid "best Price" do you mean the initial price or the final cost? Can you provide more details?**
>
> ....
>
> ▶ **Who pays the budget?**..
> ▶ **What criteria did you consider for budget allocation?**..........................
> ▶ **Do you have another preference?**...
> ▶ **What is the biggest challenge you are facing?Can you add something?**
>
> ....
>
> ....

Multiple Choice Questions

Questions that reveal preferences, priorities, and tendencies of the audience, offering a deeper understanding of their needs and desires. By asking these questions, a clear image of the transaction forms in the audience's mind, and they are placed in a position where they feel there is only one way to choose from the options you have presented.

> ▶ **Do you want to buy in full or in installments?**
> ▶ **Do you prefer yellow or black?**
> ▶ **Would you like to pick up the product in person or have it delivered by courier?**
> ▶ **Can you add something?**
>
> ....
>
> ....
>
> ....

Final Questions

These questions assess your understanding of the benefits the customer is seeking:

▶ **Under any circumstances, time is a priority for you, right?**
▶ **So, do you agree with the second suggestion?**
▶ **Is there any other issue that needs attention?**
▶ **Can you add something?**

....
....
....

Follow-up Questions

These questions help you maintain and continue the conversation with your audience while better understanding their needs and desires:

▶ **What obstacle do you face?**
▶ **What is more of a priority for you than this?**
▶ **How can we make the buying process easier for you?**
▶ **Can you add something?**

....
....
....

An important point to note is that you should know who you are talking to. Is this person the decision-maker, or is this person an influencer in the decision-making process?

▶ Effective Communication

Your customer is not just a part of a transaction. Establishing an optimal level of business communication is more important than creating a financial transaction. A customer reaches this level of connection with you when they see that, for the value they receive, they don't have to pay or compensate in any way. In other words, you prioritize your relationship with the customer over sales, which may not have an immediate tangible result but could be essential in the long term, especially for businesses with longer sales cycles and expensive products. Effective communication happens when you focus on creating interaction between the buyer and the seller instead of focusing only on selling. To establish effective communication with your customers, shift your approach from making excuses to taking action. Don't make excuses to connect with them.

In your sales campaign, keep the following in mind:

- Create content that customers are interested in, such as podcasts, articles, eBooks.
- Make sure you have a system to measure and evaluate their opinions on your products and services.
- Stay aware of their personal and business successes, and congratulate them in a unique way.
- Invite them to events that they are interested in.

Add other examples and see what resources you need to create such a relationship. Create a calendar where you track follow-ups, content created, events, etc.

▶ Body Language

The most important point in verbal communication is non-verbal communication.

The way you say something is more important than what you say. In any interaction, especially business interactions, what the audience perceives from your words is far more critical than the words themselves. In fact, in the first few seconds, the audience will mentally label you (e.g., powerful, trustworthy, suspicious, demanding, empathetic, etc.), and from that moment, everything you do or say will be judged based on that label. The truth is that while you can't control people's thoughts, you can influence their perception. People are not under your control, but they can be influenced by your behavior.

People unconsciously evaluate qualities such as credibility, trust, reliability, empathy, and power. Facial expressions, body posture, eye contact, voice rhythm, and other movements can strengthen or weaken your message.

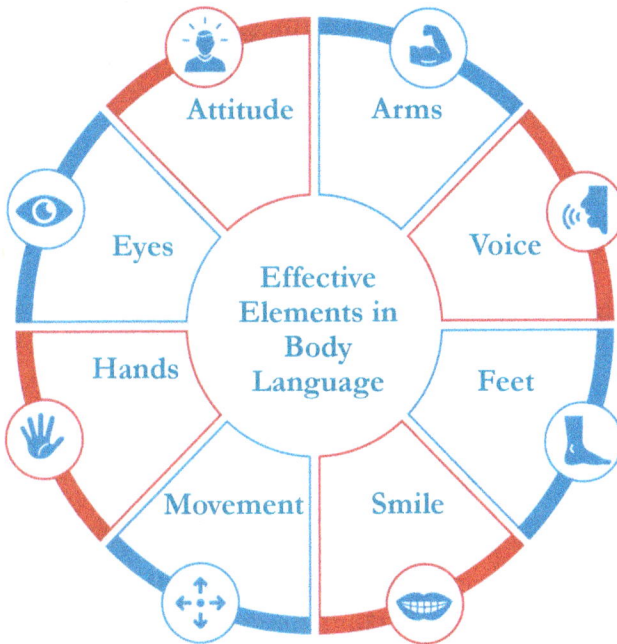

• **Attitude**

People quickly notice your attitude. In fact, all your body language reflects your attitude. Therefore, the first element you should focus on is your attitude. Before making the rules for your body language, focus on shaping your attitude. If what you say does not align with your attitude and body language, consider that the deal may be over.

• **Eyes**

Eyes have unparalleled power. Eye contact means communication through the eyes, and it does not imply control or discomfort. It's a skill to establish eye contact and stay focused with your audience. However, you must be careful not to stare in a way that makes the other person uncomfortable. Avoid looking away, as this can transmit feelings of indifference and disengagement.

• **Voice**

If you speak too quickly with your audience, they may not fully understand what you're saying. If you speak too slowly and monotonously, they may become bored. Your speech rhythm should align with your body movements.

• **Hands**

Hidden hands (in pockets, under the table, behind your back) suggest unreliability. When speaking, use your hands to emphasize what you want to draw attention to. The way you use your hands adds importance and focus on your message.

• **Movement**

You can nod your head to indicate approval when listening. When speaking, take a step toward your audience, pause, and then continue. Use clear and decisive movements. This helps instill confidence in your audience and encourages them to trust you more. However, make sure not to appear erratic or ambiguous in your movements.

- **Smile**

Smiling can be a sign of initiating an interaction. Smiles can make your audience feel more confident in their decision about you. However, you must ensure your smile is not overly forced or aimed solely at seeking validation.

- **Feet**

If you are talking or listening and tapping your feet or shifting your weight onto one foot, you send the message that you are not focused and are looking to release some pressure. To convey strength and confidence, stand with your weight evenly distributed across both feet.

- **Arms**

Avoid crossing your arms. Keep your arms open, as this helps you breathe better and appear more relaxed. Closed arms place you in a defensive position and give the impression that you are unwilling to engage with your audience.

▶ Effective Presentation

How you present something affects its perceived value. When presenting a product, your focus should be on its value, not the product itself. **People spend money only for one reason: improvement.** This could be improving their health, beauty, mood, performance, income, etc. Ask yourself, what are you doing to improve your clients' lives or work

Effective presentation elements could include:

- Creative packaging
- Unique exhibition design
- Promotional events
- Product styling
- Delivery system

410 ▶ Business Mastery

Principles of Effective Presentation:

- It is simple.
- It tells a compelling story.
- It highlights your value proposition.
- It focuses more on visualization and imagery than text and numbers.

How do you present your product?

....
....
....
....

How does your packaging contribute to the value of your product?

....
....
....
....

What related, semi-related, or unrelated products can you pair with your product?

....
....
....

How do you launch your new product? Who does this?

....
....
....

How well does your product delivery system align with your brand's reputation?

....
....
....
....

▶ Storytelling

Need is the driving force, and movement is the result of a phase difference. A story should reflect the difference and distinction that you create. What you need to give people is not information. The mistake we make is giving people product, organization, competitor, and market information to make a sale. The reality is that people don't make decisions based on information; they make decisions based on stories.

To put it simply, we can say that:

$$\text{Story} = \text{Facts} + \text{Emotions}$$

$$\text{News} = \text{Facts} - \text{Emotions}$$

The human mind is defensive when confronted with news and information. As a result, the focus and attention on what it receives diminishes, and it is forgotten. However, stories, by evoking emotions, can embed information in the minds of your audience in an engaging and memorable way. Whenever an emotion is triggered, an action follows. Stories don't need to be exaggerated or dramatized; they just need to follow a simple principle: to create an emotional response in individuals, such as joy, excitement, satisfaction, being seen, attention, motivation, understanding, friendship, hope, power, belonging, surprise, and other emotions. A professional salesperson knows well that the goal is not just "selling," but sharing. Sales are a reflection of performance.

▶ Sales Storytelling Canvas

The sales storytelling canvas can guide your thoughts for the story you create. Each part of this canvas blends with your realistic perspective and completes part of your story. Keep in mind that your story should give people insight, not knowledge. They make decisions based on insights, not information.

▶ **Sales Storytelling Canvas**

Before they buy from you:

- What challenges are they facing?
- What are they hoping for?
- What feeling are they experiencing?

Product

What was your product initially?

What changes has it undergone?

What is it like now?

Trigger Point

What is the turning point or the key factor in your story?

Main Core

What is the core factor that shaped your product?

Results

What results have you achieved?

What lessons have you learned that you can share with your heroes?

Heroes

Who are the individuals that will experience the feeling you create?

What solutions do you offer them?

After they buy from you:

What feeling will they experience after the purchase?

▶ Emotional Intelligence

Successful sellers focus not just on "being in a relationship" with their clients, but on having a deep connection at every stage of the sales process. A deep connection creates trust, commitment, and loyalty, and brings a satisfying buying experience. Emotional intelligence, like other sales skills, is an acquired ability that helps you understand both your own and others' emotions. By managing your emotional responses and aligning them with others' situations, you create a stronger relationship. Many mistakenly think that emotional intelligence is about suppressing emotions, but in fact, it's about balancing interactions in both life and business.

Daniel Goleman's Emotional Intelligence (EQ) Framework

Daniel Goleman, who introduced the concept of EQ in the 1960s, defined emotional intelligence in five levels:

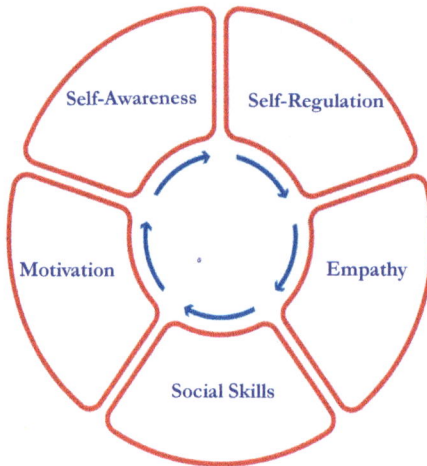

1. Self-Awareness:

Self-awareness is the ability to understand the emotions you are experiencing. A seller with high emotional intelligence knows how to manage their energy, ensuring they don't unintentionally transfer negative emotions to the customer, thus avoiding feelings of being ignored.

2. Self-Regulation:

This is the ability to adapt emotional responses to others' situations. A seller with emotional intelligence places themselves in the customer's position, enabling them to think and feel better and respond more effectively.

3. Social Skills:

Having a broad awareness of the social dynamics helps build and sustain relationships over time. Social skills enable the creation of a powerful network, which in turn opens up opportunities for sales and collaborations.

4. Empathy:

Empathy is the opposite of self-awareness. It involves understanding the emotions of your clients and adjusting your approach to meet their expectations. An empathetic seller is a seller who supports the customer, not just sells to them.

5. Motivation:

Motivation doesn't just tell you you're good at something. It doesn't give you good news or shelter you from challenges. Motivation is about your internal drive to face and resolve existing problems, improve situations, empower others, and sometimes remove obstacles. A motivated seller sees challenges as stepping stones to their goals.

▶ 27 Tips for Improving and Highlighting Emotional Intelligence

- Pay attention to the emotions you're experiencing.
- Observe your reactions during each emotional experience.
- Practice being open to criticism.
- Recognize your emotional triggers.
- Identify your emotional drivers.
- Challenge your biases.

- Move outside your comfort zone.
- Seek help when needed.
- Revisit your decisions and viewpoints (use a 360-degree view).
- Highlight and celebrate positive events.
- Don't ignore negative emotions; address them.
- Be a good listener.
- Take breaks for mental relaxation to prevent emotional outbursts.
- Be flexible with your emotions.
- Trust your insights and perspectives during difficult decisions.
- Practice realism.
- Be in a continuous learning mode.
- Initiate difficult conversations when needed.
- Instead of reacting, take time to respond thoughtfully.
- Avoid judging too quickly; reflect before forming opinions.
- Give constructive feedback to others.
- Ask others for feedback on your behavior.
- Don't expect immediate trust; build it over time.
- Be approachable.
- Travel to learn about different cultures.
- Eat healthy foods, as your diet affects your emotions.
- Welcome feedback and use it for personal growth.

▶ Financial Engineering

Successful sellers know how to craft attractive financial offers for their audiences. Financial engineering is an effective skill because it shifts focus from the input (price) to the output (value) of a product or service. For example, instead of focusing on the price tag, financial engineering techniques highlight the benefits a customer gains from the purchase, making them feel that the value they get far exceeds the price. This shift in focus is a crucial part of closing a sale successfully, as the seller shows the customer the benefits they'll receive, whether tangible or intangible, making the offer irresistible.

▶ **What is the price of your product?**

....

....

....

▶ **How do you convince the customer to pay for it?**

....

....

....

▶ **What offer can you make to reduce their perceived risk in the purchase?**

....

....

....

▶ **Can you offer alternative suggestions?**

....

....

....

▶ Critical Thinking

Critical thinking involves analyzing and objectively evaluating an issue to form a well-founded judgment. Critical thinkers do not accept solutions or ideas without evidence. They challenge their assumptions and work to refine and complete their conclusions. Salespeople with critical thinking skills believe in validating their assumptions and outcomes in order to understand the market better and overcome their biases.

On the other hand, others may accept ideas easily, make quick judgments, and spend less time evaluating the market potential and customer situations. As a result, their attempts to gain power or reach the top failure.

What stages are involved in critical thinking?

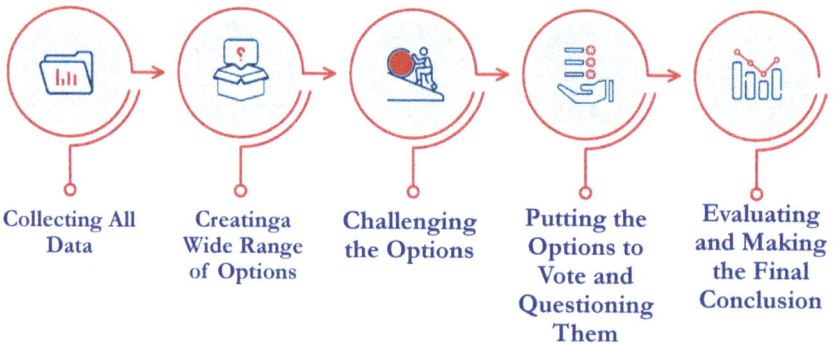

| Collecting All Data | Creating a Wide Range of Options | Challenging the Options | Putting the Options to Vote and Questioning Them | Evaluating and Making the Final Conclusion |

Critical Thinking privileges

- Refusing to accept failure and falling behind in the market
- Creating credibility and trust in the market
- Asking benefit-oriented questions
- Strengthening problem-solving skills
- Improving objection management
- Creating reassurance
- Eliminating feelings of helplessness
- Achieving the rank of top seller
- More effective communication techniques
- Creating motivation
- Helping extract crucial information

Exercise:

The series below challenges your biases, assumptions, and preconceptions, pushing you to create different scenarios and alternatives. This will allow you to have more flexibility in your execution phase.

Current	Assumption
What conflicts/issues are you facing?	**What approach do you currently have regarding each of the following?**
....	....
....	....
....	....
....	**Business growth status:**
....	....
What uncomfortable truth are you refusing to accept?	....
....	**Customer experience:**
....	....
....	....
....	**Your market position:**
....	....
....	....
How does this issue affect what you are doing for your customer?	**Organizational culture:**
....	....
....	**Your relationship with the customer:**
....	....
....	....
....	**Sales status:**
....	....
....	....

Current Status Information

Challenge	Eliminate

Reflection of Information / Blocking Biases

Challenge

What do you consider to be correct?

....

....

....

What is this issue's status from others' perspective?

....

....

....

How can you view this topic from different angles?

....

....

....

Eliminate

What biases do you have that close your eyes to creating productive solutions?

....

....

....

Write the most important points.

....

....

....

Scenarios	Alternatives

New Insights

What scenarios do you currently face?	**For each scenario, what alternatives exist at the same level?**
....	....
....	....
Good and ideal	**Good and ideal**
....	....
....	....
Moderate	**Moderate**
....	....
....	....
....	....
Bad	**Bad**
....	....
....	....

If	Then
If you are at the starting stage, what are your turning points? 1: .... 2: 3:	Where does each turning point take you? ....

Implementation

Critical thinking generates paths, solutions, and ultimately situations that you hadn't even considered before. The only way to strengthen it is by not simply passing by issues. You must take something with you in every passage.

▶ Negotiation

The negotiation table is a table of transformation.

Are you negotiating or competing? Negotiation is not a competition. That means one does not win and the other lose. I prefer to call it the art of "transformation"; not just limited to turning a deal into a sale, but much broader. Negotiation is the art of turning situations into opportunities, conflicts into agreements, and outcomes into decisions.

If winning is involved, remember that successful and prosperous deals have four winners: you, your business, the customer, and the customer's business.

Key Factors in Negotiation

Here are the key factors to always consider during a negotiation:

• Negotiation Timing

Negotiation has its specific time, which is when the customer shows interest in buying from you.

• Negotiation Content

Talking about meaningless topics wastes our time, but talking about valuable subjects is useful for both us and our audience. So, one of your most important tasks as a sales negotiator is to define what issues are worth negotiating about. You need to prioritize them based on the available time and the benefits they offer.

• Determining Flexibility Limits

Predefine your "ideal situation" and "the lowest acceptable point."

• Scoring

Start the negotiation by offering small concessions and then give larger concessions based on the deal's conditions.

• Point of No Return

Sometimes, flexibility doesn't work, and you cannot compromise on some positions. This is when your demands are not met, and an agreement at any cost is not an option. Therefore, it is essential to define in advance what you are not willing to compromise on during any negotiation.

• Agreement to Disagreement

The art is being able to decide that you and your counterpart don't align rather than settling for a false agreement. This allows you the chance for future negotiations. If you don't think about this in advance, you'll pay the price, like giving away excessive concessions, making poorly calculated offers, unplanned positions, and everything else that will cause you harm.

Here are 20 fundamental questions you must consider before every negotiation:

1. What are the topics of this negotiation?
2. What are my counterpart's interests and positions in this negotiation?
3. What are my counterpart's fears in this negotiation?
4. What are my interests and positions in this negotiation?
5. Who are the stakeholders in this negotiation?
6. What is the appropriate starting point in this negotiation?
7. How do I show my good intentions at the beginning of the negotiation?
8. Who should start the negotiation?
9. What are the likely points my counterpart will raise?
10. Do I have answers to all of them?
11. What information do I have?
12. What is the best way to present information in this negotiation?
13. What are my non-negotiables (red lines)?
14. What conditional concessions can I offer to make the deal happen?
15. What are my demands and requests for each topic?
16. How will I structure and present them?
17. How do I want this negotiation to end?
18. If this negotiation fails, what are the consequences?
19. What is the ideal length for this negotiation agreement?
20. How should we conclude this negotiation?

The biggest mistake is putting "price" or "people" on the table for negotiation. Remember that as a seller, you are selling solutions and value, not price. Therefore, what should be negotiated are the solutions, added values, and how they are presented.

▶ Persuasion

Persuasion is not coercion or wordplay. What puts you on the right path to persuasion is creating common ground. Creating a shared playing field, a common enemy, a shared benefit, or anything else you and your counterpart can discuss. In such a scenario, your counterpart sees you as their "conversation partner," and that reduces their mental resistance.

Persuasion is not limited to words.

All elements of an organization must be persuasive. Human resources, ongoing processes, the brand you build, and ultimately, the product you offer, form a persuasive chain. Since it is often said that the strength of a chain lies in its weakest link, any weakness in one section can weaken the persuasion process.

▶ Commitment Begets Commitment

We have all had this experience. If we bought a product from a place and were satisfied, we continue buying from the same source because we are convinced that "it's the real deal; this is exactly what we want." Remember, commitment always brings more commitment.

▶ Small Yeses Lead to Big Yeses

In the persuasion process, start by securing small yeses. Small yeses are the accelerators of the buying process. When the audience reaches consistent agreements with you, they are less likely to disagree with what you say in the future.

▶ Social Proof

The persuasion process is more effective when individuals see that others, similar to them, have achieved better results using your product. Social proof refers to any example of a person, group, or entity that validates your product's credibility.

Here are some examples of social proof:

1. Testimonials (customer feedback in audio, video, and text formats on online or offline platforms);

2. Success stories (demonstrating the success paths of other customers in audio, video, and text formats on online or offline platforms);

3. Social media following (quality and quantity of followers, likes, and comments);

4. Recommendations and endorsements from influencers or experts in your field;

5. Certifications and standards (anything that stamps approval on your product or brand).

▶ Is your product convincing?

....

....

....

....

▶ What stories do you have that validate your credibility? Have you displayed them yet?

....

....

....

....

▶ Who are the people who are willing to proudly speak about their experience with you? Who should you approach?

....

....

....

▶ Implicit Social Contract

It's nearly impossible that anyone has not signed this implicit mental contract: "You get what you give." When you give tangible value to a customer, they will never let you go. Values always convince them to repeat the purchase, and thus, they will continue to come back to you, regardless of the price you offer. On the contrary, if they realize that your only goal is to sell them something, they won't be satisfied with their purchase and will hesitate to buy from you again. This kind of thinking leads to seeing the customer as merely a buyer rather than someone to build a long-term relationship with.

▶ Managing Objections

We've all heard "no" at some point. When a person is not ready to do something or is uncertain, they give excuses. Therefore, objections like "the price is too high" could just be an excuse. "I'm satisfied with what I'm currently using" can also be an excuse. The important thing is not the excuses you encounter during the sales process, but understanding the root cause of the objection and planning how to address it in the customer's mind.

The objection management process has three steps: Listen, Acknowledge, and Suggest.

Everyone wants to be heard. When the customer says, "This product is expensive," don't just say, "It's expensive, but it's worth it." Acknowledge their point. Show them that you're listening. As they speak, they may express the reasons why they believe the price is too high, which in fact are the values you're offering. In the end, this might change their perspective.

When they say they are satisfied with their current supplier, don't tear down your competitor. Instead, acknowledge it and allow them to continue. As they talk about your competitor's services, they're giving you valuable information. After they've shared it, it's your turn to offer an appealing proposal. Even if you haven't provided anything yet, you've given them the feeling of being heard and valued. You've allowed them to express their concerns and priorities, which they previously showed you as objections.

Reflection Questions

▶ What objections have you surrendered to in the past?

....

....

....

....

▶ What defensive reactions have you shown that did not result in a sale?

....

....

....

....

▶ Write down three objections you most commonly face and describe what plan you have to resolve them.

....

....

....

....

▶ Closing the Sale

This is not about achieving success through steps or diagrams. This is just one moment, a decisive moment: silence. It is the time to create a safe space for the buyer to think and make a decision. While closing the sale is the last step in the salesperson's skill set, the final decision is not entirely in the seller's hands but in the buyer's. The buyer is the one who closes the sale, not you.

All you need to do up until this point is show the buyer who you are your credibility, your support, and your strength. If you have made the buyer feel satisfied before the purchase, solved their problem, and eased their pain, it is clear that they will accept you. They understand that buying from you is not the end but the beginning of a relationship and friendship. When you gain a friend instead of just a customer, the sale is certain.

Now we have reached our goal. We have gone from the root, or the "customer", through the ability of the "salesperson", to the important point, which is the sale itself. This is the essence of our story.

Section 3: Sales

Sales is anything but selling. Sales is not just taking orders; it is about forming relationships. It is about making friends and buying. Sales is the turning point of marketing. At this point, marketing moves beyond individual actions and becomes a system.

▶ Sales System

The sales system is a guiding system. Today, effective sales depend on systems, not individuals. Designing sales systems guarantees organizational profitability, and the ongoing development of these systems ensures the survival of your business.

Each system is defined by input, processing, output, and feedback. The sales system is no exception, with a focus on designing, managing, and controlling outputs. Each input is processed in line with the desired output, and it is based on the quality of the output that the processing occurs.

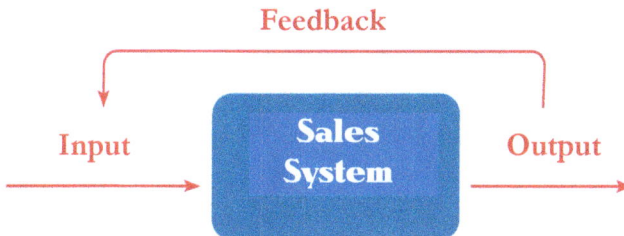

In fact, every successful sales system has five important tasks:

- Maximizing output;

- Simplifying previous processes;

- Repeatability;

- Flexibility for growth and development;

- Self-correction.

▶ Maximizing Output

I want to ask you a question. A question whose wrong answer can send a business into decline, perhaps stuck in a vicious cycle for years. The question is: "What is the successful output of a sales system?" Is it high sales volume or a large number of customers?

I have always said that in the "market school," what matters most is profit. Your sales system is not successful if it simply sells. Many businesses are not truly successful because they are not **profitable**. It is profitability that puts you on the top. The second place is simply the first loser. Free your mind. Yes, I am talking to you. Free your mind from numbers. Because profit is not just income. When I say profit, I mean financial profit, brand positioning, competitive advantage, being the first choice, visibility, and most importantly, the profit in the time we free up.

The second successful output of a sales system is creating an indelible image in the customer's mind. This is something we discussed earlier as the "customer experience." Images give the customer a story to tell. What story represents the output of your sales system? Have you designed it?

The third output is gaining an irreplaceable position in the customer's mind. This means that the customer cannot and will not let go of you at any cost, and any talk of replacing you with a competitor becomes unacceptable. This can only be achieved through genuine interaction with your team, as discussed in previous sections.

▶ Simplifying Previous Processes (Feedback Effect)

No matter how successful the sales system has been, it should not use the same old patterns for all sales processes. Doing so keeps you where you are. A successful sales system must make its outputs more efficient every time so that it can convert input into the desired output more easily in future instances. This cannot be achieved unless previous processes are simplified for use in future activities. Efficiency and simplification always come with time-saving. More time means more focus on other important matters, such as revenue streams, marketing plans, advertising campaigns, brand positioning, and talent development. Remember, even small tasks can steal the time and focus needed to do the important things.

▶ Repeatability

What happens in the sales system (with optimization) should not be considered a one-time process. Simply put, if sales are defined in the system, the process should not only be capable of one-time execution. For repeatability, documentation, sharing, and transferring experience are necessary.

▶ Flexibility for Development and Expansion

A successful sales system is not rigid and closed but is flexible and receptive to growth and expansion. This system can equip itself with new sales tools and capable teams. In general, successful systems are trainable because they believe that training is what makes them big and powerful.

▶ Self-Correction

While designing a process, no matter how large and powerful the system is, obstacles will arise, or gaps will be encountered. The sales system must be capable of alerting in such situations, identifying the bugs, and correcting them with the tools it has.

Everything you've read so far in this chapter is about how to design a sales system: understanding who your customers are not, how to position yourself in front of them, the customer journey you create, the touchpoints you establish, how to interact at each of these touchpoints, and the goal of your sales and profit. All of these are prerequisites for designing an effective sales system. What's important is the survival and life of these systems, and the life of no system continues unless it becomes embedded in the culture. Culture is not reliant on one individual, but is reflected in the behavior of the members of the organization.

▶ Write Your Five Key Takeaways from this chapter

1. ....

2. ....

3. ....

4. ....

5. ....

▶ Three steps I will immediately start:

1. ....

....

2. ....

....

3. ....

....

▶ One golden lesson to share with others:

....

....

....

....

....

....

Download all the tables and exercises of this chapter from the following website.

https://hosseintaheri.ir/bmg/

Attraction, Interviewing, and Hiring

Chapter 8:

Attraction, Interviewing, and Hiring

Recruiting is like hunting, hunting for the right candidates at the right time.

📖 **After reading this chapter, you will gain mastery over:**

- Building Competitive Work Environments to Attract Talented Individuals

- The Importance, Rationale, and Methods of Job Design

- Expressing Correct Hiring Instead of Wrong Hiring

- Writing Convincing Job Advertisements

- Effective Job Interviews

▶ **Not All Organizations Are Equally Attractive**

The process of successful hiring is divided into two parts:

"Recruitment Marketing" and "Staff Selection".

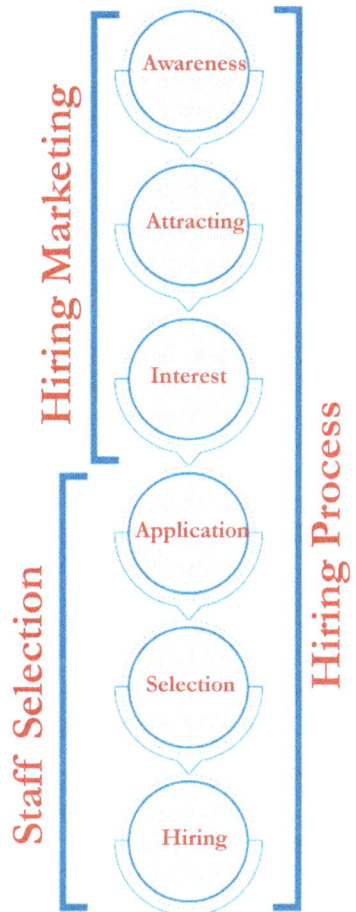

Awareness

Attracting

Interest

Application

Selection

Hiring

Hiring Marketing

Staff Selection

Hiring Process

Recruitment marketing, or attracting human resources in the entrepreneurial age, is one of the unavoidable challenges for business owners. Each of them wants to have effective and talented individuals on their teams to help foster growth. This is ideal, but how can it be achieved?

Recruitment marketing involves three stages:

▶ **Awareness and Recognition**

In this phase, your goal is to raise awareness about your company and employer brand.

▶ **Attention**

The aim of this phase is to make potential job candidates aware of available job positions.

▶ **Interest**

The final phase involves convincing selected candidates to take action and apply for the job.

The science of attracting effective individuals, or recruitment marketing, is one of the most important fields in human resources that is often overlooked. Organizations often fail to attract the ideal talent by sticking to generic job advertisements and unplanned interview sessions. These managers commonly complain with phrases like "Good talent is hard to find." Successful businesses, however, plan their recruitment channels, ad texts, and interview sessions meticulously, believing that the members of a business play a crucial role in shaping the future of the organization.

The secret to their success lies in this: **"Building talented teams and competing in the marketplace begins here."** To attract talented individuals, there are two highly effective methods:

1. **Creating Competitive Work Environments**

2. **Designing a Job Requirement Analysis**

▶ **How do organizations create competitive work environments to attract talented individuals?**

1. Building an Employer Brand

An employer brand is the most valuable asset of an organization, and building it involves shaping the reputation and image that people in society (team members, competitors, customers, and the public) have of your organization. It represents the extent of attraction and value that the organization offers to employees. Furthermore, it reflects how a business is perceived as a desirable workplace and directly or indirectly influences the recruitment, retention, and engagement of people within organizations. The employer brand can be developed through actions such as focusing on employees' mental well-being, showcasing team successes on websites and social media, storytelling, reflecting the organization's mission to serve the community, and creating a unique work environment with high-quality tools. Any company that thinks about building such an environment successfully attracts the talent it desires.

2. Creating Educational Opportunities

Training keeps your team updated and equips them with new skills and knowledge. People who see learning as a lifelong responsibility will be attracted to companies that support them in this regard. Additionally, the participation of employees in various training courses reflects the organization's commitment to their growth.

3. Creating an Inspirational Work Environment

The principle of inspiration stems from the principle of benefit, where individuals feel that something is added to them and benefits them. It's about knowing the playing field and how much support the rules of the game provide. Inspirational environments support creative and innovative ideas, encouraging independent thought and fostering discussions and brainstorming. These environments also embrace mistakes and risks, as long as the opinions align with the organizational teachings. An organization can create an inspiring environment with inspirational leadership, where the actions of each individual are visibly impactful. People strive for better results when they see the outcomes of their efforts.

4. Using New Technologies

Implementing new technologies in the workplace facilitates processes. Improving internal communication using up-to-date tools, utilizing business intelligence (BI) systems, and overall technologies that save time and increase work quality, are powerful factors in attracting skilled human capital.

5. Maintaining Organizational Mental Health

Organizations that successfully attract talent are those that focus on their employees' mental well-being. Professional managers work towards ensuring:

- Providing adequate resources before expecting any deliverables from the team.
- Building effective communication and organizational culture.
- Leading without micromanagement.
- Guaranteeing job security.
- Helping employees address their weaknesses and develop their strengths.
- Being clear and transparent.
- Listening actively.
- Setting a good example.

6. Creating a Collaborative and Innovative Organizational Culture

An organizational culture can be seen as the foundation of organizational cohesion, goal achievement, and the development of both internal and external communications. Companies that design their organizational culture around collaboration, unity, and innovation are far more attractive to talent.

7. Developing Public Relations

Organizations can demonstrate their power in their interactions by building effective public relations with the community. This includes participation in events, communication with various media (online, radio, television, print), and engagement in social and environmental activities. Effective public relations can significantly contribute to attracting skilled and interactive workforce. Competitive strategies for building attractive work environments are often overlooked by many business owners and human resource managers, but for a business owner, it is crucial to realize that the era of traditional recruitment is over. Individuals no longer settle for a simple job advertisement; they want to be a part of a society that is innovative, forward-moving, positively interacts with people, and is well-known.

▶ How do organizations identify job requirements to attract talented individuals?

Apart from competitiveness, analyzing the needs for skilled labor can greatly assist in meeting job requirements, ultimately attracting effective individuals. Below are four exceptional methods to conduct this process effectively:

1. Interviewing the Current Team and Managers

Ask your current team about the tasks, skills, expertise, and resources needed for their jobs. Imagine that you are hiring them again and ask them to envision such a scenario. Their experience working within your system will provide the best insights on what the organization needs to build a competitive work environment. Ask them what makes the environment more attractive. Similarly, in interviews with your organization's managers, repeat this scenario and ask them about their challenges with teams. Have them identify the strengths and weaknesses of team members over time and report on how strengths have evolved while weaknesses hindered results.

2. Market Research

Conducting market and industry research will give you an understanding of the current and future job requirements in your industry. Examine what advantages your competitors have over your organization that make them more attractive to candidates. What needs do they fulfill that you might have overlooked? Why are their teams always on board with them in all circumstances? What media do they use, and what are they providing their employees that you are not?

3. Reevaluating Job Descriptions and Responsibilities

Review the responsibilities and job descriptions for your team. This includes both main and secondary duties, activities, complexity levels, time requirements, skills, working conditions, communication, work relationships, environment, and scheduling. Ask yourself what resources and equipment you have provided them with.

4. Feedback from Customers and Users

Getting feedback from your customers and audience is essential since the outcome of your organization's mission depends on them. Evaluating their opinions tells you what your team needs to do to receive more positive feedback. Now you have a set of criteria and characteristics that your ideal candidates would like to see and understand in the work environment. In fact, analyzing job requirements helps you see your company from the perspective of the individuals who want to work for you. This will prepare you to design more effective recruitment advertisements and better interview processes. It will also help you identify and attract talented individuals based on how well they align with your job requirements.

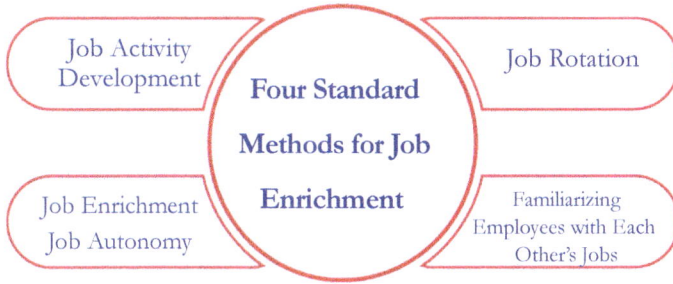

Job Activity Development

Job Rotation

Four Standard Methods for Job Enrichment

Job Enrichment
Job Autonomy

Familiarizing Employees with Each Other's Jobs

According to the checklist, answer the questions for each of the four methods:

Job Rotation:

▶ Can you arrange for each member of your team to rotate between different roles within the organization every few hours, days, or weeks?

Yes ☐ No ☐

▶ Is job variety beneficial and satisfying for some people?

Yes ☐ No ☐

Job Activity Development:

▶ Can you arrange for each member of your team to perform several similar tasks instead of just one?

Yes ☐ No ☐

▶ Is job variety beneficial and satisfying for some people?

Yes ☐ No ☐

▶ Could factors like restlessness or excessive job changes have a more significant negative effect on some people?

Yes ☐ No ☐

Job Enrichment:

▶ Can you arrange for people to take on more responsibility for making decisions about goals or ways to accomplish tasks?

Yes ☐ No ☐

▶ Can people receive feedback to monitor their performance?

Yes ☐ No ☐

▶ Can people take on higher-level tasks?

Yes ☐ No ☐

▶ Can people use new skills and expertise?

Yes ☐ No ☐

Job Autonomy for Teams:

▶ Can you give your team more responsibility for planning, organizing, or controlling their work independently?

Yes ☐   No ☐

▶ Could closer work relationships among team members benefit the group?

Yes ☐   No ☐

▶ Could some people be dissatisfied with having closer work relationships?

Yes ☐   No ☐

What Makes a Job Satisfying?

Here are some aspects to consider when designing jobs for individuals. Think about how they relate to each of the members of your group:

▶ Is the job a part of the whole and has a clear impact on providing services or the group/organization?

Yes ☐   No ☐

▶ Does it have value to be done?

Yes ☐   No ☐

▶ Does it give the person enough freedom to decide how to perform their tasks?

Yes ☐   No ☐

▶ Does it provide a good environment for learning and growth?

Yes ☐   No ☐

Keep in mind that individuals are different, and what seems appropriate or sufficient for one person may seem either too much or too little for another. However, we ask you to name individuals from your organization who are receptive to your efforts to improve their jobs.

Review of Possible Advantages and Disadvantages

Below are the possible advantages and disadvantages regarding job enrichment for employees. Think about your own situation and see which ones relate to job rotation (R), job development (D), job enrichment (E), and team autonomy (A):

	Advantages / Disadvantages
➤ Productivity	➤
➤ Quality of work	➤
➤ Flexibility	➤
➤ Use of time	➤
➤ Employee retention	➤
➤ Job satisfaction	➤
➤ Team morale	➤
➤ Need for managerial supervision	➤
➤ Communication with management	➤
➤ Cost management	➤
➤ Other factors	➤

▶ Job Design

You need to understand that when your work is running smoothly, it is the weaker employees who cause the most harm. I've always said, and I'll say it again, that the strength of a chain depends on its weakest link. Don't get it wrong. Human resources are not your biggest asset, but worthy human resources, which I prefer to call human capital, are your greatest asset. This is because humans, despite having equal values, often fail to act on them. Therefore, in order to effectively hire human capital, you need to design their role or, in other words, their job.

▶ **What should we do to make jobs more desirable for employees?**

The old and traditional view in businesses was that if an individual was responsible for just closing a box, their speed would increase, and they would do this task more efficiently over time. But, over the past half-century, the concept of "job design" has evolved. Historically, the goal of job design was to make work faster, cheaper, and more efficient. However, over the last few decades, job design has shifted its focus from the work itself to the worker and has pushed business owners to answer a critical question: *What can we do to make a job more appealing to the employee?* As entrepreneurs, we see a job as a collection of duties, activities, and responsibilities, while job design is about finding the right combination of duties, activities, and responsibilities for each position. Job design for human capital should be done in a way that eliminates all the negative aspects of their job.

▶ **Goal of Job Design:**

1. Maximizing Job Satisfaction:

What factors can increase an employee's job satisfaction?

- The job should not be simple, monotonous, or repetitive.
- The job should be creative.
- It should require thinking and problem-solving.
- It should offer diversity and freedom.
- It should provide opportunities for growth and advancement.

2. Maximizing Job Motivation:

How can a job increase an individual's intrinsic motivation to perform it? How does a job make employees passionate about it?

3. Defining Competency Standards:

What competencies are required to be hired for such a job?

4. Reduction:

What aspects of the job should be minimized?

- Reducing the gap between the job and the employee.
- Reducing job-related stress.
- Minimizing absenteeism, tardiness, and turnover.

5. Efficient Performance:

How can we enhance individual performance and output? Before exploring job design methods, let's review a few concepts:

▶ **Job:** A job is a set of tasks, activities, and responsibilities.

▶ **Job Design:** Job design is about finding the right combination of tasks, activities, and responsibilities for each job position in a way that eliminates all the negative aspects of an individual's job.

▶ **Responsibility:** A person should be able to recognize the importance of their tasks and understand how they affect the organization's goals.

▶ **Authority:** Authority complements responsibility. We cannot hold individuals accountable if we do not provide them with the necessary authority. Giving authority to organize and control matters within defined parameters is essential.

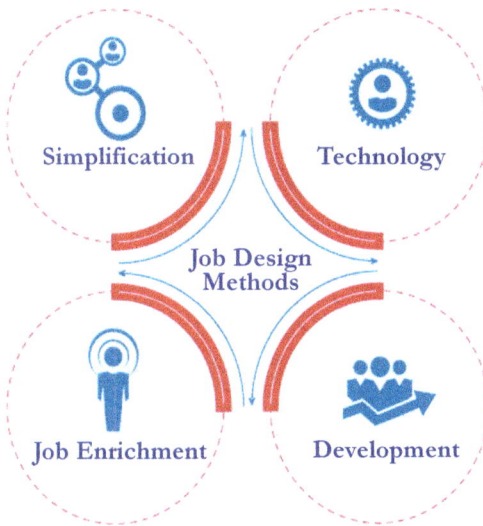

1. Simplification:

Simplification involves breaking down a complex job into its smaller components, assigning each part to an individual who will continuously perform it. Over time, the individual becomes skilled at the task, leading to the best possible results. This method enhances organizational productivity by focusing on efficiency and reducing task complexity.

▶ **Advantages:**

- Reduced physical and mental stress, and anxiety.
- Elimination of unnecessary processes and activities.

▶ **Disadvantages:**

- Job monotony.
- Constant fatigue.
- Normalization of work processes.
- Reduced attention.
- Increased personal errors.

2. Job Rotation:

Job rotation involves rotating employees through different roles within the organization. This gives individuals the opportunity to experience various tasks and departments, providing variety and flexibility in their daily work.

▶ **Advantages:**

- Increased awareness of other organizational tasks.
- Development of multi-level skills.
- Discovery of hidden talents and potential.
- Matching employees to tasks that better align with their skills and preferences.

▶ **Disadvantages:**

- Reduced cohesiveness and team integration.
- Fear of not performing assigned tasks correctly.
- Constant work interruptions.
- Frequent misunderstandings.

3. Job Enrichment:

Job enrichment involves increasing the responsibilities and authority of employees, making their jobs more meaningful and challenging. This method aims to boost job satisfaction by giving employees more autonomy and opportunities for growth.

▶ **Advantages:**

- Creation of challenges that increase personal capabilities.
- Increased willingness to accept new responsibilities.
- Reduction in managerial layers.
- Increased motivation and better performance.

4. Job Development:

Job development focuses on assigning additional tasks to employees without increasing their authority. Employees take on more responsibilities in their existing roles, which can lead to improved adaptability and flexibility in their work.

▶ **Advantages:**

- Responsibility for similar tasks.
- Scheduled training and learning opportunities.
- Increased job flexibility and adaptability.

Job Design Table

Job Title	Job Position
Duty	**Knowledge of Task**
Responsibilities	**Skills**
Personality	**Expertise**
Authority	

► Hiring

Ask yourself:

- What costs have you incurred due to hiring weak employees?
- Do you often wait until you are disappointed with people before thinking about replacing them?
- What have you done to prevent weak individuals from entering your team?
- Do weak team members often get fired or quit?

Now it's time for hiring. It's like hunting , hunting for the right candidates in the right places. Often, business owners, when they reach a point of frustration, want to hire quickly. But if you don't address the right time for hiring, you're making a mistake. The best time for hiring is *always*. You should always have a flow of talent coming into your company. And not just for those who are unemployed. In fact, the best talent you can hire is likely already employed in other organizations.

Before we talk about effective hiring methods, I want to introduce a new concept in human capital. A concept that is as crucial in hiring as customer marketing is in business. The concept of "Hiring Persona," which you should always think about. What kind of people do we want to accept into our organization? What traits do they have that can create opportunities within our organization? What skills should they have? What are their job preferences? What content do they follow? What have been the factors behind their past successes? What are the reasons for their frustrations?

The Hiring Persona canvas is something that can be vital in navigating the challenging hiring process, making it more efficient and effective.

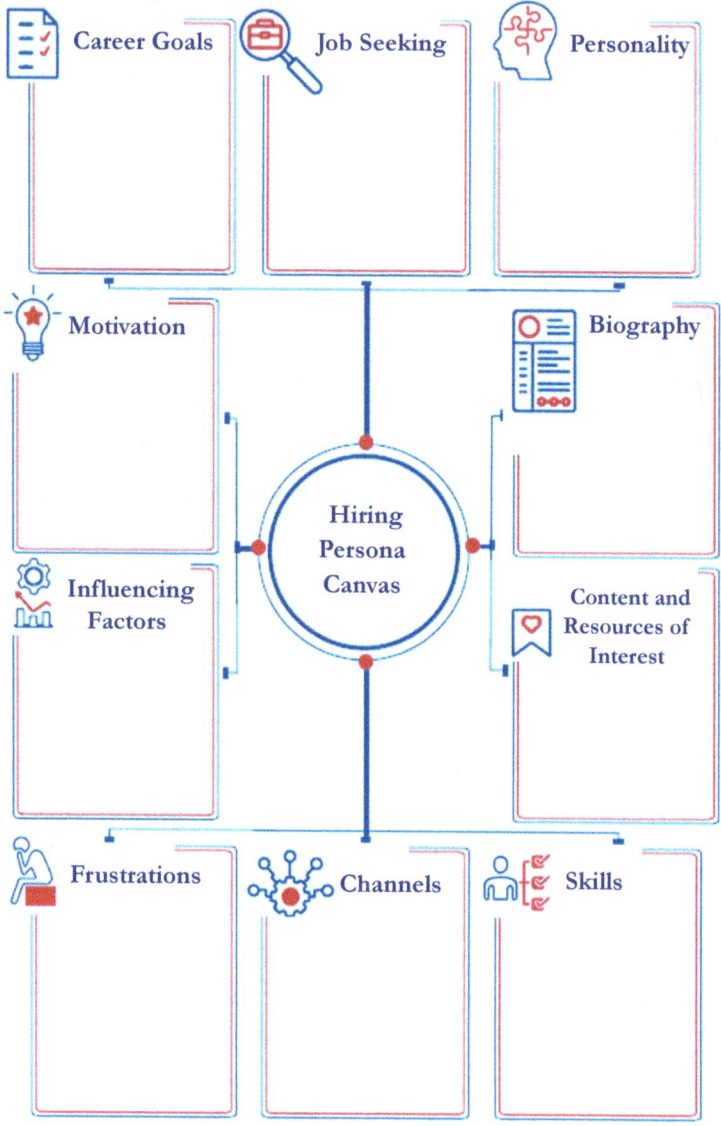

Career Goals

Job Seeking

Personality

Motivation

Biography

Influencing Factors

Hiring Persona Canvas

Content and Resources of Interest

Frustrations

Channels

Skills

Biography

Write a brief biography of a hypothetical person you want to hire, considering your organizational environment and culture.

- Gender:
- Age:
- Interests:
- Hobbies:
- Family status:
- Geographical location:

Personality

- What is their personality like?
- What values do they hold dear?
- What are their ethical qualities?
- What are their non-negotiables?

Skills

- What skills and abilities do they have?
- What tasks can they do for you?

Job Search

- What kind of job are they looking for, and what characteristics does it have?
- How does the desired job meet their needs?

Career Goals

- What goal are they pursuing?
- What career vision do they have for themselves?

Frustrations

- What frustrations have they experienced in their previous work environments?
- What needs have been ignored in their past jobs?

Motivation

- What is their main motivation?
- What drives them to work?
- The most important reason they come to your company every day is...?

Content and Resources of Interest

- What are they interested in learning?
- What content do they follow for entertainment?
- Which social networks are they most active on?

Influencing Factors

- Who influences them and their decisions?
- What factors or conditions affect them?

Completing the Hiring Persona Canvas

By completing the hiring persona canvas, you become more aware of what role is missing in your organization.

In general, the best employees:

- Want to be the best at their job.
- Take on high levels of responsibility.
- Have a positive mindset.
- Make the best use of their time.
- Have good interactions with other employees.

▶ Hiring Methods

Now, let's talk about hiring methods that are more effective and yield faster results compared to traditional methods.

▶ Transform Employees into Talent Scouts

Turn all of your employees into talent scouts. Due to the experience they have in your organization, your employees can recommend suitable candidates to you. You can even reward them for helping with talent acquisition. Pay half of the reward when the hiring process starts, and the other half after six months of successful collaboration with the hired individual. Also, ask them to share your organization's job posts on their social media pages. The benefit of doing this is that when a job post is shared by someone already working in your organization, it reflects their satisfaction with working for you.

Your website is an Overlooked Hiring Tool

▶ Blog

At the end of your job posts, ask users to fill out the hiring form if they are interested in joining your team.

▶ Checklist

Ask users to submit their hiring information before downloading checklists and eBooks.

▶ Landing Page

Create a landing page titled **"Join Us"** or **"Become a Part of Our Team"**:

- Create a video showcasing your work environment, team members, and defined processes.
- You can also interview successful employees in your organiza-

tion or those who feel connected to it and share their feedback in video form on this page.

- Some of their feedback can be displayed as testimonials with photos and text.
- Add a form to collect contact details from individuals interested in joining your organization.
- Create a "Job Opportunities" section on this page and continuously update it.
- This page should answer four key questions:
- What does your company do?
- How are values defined in your work environment?
- What culture do you follow?
- What is your organization's mission?

▶ Emails and Text Messages

You can send emails and text messages to previous applicants. Show them your updates by sending links to your website or social media pages.

▶ Social Media

The growing use of social media platforms like Twitter, Facebook, LinkedIn, and Instagram allows organizations to post job opportunities. This method provides access to a larger pool of potential candidates. Additionally, organizations can use the targeting capabilities of these platforms to show job postings only to individuals who meet the required criteria.

For example, LinkedIn is an ideal platform to find top talent because it's the social network where most professionals engage, and its content revolves around brands and teams actively working within various organizations.

Some strategies to get started on LinkedIn:

- **Create an Employer Page:**

If your organization doesn't have one, make sure to create it. This page can describe the company, its activities, and available job opportunities.

- **Use Search Tools:**

LinkedIn provides advanced search tools for finding candidates that match your needs. You can use filters like location, industry, experience, and skills to tailor your search.

- **Follow Industry Professionals:**

On LinkedIn, there are pages related to your industry. By following these, you can connect with professionals active in your field and find suitable talent.

- **Use Ads:**

LinkedIn allows you to run targeted text or image ads that will appear to users meeting your criteria. You can leverage this to build your brand and attract the right talent.

- **Industry Events, Conferences, and Trade Shows**

Networking with people active in your industry can always help you find the right talent. At these events, you can directly engage with industry experts, attracting potential candidates while boosting your company's brand.

- **Collaborating with Universities and Educational Centers**

Universities and educational centers are filled with young talent eager to learn and gain skills. Hosting workshops or attending them gives you the opportunity to engage directly with professors and students, attracting top talent to your organization.

• Internal Hiring

Internal hiring means sourcing talent from within your organization. Sometimes, you don't need to hire externally, as you can discover hidden talents and potential within your existing team.

• Job Boards

The final method we'll discuss is one you're probably already familiar with, job boards like Jobvision, Iran Talent, Eestekhdam, and Jobinja. These platforms allow companies to post job openings online. Job seekers can search for jobs based on skills, location, and other relevant factors. Most job boards also provide features like online resume submissions and direct communication with employers.

▶ How to Write a Convincing Job Advertisement

The most important goal of a job advertisement is to attract candidates who are not only looking for salary and benefits but are also interested in challenges and growth opportunities. You don't want candidates who are just looking for a paycheck, but those who thrive on challenges that help strengthen both the organization and themselves.

A convincing job advertisement is the most critical part of your hiring marketing. It's the pivotal moment that persuades individuals to accept your unique offer.

Let's compare two different job advertisements:

Sales Recruitment

A reputable company in Isfahan with years of experience is looking to hire a motivated and talented individual for their sales department.

▶ **Requirements:**

1. At least two years of relevant experience;

2. Motivation for growth and advancement;

3. Honesty and ability to work as part of a team.

▶ **Benefits:**

1. Free training, health and supplementary insurance;

2. Retirement benefits;

3. Monthly commissions.

Hiring a Salesperson

Our main concern is the growth of our team and its members. Given our responsibility within the organization, we now recognize the need for a person who can manage different situations and complete our superhero team. If you are also looking for growth, we have created an environment with resources and equipment that will help you work through the challenges together. Please send us your resume to get in touch.

By the way, you can find the company's website, Instagram, and other social media links at the bottom of this advertisement. We believe that if we consider it our right to receive your information and resume, you also have the right to know which company you are sending your resume to.

Now that we've looked at these two examples, answer the following questions:

- If you were an applicant, which job ad would you respond to?
- Which ad would attract a skilled candidate?
- Which ad would filter out unqualified resumes?
- For which ad would only those without a job apply?
- Which ad would attract resumes from people who are currently employed?

An effective job ad must clearly communicate the value of working with your company. It should show that your company is always growing and expanding. It should indicate that your team is collaborative and creative, passionate about continuous learning and developing their skills. Your ability to find and hire the right people is the key to increasing your influence and expansion in the business.

▶ Job Interview

The interview session can be considered a "session for impressions." The interview process is a crucial step for the progress and development of any organization. When we look at the numbers, the significance of this matter becomes evident.

For example, globally, the average cost of hiring is around $3,300 per employee each year. In addition to this staggering number, reports show that up to 80% of a company's turnover is caused by poor decisions during the hiring process. Moreover, research by CareerBuilder has found that 74% of employers have made poor hiring decisions, which usually results in increased costs and reduced productivity within the organization. The question is, what is the main reason for hiring the wrong person? The answer lies in several factors, but certainly, one of the most significant is the lack of an effective and optimized interview strategy.

► Why Do We Make Hiring Mistakes?

Selection and recruitment play a crucial role in the success or failure of an organization. You must understand that poor hiring costs significantly (3 to 6 times the annual salary). Therefore, it's important to identify the factors that lead to poor hiring decisions and be aware of them to ensure a more effective hiring process.

1. We Hire Based on Resumes Only

Resumes, especially long ones, are often seen as a measure of effective hiring. However, interviewers who focus only on resumes and ignore the rest of the interview details can miss important factors.

2. We Fall for the Halo Effect

Many interviewers are guilty of this: They get impressed by one specific trait of the candidate during the interview and end up ignoring the other crucial aspects. The Halo Effect suggests that interviewers can overemphasize one positive trait and make decisions based on that alone.

3. We Rush to Fill a Vacancy

Hiring under pressure usually results in poor decisions. Often, when a vacancy arises, we rush to fill it without thoroughly understanding why the previous employee was underperforming. This leads to a high likelihood of making the same mistake again, costing the organization in terms of time and resources.

4. We Ask the Wrong Questions

Often, interviews end with generic, overused questions that do not truly assess whether the candidate will fit within the organization. You should be asking questions that help you understand if you can work with the individual in the long term and assess their behavior in different job-related situations.

5. We Lose Control of the Interview

Interviews should not be a platform for showcasing the company. Many interviewers spend too much time talking about the company's glory, instead of listening and assessing the candidate's fit for the role.

6. Interview Fatigue

When an interviewer conducts too many sessions, they can experience fatigue. This can affect their judgment, leading them to accept candidates quickly without thoroughly considering the individual's qualifications, just to end the interview process.

The interview can be divided into three stages: before, during, and after the interview.

▶ Pre-Interview

Before conducting an interview, you need to have a clear understanding of your goals. Ask yourself, What do you aim to achieve through this interview? Why do you want to interview the people you have selected

Common goals for interviews typically include:

- Evaluating the candidate's skills and abilities to determine if they match the job position;
- Assessing the candidate's adaptability to the company culture and environment;
- Verifying the information provided by the candidate in their resume;
- Understanding the candidate's motivation for wanting to work at your company;
- Setting expectations for the new employee;
- Analyzing responses and reactions of the interviewee to assess their weaknesses and strengths;

- Assessing the candidate's future career goals.

How to contact the candidate for an interview:

Just as organizations have the right to review a candidate's resume before the interview, candidates also have the right to know which company they are being interviewed by. When reaching out to invite someone for an interview, ensure the following steps are followed:

- Your first contact shouldn't only be about setting the interview time and sharing the address. This approach might lead to the candidate not showing up at all.

- Have a friendly initial conversation with the candidate.

- Tell them that you chose to contact them from a pool of applicants. This shows the candidate that their resume was reviewed and adds value to the interview.

- Introduce your organization and ask the candidate to research your company before the interview.

- Send them the company's website and active social media links after the call.

- Always thank the candidate for their time and express excitement about meeting them.

▶ Preparing for the Interview:

Be prepared to answer the typical questions a candidate might have, such as salary, work hours, work environment, benefits, and promotion opportunities.

To make the interview process smoother, you can prepare a list of frequently asked questions along with their answers and provide them to the candidate beforehand.

▶ During the Interview

The interview session should not be a competition between resumes. It should focus on "behavior analysis" and solving problems. You should focus on understanding how both parties can resolve issues in different situations. An interview is an evaluation of the mutual understanding between the two parties about the work relationship.

Use a pen to write down responses. A candidate without a pen is a red flag for you, as it indicates a lack of preparedness. A strong interviewer asks insightful questions that focus on problem-solving abilities. Do not spend more than three minutes introducing the company or talking about the hiring goals. Instead, dedicate the rest of the session to asking questions.

Keep in mind that not all candidates need to meet with the CEO. In many cases, middle managers or team leaders are more effective in conducting interviews.

Questions to Ask During the Interview:

Avoid broad questions. Focus on specifics to get detailed answers about their skills. For example, present challenging work situations and ask how they would solve them. If the role is analytical, prioritize questions that test reasoning rather than memorization.

Prepare three to five real job situations and be ready to present them during the interview. Analyze the candidate's response to these examples, focusing on problem-solving abilities. Pay close attention to the candidate's reactions. You are not just assessing their answers but also their thought process and reasoning behind the solutions.

Types of Interview Questions:

Interview questions come in various types, and their focus may change depending on the job's nature. You can focus on behavioral, analytical, or psychological questions depending on the role being discussed.

By maintaining a clear focus and asking the right questions, you can better understand the candidate's suitability for the role and the organization.

Psychological and Analytical Interview Questions:

How do you see your future with this organization?

....

....

....

Where did you see this job posting?

....

....

....

What made you send your resume to our organization?

....

....

....

....

How much do you know about us?

....

....

....

....

What commitments would you like your supervisor to make to you?

....

....

....

Which of your skills would you like to improve, and how do you plan to do so?

....

....

....

Why should we hire you?

....
....
....

What achievements are you most proud of?

....
....
....

What salary range do you think you should be offered?

....
....
....

Why should we accept the salary proposal that you're asking for?

....
....
....

What level of performance would make you feel very satisfied?

....
....
....

If you had a conflict with a colleague, how would you resolve it?

....
....
....

If someone doesn't cooperate with you and has a negative opinion about you, how would you encourage them to work together?

....
....
....
....

How do you manage your time?

....

....

....

Can you describe a situation where you planned something and successfully reached your goals?

....

....

....

How do you make decisions when you need to choose between two important opportunities?

....

....

....

What are your thoughts on working during weekends or holidays?

....

....

....

Why did you leave your previous job?

....

....

....

If we contact your previous managers, how would they describe you?

....

....

....

Have you applied to work at any other companies?

....

....

....

If you could work for any company, where would you want to work?

....

....

....

What is your biggest strength?

....

....

....

How do you react in the face of failure?

....

....

....

How do you manage situations when you're extremely angry?

....

....

....

What is your biggest weakness?

....

....

....

Can you tell us about a time when you exceeded expectations while working on a project?

....

....

....

What did you like most about your previous job?

....

....

....

....

Which companies have you had the most and least success with, and why?

....

....

....

How did you make time for this interview? Does your boss know where you are right now?

....

....

....

....

Can you describe a situation where you impressed others?

....

....

....

If you were asked to do something and didn't know how to complete it, what would you do?

....

....

....

One of our goals is ... Can you provide the most relevant experience you have in this area or a similar one?

....

....

We know everyone makes mistakes. Can you share an example of a mistake you made and the lesson you learned from it? (Assessing honesty)

....

....

....

....

One of our goals is ... If you were hired, what plans would you have to achieve it?

....
....
....

What hobbies or leisure activities do you pursue?

....
....
....

How do you think our company could improve its performance?

....
....
....

Have you ever considered becoming an entrepreneur?

....
....
....

▶ Response to Final Interview Questions:

Just as you are looking for skilled and talented individuals, candidates also have questions for you. They want to evaluate whether your business is the best among the available options. Therefore, allow the candidate to ask questions, and be patient in answering them. It is advisable to ask if they have any clarifications or concerns they would like to raise at the end of the interview. This could lead to the candidate bringing up important points that you may not have thought of.

Key Points to Remember:

Take Notes: Even if you have a strong memory, it's unlikely that you'll be able to remember all the details of every candidate's qualifications. Therefore, taking notes during the interview will not only help you capture accurate details but also show the candidate that you are professional and attentive. This becomes especially necessary as the number of candidates increases. Effective note-taking helps during the final evaluation.

Avoid Generalizations: Avoid writing general remarks; these make the evaluation difficult. For example, if you're noting something about confidence, rather than simply writing "the candidate is confident," mention specific behaviors that demonstrated their confidence.

End the Interview Positively: At the end of the interview, inform the candidate when they can expect to hear the final result. In many companies, candidates are not informed about the outcome of the interview. Be sure to mention that you will contact them by a certain date via phone, text, or email.

Rejection Communication: If the candidate is not selected, it's a good practice to send a rejection letter explaining the decision. Be clear and transparent about the reasons. If possible, let the candidate know their resume will be kept on file for future openings. Though this might seem simple, it gives a professional image of your company and leaves a positive impression on the candidate.

Key Do's and Don'ts in an Interview:

Do's:

- Be clear and articulate.
- Greet the candidate with a firm handshake, if possible.
- Listen attentively to their responses.
- Introduce yourself confidently.
- Address any concerns or questions they have.
- Use polite phrases like "please" and "thank you."
- Thank the candidate for their time at the end of the interview.

- Occasionally, repeat their words to ensure you've understood correctly.
- Be punctual for the interview.
- Control the flow of the interview; don't let the candidate guide it.

Don'ts:

- Never mock the candidate's responses.
- Do not allow the candidate to control the direction of the interview.
- Manage your own emotions; avoid causing unnecessary stress for the candidate that might hinder them from presenting their skills in the best way possible.

▶ After the Interview

Evaluation: After the interview, evaluate the candidate based on a structured framework. Using a numerical scale for each key quality can help in the assessment.

Additionally, qualitative assessments like "excellent," "good," or "fair" can also provide useful feedback.

▶ Thank You Letter

A thank you letter or follow-up email can significantly improve your company's reputation in the eyes of job applicants. In this letter, thank the candidate again for attending the interview, and provide the timeline for the result. If applicable, provide details on when they will hear back from you.

▶ Offer and Onboarding

If you've selected a candidate, begin the offer process. Discuss salary and benefits with them and provide them with details about the company and the position. Introduce them to the organization's values, the job's responsibilities, and the corporate environment.

Onboarding phase or orientation typically consists of three parts:

- Explaining the organization's mission, core values, and objectives.

- Familiarizing the new employee with aspects such as salary, benefits, leaves, business trips, and other organizational policies.

- Providing a job description and outlining responsibilities to the new employee.

- Introducing the new employee to the workplace environment and different departments.

- Presenting the new employee to colleagues.

Typically, during the initial onboarding phase, a mentor or experienced employee guides the new hire, which is referred to as the "honeymoon period." The more you familiarize the employee with their role during this time, the better their performance will be in the future.

▶ Test:

Improving Problem-Solving Skills with Answer Key and Thinking Guide

It is recommended to record the time required to complete each step of the exercises and note it at the end of the exercises. Try to increase your speed as much as possible.

● Problem-Solving Skills

Problem-solving is a skill that is often required in our daily lives, where we face challenges and need to find solutions quickly. Some of these problems are easy to solve, but others require creative and logical thinking. Developing this mindset will help you:

1. Look at problems from different angles: You will be able to analyze a problem and understand how its parts connect with each other. Sometimes the solution lies in these hidden connections.

2. Evaluate the strengths and weaknesses of the solution: You will assess whether the consequences of choosing this solution outweigh the benefits. Can you overlook the negative consequences to achieve the positive outcomes?

3. Visualize the problem as a story: Imagine yourself as the main character in a story, where you have multiple choices to resolve the problem. What actions will you take, and how will they impact the story?

4. Empathize with others involved in the problem: Put yourself in the shoes of others who are also affected by the problem. Consider how your solution would impact them and if it would help them as well. You could even seek their advice and opinions on the matter.

1. Write a short story using the following words. Each word must be used only once in your story:

Power, Development, Leadership, Partner, Dismissal, Growth, Pen

....

....

....

....

....

....

....

....

....

....

....

....
....
....
....
....
....
....

2. In this exercise, you are given twelve pairs of words. Read them carefully for ten minutes and try to find connections between them.

Then continue with the exercise:

Notepad Company	Chain Picture Frame	Corporation Ring binder	Flowerpot Library
Pen Clock	Mug Warehouse	Recruitment Wallpaper	System Hotel
Hand Decision	Position Drawer	Telephone Negotiation	Newspaper Winner

Group the following words in pairs, similar to Exercise number 2.

Notepad, Company, Telephone, Flowerpot, Pen, Picture Frame, Clock, Mug, Corpration, Chain, Winner, Decision, Warehouse, Hotel, System, Folder, Wallpaper, Bookcase, Recruitment, Negotiation, Drawer, Newspaper, Hand, Position

3. Try to choose the path that leads you to the destination

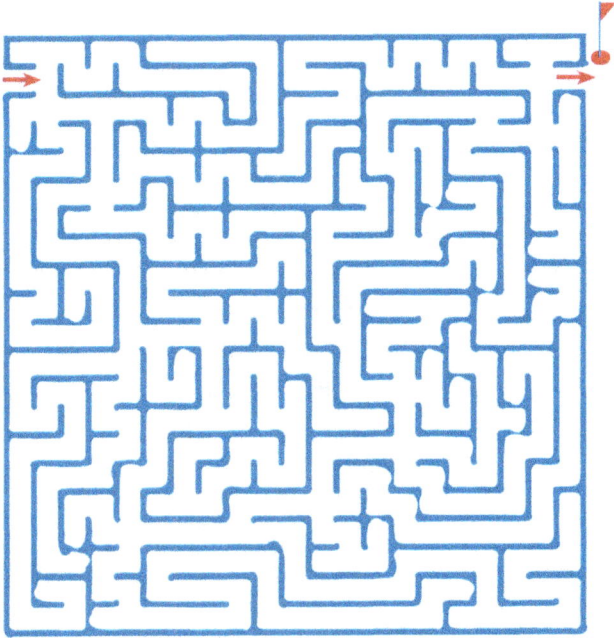

4. Look at the images below for two minutes, then go to the next page.

Based on the exercises on the previous page, complete the faces.

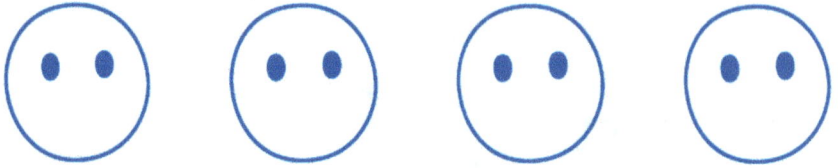

5. Carefully look at the first and second images. In this exercise, you should try to place the discs from the first image onto the rod like in the second image with the fewest moves. Be careful that you can only move one disc at a time, and you cannot place a larger disc on top of a smaller disc.

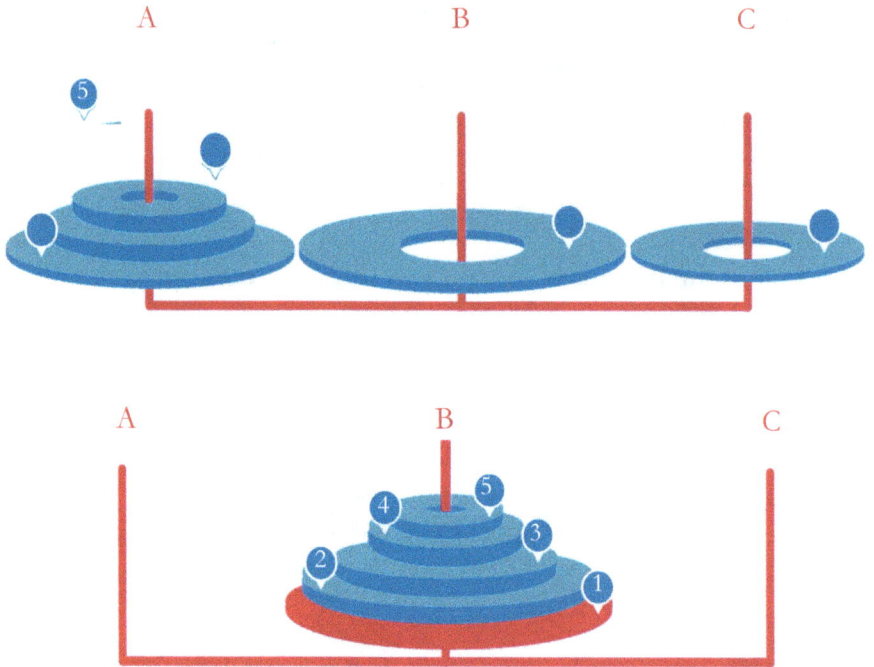

▶ **Answer Sheet**

Problem-Solving Skills Test:

Date of Exercise Completion:

Time Taken for the Exercise:

Number of Mistakes:

Main Weaknesses:

Strengths:

Answer to Question 3

Answer to Question 5

Disc 5 to rod B ☞ Disc 4 to rod A ☞ Disc 2 to rod B ☞ Disc 5 to rod B ☞ Disc 4 to rod C ☞ Disc 5 to rod C ☞ Disc 3 to rod B ☞ Disc 5 to rod A ☞ Disc 4 to rod B ☞ Disc 5 to rod B

▶ **Write your five key takeaways from this chapter:**

1...

2...

3...

4...

5...

▶ **Three steps I Will Immwsiately Start:**

1...

2...

3...

▶ **One Golden Lesson to Share with Others:**

....

....

....

....

....

....

Download all the tables and exercises of this chapter from the following website.

https://hosseintaheri.ir/bmg/

Team Building

Chapter 9:

Team Building

A team means the collaboration of individuals to create new value.

📖 **After reading this chapter, you will gain mastery over:**

- Why and how to build a team
- Types of organizational teams
- The bystander effect
- Acceptance and adjustment of conflict
- Types of rewards

'Team' is not just a word. It is not merely a group of individuals forming an organization with a shared goal. Rather than considering a team as the organization's mastermind, I prefer to see it as "the beating heart of society"; people who, together, are the lifeblood and survival of themselves, their organization, and the community of their customers. As Carlo Ancelotti says, 'The essence of every coach's job is to take care of the team, help the team grow and progress, celebrate victories, and be there with the team after defeats.'

In business, the team has great importance, and players also play a significant role because you can never be a winner alone.

▶ Why should we build teams?

When the 'why' of something is clear, the 'how' becomes obvious. When the individual goals of everyone in an organizational community align with the goals of that organization, the result of achieving those goals, whether individual or organizational, is much quicker. In today's competitive economy, assets and capital used to be defined differently than in the past. In 1930s, land and physical assets were considered competitive advantages. This means that if someone worked on land and performed physical labor to increase its productivity, they were considered a winner, even if their work did not require thinking.

Teamwork, on the other hand, is not achieved by the work of one person alone. In the 1940s, optimal productivity from land was achieved only when workers were employed in their fields, and by increasing their activities, they were able to produce more. In the 1950s, in addition to land and workers, capital was also necessary to increase the speed of farming or factory production. The emergence of industrial production was a pivotal point in human history. This phenomenon brought about an extraordinary competitive advantage by eliminating tiring physical labor and introducing new production methods.

In the 1970s, the issue of quality came into play, and goods needed to be produced with high quality and professional services in order to be sold in the market and delivered to people. Competitive advantages were changing across different sectors. No longer was having land, workers, capital, and quality enough. The real art was in services. This meant that organizations had to think about how to gather more information about the market and their customers' needs.

After that, merely having enough information was not enough. What mattered was the ability to extract what they wanted from that information."

Competitive advantage increases the complexity of efforts.

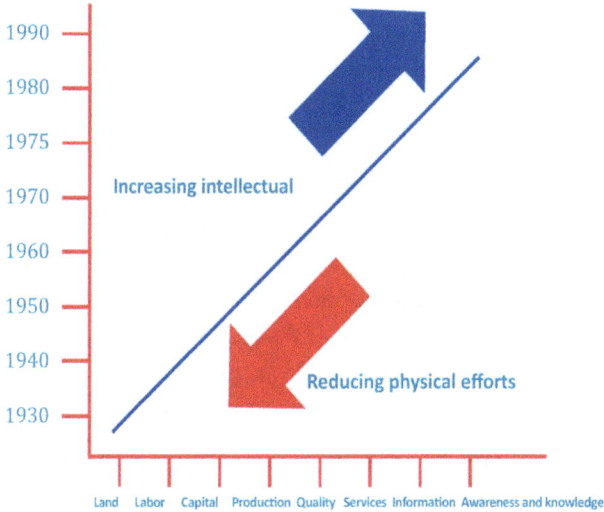

You know that individuals have needs, and you must be able to align your organization with these needs. We all have needs that make us join teams. Below are the factors that drive individuals to join teams:

- Security
- Status or position
- Feeling of worth
- Belonging
- Power

• Goal fulfillment

Why do people join teams?

Security

Note: When people are with us, we feel that they are taking care of us, and this is the need for security.

Action: Show them that you are with them to reach the highest level of energy, motivation, and commitment in their work, and that you are there to help solve their problems.

Status or Position

Note: Many individuals need a position in order to secure their social standing and have a space for themselves in the workplace.

Action: Create positions for your team members and help them reach these positions. A position they would find hard to lose. When individuals gain a position, they tend to want to advance, grow, and enhance it. Creating positions acts like a strong magnet; it not only keeps the individual in the team but also excites other team members or even new recruits to work with you.

Feeling of Worth

Note: The feeling of worth comes from being seen and achieving results. When individuals see that their results contribute to others and, in turn, impact an organization, they feel valuable.

Action 1: Involve your team members in decisions and processes. Let them see themselves as a key factor in successes and part of the results.
Action 2: Let them see the impact of their work in your system, making it visible to their families as well. When their families recognize the value they are creating, it sets in motion a cycle of voluntary and creative effort from them.

Belonging

Note: Humans are naturally attached to something. What you create in terms of belonging is crucial. A common misconception is that people join teams simply for money. However, the need of individuals goes beyond this.

Action: As a team leader, get your team members used to a work style that is reciprocal, so that they cannot and do not want to work outside of this. Providing job security, offering status, and creating a sense of worth will help foster this sense of belonging.

Power

Note: People feel more powerful when they are together, which is why they join teams. This power can be experienced in the form of knowledge, influence, authority, and a sense of peace. Being together amplifies experiences, increases their impact, and creates stronger arms for their organizations by eliminating deficiencies.

Action: Teams must be empowering. Share experiences and create dynamic spaces that go beyond just meetings. Encourage the flow of energy and power and stay away from negative individuals.

Goal Fulfillment

Note: A goal is not simply victory; it is the development of victory. It always has to be about growing towards success. Aligning individual goals with the organization's goals fulfills this need.

Action: Do not belittle the organization's main goal. Do not tie it solely to financial benefits. Connect it to the benefit of the community. This is where your team will work with heart and soul.

Discuss these six factors with your team members: What can I do to increase your security? How can I improve your social status (position and rank)? What can I do to make you feel valued? What resources can I provide for you? What kind of training do you need? Do you need advice? What can I do to make you feel more powerful when presenting the price to the customer? What can I do to help you proudly present our product? How can I help you achieve your goals? How can you help us achieve our goals?

It's important to focus on the right questions. If you focus on these six, your role with the team will be clear, and the team will function more effectively.

As I mentioned earlier, what works best when setting goals is "alignment." I organized a meeting with my team and talked to them about why they are here in our organization. The turning point in the meeting was when I said: "Anyone who works in this company should not be here for me, my pocket, or their own pocket, but to help improve our business together. Our goal is to remove the fear of action from managers. Our goal is to create power and revitalize businesses. In doing so, the blessing will flow into all of our lives. That is our main goal."

The criteria for individuals joining or not joining organizational teams are these six factors. It is possible that a company has worked so well on providing security or creating a sense of value that this alone attracts people to join the team.

Exercise: What advantages do you create in these six areas that enhance each of them?

This table should draw a model for your organization so that by writing the advantages you create, you become more aware of them, improve them, and ultimately make your team more effective. These six columns of team-building are crucial because they determine where and in which organization individuals should come together.

	The advantage you have created	The advantage you should create
Security		
Status or Position		

Belonging

Feeling of Worth

Power

Goal Fulfillment

Why Should We Build Teams?

After reading this section, think about why team building is necessary. Sometimes, we want to go fast, we want to achieve a big vision, and we want to move alone. John Wooden, one of the greatest basketball coaches in the world, says: "If you want to go fast, go alone; but if you want to go far, you need a team."

▶ Skill or Position?

Suppose you want to build a team and there is a need for a graphic designer in that team. This position is open in your organization. There is also someone in your organization who is not a graphic designer, but with the training they've received, they can design a relatively good PowerPoint presentation. Now, the question is, why do you want to build this team? Do you want to fill that position, or do you need the skill?

Team building is based on skills, not positions. This is why sometimes things don't move forward in your organization. Because when you try to fill open positions, you haven't addressed the skills gap. Without considering skill, you may have filled positions but not solved the problem. When you consider skill, instead of focusing on filling a job, you focus on providing the necessary training for the right skills. In some organizations, when the number of people decreases, the team still functions better because the people who remain have better skills. Simply put, one person can be as effective as three. So, when you hire someone, make sure they have the necessary skills. A person in your organization needs three things: tools, skills, and prerequisites to achieve results. For example, if you hire a graphic designer, they need the tools like a computer and graphic design software, as well as the skills to use these tools. Once you provide these tools and training, the person will be able to produce the desired results, and over time, the quality of the output will improve. If you're hiring someone and training them, it should be based on skill development, not just filling a position.

▶ From Synergy to Co-creation

If the team has the right skills and positions, it will create synergy and prevent waste of organizational resources, such as financial and time resources. In many organizations, I see that although the organization has clear goals, each person does their own work in a direction they prefer, and there is no alignment or coordination in thought, skills, and performance. The organization hasn't made an effort to align the team with its goals. It's clear that in such organizations, resource wastage is high. Waste of resources prevents achieving the goals in a timely manner, and money, time, and energy are wasted. In a team where synergy exists, ideas are aligned, and synergy is created. This results from exponential collaboration. Essentially, you form a team so that you can reach your higher goals faster and more efficiently through synergy.

The Key Characteristics of a Team

A team should have several key characteristics:

- They should have complementary skills;

- They should share common goals and approaches;

- They should have adaptive and complementary dependencies with each other;

- They should participate in the exchange of information and knowledge;

- They should encourage and motivate each other.

First, team members should have complementary skills, even if they are in different positions. For example, one person may be in the warehouse, another in sales, and another in customer service. These members should have complementary skills. Each person's work should complete the other's. They must have common goals and a shared approach. They should also have adaptive and complementary dependencies, meaning they can adjust their skills, thinking, plans, and ideas to each other. At times, they should compromise on their positions and at other times, they should strive to convince one another. This is how you can work in teams. If you only stand firm on your own positions and follow your own path, you won't be able to align with others. Just like in the diagram, if every team member moves in their own direction, the dependencies will not function effectively. Everyone will be speaking their own ideas and opinions. However, they must participate in the exchange of information and knowledge and be generous in sharing them. After all, the cost of the information and experiences they have acquired has been paid by the organization. Therefore, when one person acquires this knowledge and shares it with others, the cost is spread across the team.

Members must also be encouraging, supportive, and empathetic. They should be able to congratulate each other. In an organization where people encourage each other, they feel better about each other's achievements.

If you do not have these elements, then you do not have a team, but rather a group. A group is not the same as a team. A group lacks the characteristics of a team. In groups, resources are wasted, while in teams, due to synergy, costs turn into income and profits. If you spend money that generates revenue, then this expense is justified and permissible.

▶ What You Need to Build a Team:

Training (T), Integration (I), and Collaboration (C).

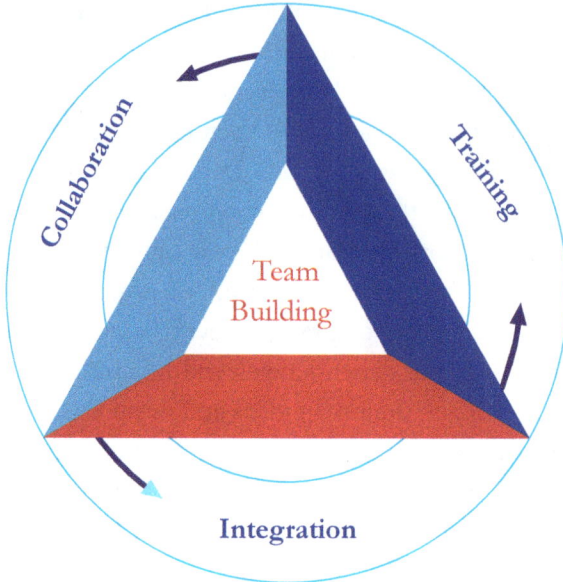

Training creates integration, and integration leads to synergy. Synergy keeps people aligned both mentally and operationally, working together in a shared direction. A team is where there is training, integration, and participation. From tomorrow, when you think about your team, consider what you've done to train them. How much have you taught them? How many plans or rules have you created to make sure the team works in harmony? What have you done to encourage greater participation?

▶ Training:

● Acquisition and Transfer of Experience

The first important thing in training is to create an environment where people can learn from others' experiences and not repeat the mistakes of others. You, as a business owner, have experience, and you transfer this experience to your team. For example, if you were to teach a child, would you teach them how to eat properly, or would you share your own experiences of eating? Therefore, training can be seen as "transferring experience." Share your experiences with your team and create an environment where they too can share their experiences with others.

If you don't train your team, they won't grow. Because they will get used to doing small, simple tasks and will always rely on you, like robots. When you teach them and mentor them, you unleash their talents and develop their skills.

How sad it is when a manager asks me, "What should I do if I train my team and they leave my company afterward?" I respond, "What if you didn't train them, and they stayed? That would be a disaster." My sadness comes from the superficial view some managers have about their teams.

Let's look at this issue from another perspective:

Scenario 1: After you provide training, the individual leaves your company for another and applies what they learned.

Scenario 2: You don't provide any training, and the untrained employee stays in your company and eventually destroys your system.

Question: Which scenario causes you more harm?

You might stop focusing on skill-building because you're afraid of losing the individual you've trained. But you must understand that in today's world, no knowledge or skill is permanent. You can continually train, educate, and make your organization stronger and more fruitful.

Mental and Operational Skills

• **Mental Skills:** These are the abilities required to think, focus, and make decisions that form a clear mental or visual map of the path ahead.

• **Operational Skills:** These are skills that help manage priorities. Prioritization involves calculating the return (time, cost, profit, and credibility) of each task. The more individuals in your team improve their operational and mental skills, such as communication, behavior analysis, conflict resolution, and crisis problem-solving, the more capable you and your team will become. Skill should generate power. In fact, developing mental and operational skills increases the team's mental and operational power. The result of this power is turning resources into opportunities, which is one of the most outstanding features of competitive businesses. Create conditions where, in addition to the training they receive from you, your team members also teach others. The most important method of learning is teaching. They will understand that teaching what they've learned leads to a deeper and more lasting understanding of the concepts.

• **Self-Assessment:** Create conditions for self-assessment. Teach them to grade themselves before you do. They should be able to track the quantity and quality of their work and rate themselves based on previously defined standards. Self-assessment is not complicated; it simply requires individuals to evaluate their performance and thinking. It is an alignment and synergy factor. To align your goals and expectations with your team members' objectives and motivations, you need clear criteria for assessing satisfaction on both sides. These criteria should clearly indicate what factors cause satisfaction for you and what factors cause satisfaction for your team members.

• **Promotion:** Give this book to your team members to read. When you do this, this collective learning is a form of training. Training has one meaning: lifting others up. Anything you do to elevate others means training them, and that's the "T" in the word "team."

► **Integration**

What is meant by integration includes:

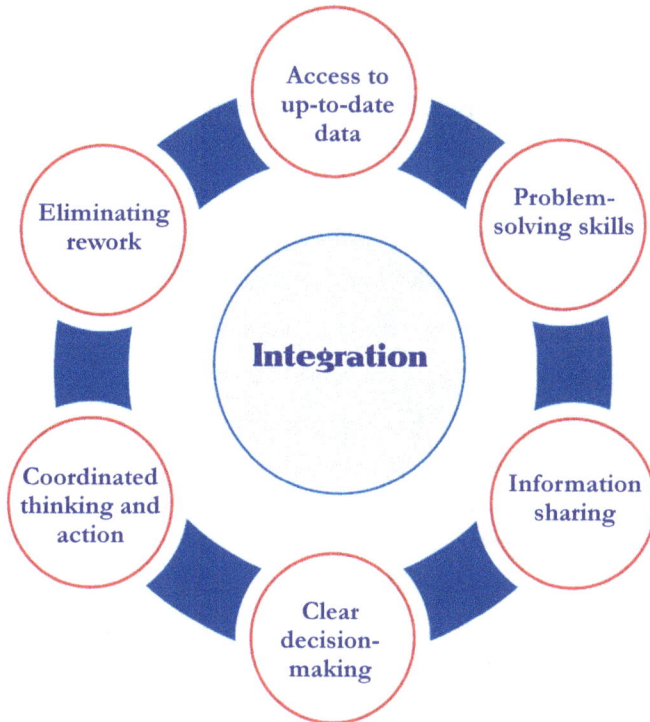

Integration can be seen as coordinated thinking and action. Team members are trained to eliminate rework. When you achieve integration, you can create collaboration. Where can you find rework? From experience and training. You can see that all the components are interconnected. Integration means creating multi-skilled individuals in your team so that, if you define a project, your team members can work together to execute it. In team projects, they understand how to pass the ball to each other and how to score. This is integration. In integration, I, as a manager, make decisions, middle managers make decisions, and so do the individuals in each department. Meanwhile, the boundaries of decision-making are precise, and everyone knows how to act in their role at any level. In integration, you can also critique problem-solving skills. When people want to synchronize with each other, what should they do so that they ask fewer questions and don't waste time on unnecessary discussions? As a result, their time is spent on action. In integration, sharing information at various levels is very important. You need to define clear access levels for each person. An important factor in integration is the credibility of the data that reaches the organization, as it helps improve working conditions, make correct decisions, and ultimately enables individuals to achieve appropriate results. An organization where everyone moves in different directions and bumps into walls is also a disorganized one. Therefore, the more aligned the organization is, the more integrated it will be.

▶ Collaboration

There are a few key points regarding collaboration:

If team members cannot collaborate, the training you've invested in them is wasted. Collaboration means increasing the social capital of an organization. It means boosting trust, fostering a sense of responsibility, and creating a supportive environment within the organization. It means embracing and supporting the security, status, time, and ideas that individuals contribute. **In collaboration, your job is to manage communications, communication that should neither be too intertwined nor too distant.** In bureaucratic organizations, due to poor communication management, collaboration tends to be low. Managers in such organizations often don't participate; they don't interact within the organization or with the external market. They don't know how to improve and manage these communications.

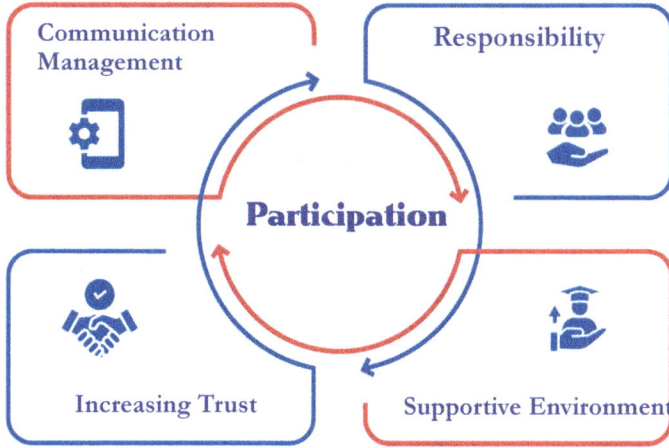

It is important to note that collaboration and coordination are not the same as participation. People often think that if they are in coordination, they are participating. This is not the case. The definition of participation is clear: it means that individuals work together to create something new and reach common perspectives for that goal.

The key point is the effort to create something new in a non-individualistic way. In other words, it is something that belongs to everyone and keeps all team members together. Coordination and cooperation are subsets of participation. Coordination is about sharing information and resources to support a common goal. While participating to create something new, coordination must exist, and information and resources must be shared to achieve that goal. Many organizations are coordinated but do not participate. Information circulates among everyone, but it is not directed towards supporting a common goal.

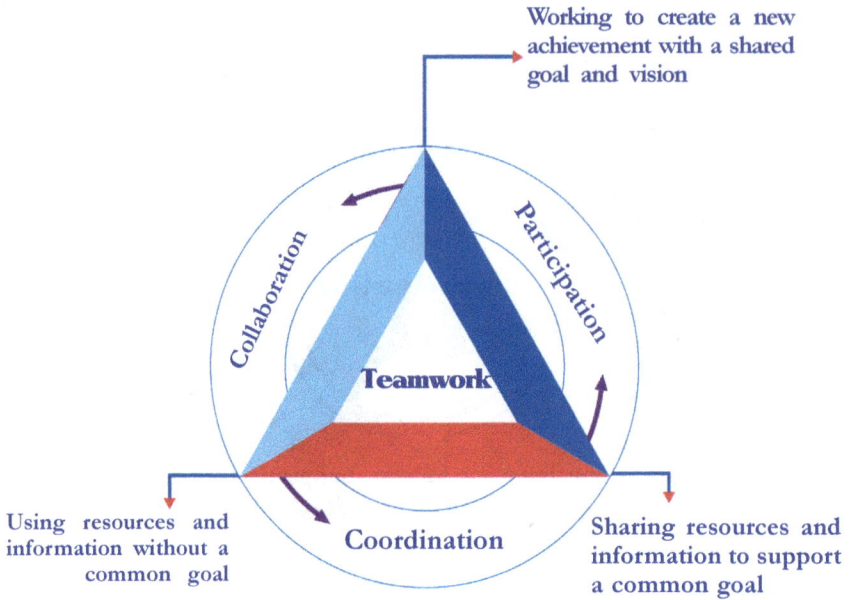

In many organizations, there is collaboration, but there is no participation. Resources and information are shared without having a common goal; however, in collaboration, there is no deep trust, no supportive environment, and no well-organized communication.

In coordination, information and resources are shared in such a way that each member of the organization can find their role in supporting the organization's goal. Coordination is about teamwork in executing plans, and it does not involve creating or developing something new.

In participation, people work together to create something new, whereas in coordination, they are only working together to execute tasks. Collaboration, coordination, and participation are all aspects of teamwork but differ significantly from one another.

Increasing Team's Capability

What skills should your team develop in the coming three months in various departments?

....
....
....
....
....
....
....

How are the experiences within your organization documented and how are they communicated to team members?

....
....
....
....
....
....

What actions are taken to eliminate redundancies within the organization?

....
....
....
....
....
....
....
....

▶ Bludorn Questionnaire

Evaluating Participation and Engagement of Individuals in the Organization

---

1. We like to do several activities at once:

Strongly disagree	Disagree	Neutral	Agree	Strongly agree
☐	☐	☐	☐	☐

---

2. We prefer to complete parts of several projects rather than completing one project in full:

Strongly disagree	Disagree	Neutral	Agree	Strongly agree
☐	☐	☐	☐	☐

---

3. We believe that individuals should try to do many tasks at once:

Strongly disagree	Disagree	Neutral	Agree	Strongly agree
☐	☐	☐	☐	☐

---

4. When we work alone, we usually work on several projects at once:

Strongly disagree	Disagree	Neutral	Agree	Strongly agree
☐	☐	☐	☐	☐

---

5. We prefer not to do just one task at a time:

Strongly disagree	Disagree	Neutral	Agree	Strongly agree
☐	☐	☐	☐	☐

---

6. We believe that individuals put in their best effort when they have many tasks to complete:

Strongly disagree	Disagree	Neutral	Agree	Strongly agree
☐	☐	☐	☐	☐

7. **We believe that the best way to work is to complete several tasks before starting a new one:**

Strongly disagree	Disagree	Neutral	Agree	Strongly agree
☐	☐	☐	☐	☐

8. **We believe that the best thing for individuals is to have several tasks to complete:**

Strongly disagree	Disagree	Neutral	Agree	Strongly agree
☐	☐	☐	☐	☐

9. **We like to work on more than one task at a time:**

Strongly disagree	Disagree	Neutral	Agree	Strongly agree
☐	☐	☐	☐	☐

10. **We prefer to work on completing parts of different projects every day rather than completing one project in full:**

Strongly disagree	Disagree	Neutral	Agree	Strongly agree
☐	☐	☐	☐	☐

	Strongly agree	Agree	Neutral	Disagree	Strongly disagree
Score	5	4	3	2	1

Lower Score Limit	Average Score Limit	Upper Score Limit
20	35	50

- Score between 35 and 50: Indicates a strong tendency to perform multiple tasks simultaneously, with high participation.

- Score between 20 and 35: Suggests a moderate tendency to handle multiple tasks simultaneously and a willingness to participate.

- Score below 20: Indicates a low inclination to perform multiple tasks at once, with a preference for independent work.

▶ What types of teams should you build?

The first question was why you should build teams, and now the question is what types of teams should you build?

The types of teams are:

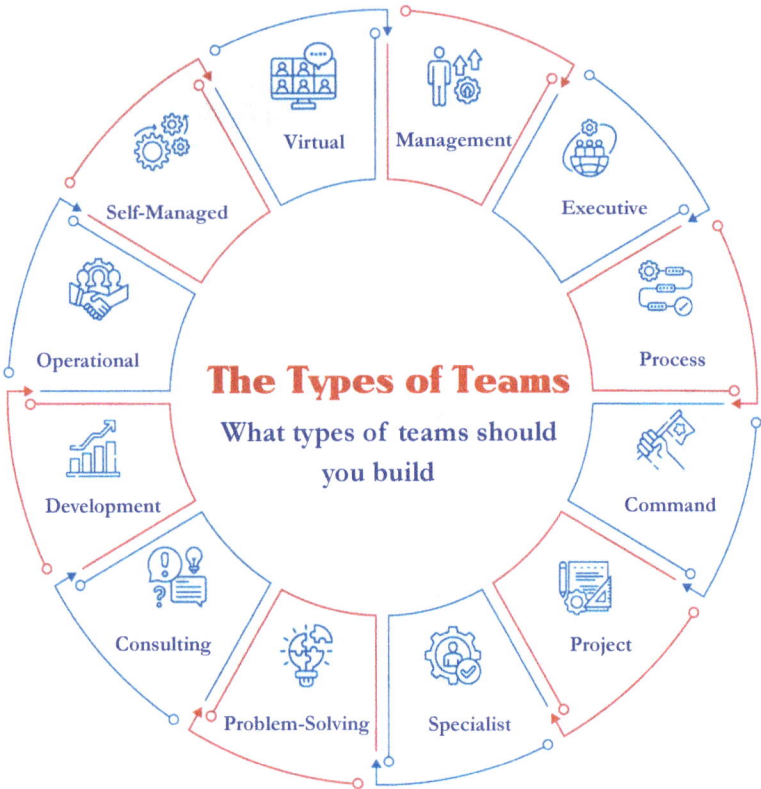

The Types of Teams

What types of teams should you build

Virtual · Management · Executive · Process · Command · Project · Specialist · Problem-Solving · Consulting · Development · Operational · Self-Managed

Now, the question is: What types of teams should we build in our business? What teams should be internal teams of the organization, and what teams should be outsourced teams?

There are twelve types of teams:

1. Executive Team:

Their task is to execute work. In an organization, one or two people are assigned to execute tasks.

2. Process Team:

These teams handle the main processes of organizations and refine them. For example, IT teams are part of process, specialized, and virtual teams. Therefore, a person may be part of multiple teams.

3. Command Team:

Their task is to provide leadership and guidance. They work with other members to drive plans forward.

4. Project Team:

When a project is defined in the organization, members of the project team work on it. Project teams can overlap with executive and process teams.

5. Specialist Team:

These teams consist of individuals with various expertise and gather to complete specialized tasks.

6. Problem-Solving Team:

These teams come together to solve issues, exchange ideas on work processes, and provide proposals to improve methods. For example, if there's a problem in a city project, the problem-solving team is responsible for resolving it.

7. Consulting Team:

These are outsourced teams. For example, for handling tax matters, instead of hiring in-house employees, you might consult with an external specialist team.

8. Development Team:

Their duties include market development, product development, human resources development, and communication development.

9. Operational Team:

Unlike the executive team, whose tasks and methods are precisely defined by higher authorities, operational teams determine their own tasks and methods. They have more autonomy in selecting the appropriate tools and methods for completing their tasks.

10. Self-Managed Team:

These teams handle responsibilities such as procurement, services, and housekeeping. For example, in my own organization, we provide training to the services team and let them handle maintenance tasks independently without needing to consult with management.

11. Virtual Team:

This team consists of individuals who may be geographically distant but are connected by the internet. They work together remotely, and their primary role is to find the best specialists for a project without considering where they are located.

12. Management Team:

This team consists of the organization's key decision-makers, such as the CEO, middle managers, and business owners. They discuss organizational concerns, financial issues, threats, opportunities, and human resources matters.

Team-building is not limited to internal teams only; it includes the creation of teams both inside and outside the organization that contribute to the growth of your organization, work towards your shared goals, and create synergy. Regardless of whether your business is small or large, you need to have all twelve of these teams. In some cases, functions like finance, sales, and public relations may be integrated into a single team, such as a market development team. The finance and sales teams may collaborate to collect debts. Is it possible for the finance department not to support the sales department? Or for the marketing or commerce department to participate in a trade show without the finance team being involved, saying, "spend however you like"? That would never happen. This isn't just responsibility in terms of accountability, it's a duty.

One team that should always be considered in team-building is the legal advisory team, which should be used with the understanding that it's a consulting team.

How are teams different from groups?

Needs

In a Group

People come together in groups to fulfill their material and physical needs. Once their emotional needs are met in the group, they are satisfied.

In a Team

People gather in teams out of the need for survival, competition, and fear of external power that could destroy the team from outside. Security and dependence are more important than emotional attachment, as belonging and a sense of attachment are crucial. You might simply like someone, but you trust someone else and feel secure around them. In fact, trust means you like and accept the other person. Trust is the foundation that teams rely on to succeed.

Goals and Aspirations

In a Group

A group that shares a common vision and goals can achieve them with effort and teamwork, even if they face challenges and obstacles along the way.

In a Team

They don't just focus on goals and visions; they also aim for progress and development within the team. They are idealistic and committed to their goals.

Principles and Initiative

In a Group

Groups have common principles and values.

In a Team

In a team, there is initiative and social utility. Social utility means that the work done in the team benefits others as well.

Communication

In a Group

Communication is minimal in a group.

In a Team

In a team, communication is widespread. The more a team plans for communication, the less coordination is needed in the future, increasing team participation. For example, members of a surgical team communicate extensively, but once they enter the operating room, they don't keep checking or asking each other questions. Coordination has already been done, and now it's time to act. This is the essence of participation, and it shows the difference between a group and a team.

Groups and Combinations

In a Group

In groups, members tend to create smaller groups

In a Team

They combine with others to get better results in teams.

Identity

In a Group

People in groups don't usually try to express their true identities. They hide their true selves so that if something goes wrong, the blame isn't on anyone specifically.

In a Team

In teams, they reveal their true personal and work identities.

When all these things happen, it is the team that wins, not the individual.

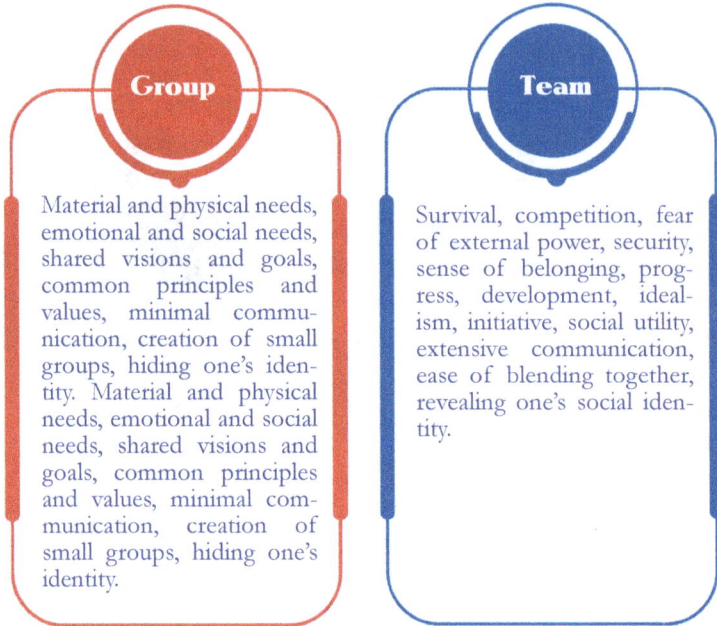

Group	Team
Material and physical needs, emotional and social needs, shared visions and goals, common principles and values, minimal communication, creation of small groups, hiding one's identity. Material and physical needs, emotional and social needs, shared visions and goals, common principles and values, minimal communication, creation of small groups, hiding one's identity.	Survival, competition, fear of external power, security, sense of belonging, progress, development, idealism, initiative, social utility, extensive communication, ease of blending together, revealing one's social identity.

▶ Team Building

For effective team building, the following points should be considered:

1. Bystander Effect

The first thing you need to do in team building viral or share responsibility. The "bystander effect" occurs when people are seen taking responsibility for their work. For example, during one of my trips to Anzali[1], I saw a group of people wearing uniforms with white gloves, carrying garbage bags, and cleaning the beach. Watching their responsible actions made me feel responsible too. As a result, I took a plastic bag and started picking up garbage.

1-Anzali: A port city in northern Iran, located on the Caspian Sea

When you, as the team leader, accept responsibility for events, problems, and crises, this encourages others in the organization to do the same. The more responsibility is visible in the team, the more the organization's culture is built on responsibility. I have fostered a "responsible team" in my organization. Thus, every new member who joins the system unconsciously learns and repeats this responsible behavior by observing the actions of the team members. This phenomenon is called the "bystander effect."

2. Discipline Furnace

The second important task is to establish a discipline furnace in the organization. Discipline means doing the right work at the right time for the right reason. When you enforce discipline in the organization, talent turns into ability, and skills are created. People learn to use their time, energy, and resources effectively. Sometimes, as the leader of the organization, I would arrive at the office at 7:30 AM. Over time, employees who used to arrive between 8:00 to 8:30 AM started to consistently show up by 8:00 AM. In the discipline furnace, talent is transformed into ability, just as clay is turned into brick in a furnace. Ability, power, and endurance are the strength of an organization. Imagine someone with talent, but not yet "hardened" in the discipline furnace, just like raw clay. When they join a team that is integrated, participative, and well-trained, what happens? They become solid, and their talent transforms into ability.

3. Alliance and Consensus

People are both "partners" and "allies" They are partners because they participate, and they are allies because they must move in the same direction and towards a common goal. In a team, the first step is to work together so that later they can win together. Until they can work well together, they cannot win together. Partnership means participating, and consensus means moving towards a specific goal to reach a position that everyone agrees on. Look at the teams that lift the championship cup. Even their body language is unified, and their happiness is similar. They are aligned both in the journey to winning and in the joy of winning. Their story of victory and championship remains in history because they managed to work together and then win together.

4. Making Individuals Responsible

Responsibility means that from the moment you commit to doing something, you do not abandon it until it is finished. Responsibility is a quality, and it elevates the quality of our actions. Correct and responsible actions elevate the quality of relationships within the organization. In other words, responsibility enhances the power of the team.

5. Lack of Transparency

One of the problems that create issues in teamwork is the lack of transparency. Be clear with people about what you want and where you want to go. Tell them what benefits come from participation and teamwork. Lack of transparency is a major cause of demotivation in many teams. Demotivation harms the team.

Discuss with your team and clearly tell them what you want to achieve and where the organization is headed.

Explain the role each person plays in reaching that position and how it benefits both you and them. When transparency is low, conflict arises, and participation decreases. This leads to a breakdown in unity, like in an image where arrows are pointing in different directions. If team members have not learned to be transparent and move forward together, everyone will head in their own direction.

6. Feeling of Value

You need to give your team the feeling of being valued. Help your team to become the champions of your clients. Make the tasks you assign to them meaningful. Give meaning to the work and performance of the organization. Tell your team members how their work improves people's lives. For example, tell them that by installing each surveillance camera, they protect the achievements of a father and a family. Tell them that by packaging this nuts product, they contribute to a family's happiness as they enjoy it.

As we mentioned before, one of the reasons people join a team is that they want to feel valued. By giving meaning to their work, this sense of worth is created.

It's through such beauty and simplicity that you can make work meaningful. When people's work becomes meaningful, they feel valued.

7. Social Loafing

"Social loafing" is a form of collective slacking off. It's not an individual phenomenon but a collective one. Why does someone throw garbage on the beach? Because they see others doing it. Why does someone not pick it up? Because they see others not doing it. Why does someone not stand up? Because they see others sitting too. This needs to be prevented.

As mentioned before, hiring should not just be about filling positions, but also about taking simultaneous actions and utilizing the synergistic benefits of the team.

In a tug-of-war experiment, two groups were chosen and a person from each side was attached to a dynamometer. Each person exerted their maximum effort to pull the rope. Then, more people were added to each side, but the dynamometer showed that as the number of people increased, the force exerted by each person decreased significantly because, due to the presence of others, each person did not use their full strength.

Another example is when you want to move a table. If ten people surround the table, it still doesn't move properly. Some may only place their hands on the table and not contribute force. This means the total force exerted is less than expected.

This phenomenon does not only occur in physical tasks but also in thinking. Sometimes, due to collective laziness in an organization, intellectual work does not take place because everyone assumes that others are thinking, so they feel no need to think themselves.

8. Me, Us, or Them?

In a team, "I" does not exist. A team is not a personal territory. It is formed so individuals can showcase their "we" mindset.

In a team, it is not about which individual is more important. All are equal. Just like in an orchestra, everyone practices, and if one person plays out of tune, the whole song is ruined. It is not about which instrument is more important. What matters is the team.

If someone in the team says "I," remove them from the team. The team belongs to everyone, not a specific individual, because the common goal that they are striving for belongs to everyone.

9. Acceptance and Conflict Resolution

In a team, you must accept conflicts. Acknowledge that there are differences in opinion and work to resolve them. Conflict and disagreement are inseparable parts of any human gathering. Even at a wedding or family picnic, there are disagreements, let alone a team where individuals are not family members, come from different cultures, and have different upbringings. When we say they should be trained, it means they should be trained based on organizational behavior and culture. When conflict arises, it is crucial to create an environment where neutral and unbiased conversations can take place. Don't defend anyone, and let people resolve their issues with each other. The issues that reach the management room didn't appear today; they have developed over time and those involved have not yet been able to solve them themselves.

10. Synergy

Teamwork should help members achieve goals that are not possible alone. People come together in a team to achieve the goals we set earlier for the team. You need to create an environment where individuals feel they can reach their goals alongside you and get their share. This way, team members won't leave you. If they do leave, they will always miss being part of your team. Build a shared goal with your employees and customers. If a customer knows that the growth and security of their system are in your hands, they won't leave you and will easily tolerate any issues that arise. Remember, synergy means that the whole is more valuable than the sum of its parts.

11. Feedback Culture

Create a feedback culture within your team. If you don't give feedback to employees, they will develop anxiety and doubt. They will ask themselves if they are really doing their job well. People want to know that they are doing things correctly. It's up to you to plan for this. Occasionally, gather feedback from your team or give them feedback.

A business's speed increases with a culture of feedback. Team members will feel important. To make this feeling repeat, they will perform better and better. This is a form of recognition. In the training section, we mentioned self-evaluation. Giving and receiving feedback is also a form of evaluation.

12. From Job Descriptions to Task Allocation

There is a difference between a job description and task allocation. When writing a job description, you must also assist with the quality execution of the tasks. Have you ever wondered why many job descriptions in organizations aren't implemented? Because you don't discuss them with your team or gather feedback. Agree with your team on the tasks you assign to them and then break them down into smaller tasks. **By relying on this method, you will witness an improvement in the culture of responsibility and the executive management capabilities in the organization.**

13. Organizational Culture

Organizational culture means setting boundaries for informal and personal behaviors. When you go to a stadium, the environment and atmosphere there make you behave in a certain way. When you go to a theater, the atmosphere there makes you behave differently. In the stadium, you align with the crowd's cheers and movements, but in the theater, you remain silent. Organizational culture determines how the members of the organization interact with each other, how leaders interact with employees, the values, rules, dos and don'ts in team work and team building.

As mentioned before, one of the priorities of individuals is to ensure their own security. Therefore, organizational culture must be designed in a way that ensures the protection of individuals' privacy and security. The working environment can be formal but still enjoyable.

14. Reward System

The goal of the reward system is to appreciate competencies, not to bribe. Through rewards, you show individuals that their efforts are noticed, and being noticed is the most valuable feeling for a person. The feeling of being noticed is directly related to the feeling of being valued. The reward system is one of the sources of power for an organization. Try to offer diverse and motivating rewards, not repetitive and predictable ones.

In general, rewards are divided into the following seven categories:

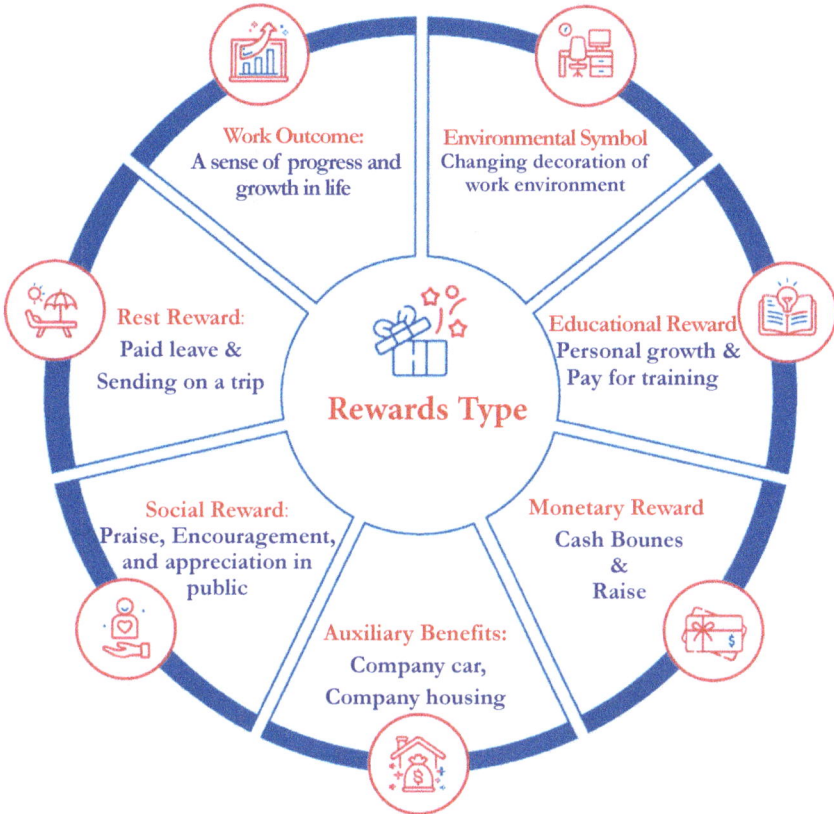

15. Unique Communications

People have different personalities and communication styles. Try to have a unique relationship with each person. Employees are not clones, so they should not be treated the same way.

▶ Individual Mood Test

This test is for assessing individuals' mood or personality traits. You can have your team take this test so they can better understand themselves. Look at the options below, choose one, and then draw it.

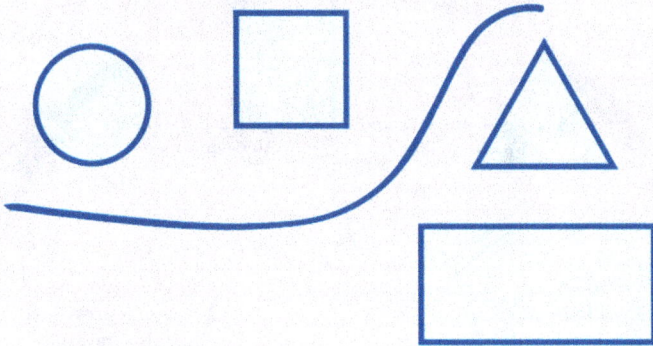

Circle

▶ Characteristics

- People who choose the circle are sociable and talkative.
- They do not have a harsh tone. They are very kind, and when they face issues in team communication or with clients, they try to control the situation through talking.
- In life, their top priority is relationships.
- If given a task, they will talk about it as the responsible person until the necessary coordination is achieved. As a result, they make good employees.

▶ Job Positions

- Receptionists
- Secretaries
- Customer Service

Square

▶ Characteristics

- They only feel at ease in a stable environment. As soon as the environment is disrupted, their calmness is disturbed, and they want to leave.
- Their career path is entirely clear because they have mapped it out repeatedly.
- They are very logical and extremely conservative.
- They like everything to be neat and organized.
- They are very responsible.
- They are excellent finishers and are suitable for tasks that need to follow principles.

▶ Job Positions

- Auditors
- Inspectors
- Project Managers
- Purchasing Managers

Triangle

▶ Characteristics

- They are very goal-oriented and perform tasks with a clear purpose.
- They enjoy planning ahead before starting work and always keep a notebook to jot down ideas.
- They like tasks or work where there is development.
- They are interested in large-scale and long-term projects.
- They are good at organizing groups (e.g., a film director).

- They are the best at executing ideas.

▶ Job Positions

- Production Managers
- R&D Managers
- Content Producers

Rectangle

▶ Characteristics

- They are very principled.
- It is important for them that everything is done the way they have learned.
- They like order and prefer to organize everything precisely, ensuring the tasks are executed properly. This makes them explore all possible ways to do the work.
- If given a task, they will organize it from start to finish in a way that no one can criticize it. If the organization breaks down, they will follow up continuously.
- They explain every task they want to do.

▶ Job Positions

- Managers and Executive Teams

Curve

▶ Characteristics

- Creativity is their key feature.
- They often try to do things differently and innovatively.
- Order and routine are boring for them.
- If given a task with specific instructions, they will still do their own thing and follow their own path.

- They are always in search of new ideas.

▶ **Job Positions**

- Advertising Companies

- Organizations that need innovation and product/service design

More than any other factor, the success of your business is determined by the people working for you. All tasks are done by teams. The work of the manager is the result of the team's work, and success requires excellent performance from each team member.

▶ **Write Your Five Key Takeaways from This Chapter:**

1. ....

2. ....

3. ....

4. ....

5. ....

▶ **Three Steps I Will Immediately Start:**

1. ....

2. ....

3. ....

....

▶ **One Golden Lesson to Share with Others:**

....

....

....

Download all the tables and exercises of this chapter from the following website.

https://hosseintaheri.ir/bmg/

Finance and Profit

Chapter 10:

Finance and Profit

Working does not create wealth; financial management does.

📖 **After reading this chapter, you will gain mastery over:**

- The concept and importance of financial management
- The role and impact of financial software
- Business Mastery vocabulary in financial and tax accounting
- Financial models
- Categorizing financial ratios

In all of our businesses, we often face time and money shortages. Therefore, one of the primary goals for all businesses should be achieving financial growth. To achieve this goal, business owners must understand the potential consequences of their managerial decisions in relation to various financial aspects, such as profit, cash flows, financial risks, and more. When we talk about a financial system, it means an efficient management system of financial resources, including money, credits, debts, investments, and assets, aimed at helping the organization achieve predetermined goals and balance its revenues and expenses.

The goal of designing a financial system is to provide accurate information, extract documented data, and process them so that managers can make appropriate decisions based on the current economic conditions. In order to generate income, inventories of supplies, equipment, facilities, wages, sales volume, purchase management, liquidity management, debts and receivables, and the budget for growth and profit must all be measurable and calculable at any given time. This enables financial planning according to the prevailing environment in the organization and the market.

Effective financial management helps managers make the best use of resources, perform their obligations correctly, and achieve long-term financial stability.In fact, financial management is based on methods of managing a business, which involves adopting policies that not only help an organization progress financially but also allow individuals and shareholders to benefit from good returns. **Warren Buffet,** one of the greatest American investors, said in one of his speeches:

"Never think that working can make you rich. It is financial management that can lead you to wealth."

The main goal of the financial system is to manage the resources and expenses of an organization in such a way that it increases the value, wealth, and profit of its stakeholders. This goal is based on three main pillars: financial planning, financial control, and financial decision-making. Adhering to these three pillars places a business on the path of profitability and sustainability. Keeping records, analyzing cash flow, and planning for capital creation are three major tasks for businesses.

Many organizations believe that financial management only means accounting recordkeeping and reporting, thinking that with accounting software, they can fully manage their finances. However, the real profitability of your business is much greater than its current results. All business activities can be expressed in numbers. Numbers do not lie, and measuring this aspect is essential for business success. What do these numbers mean for your business?

Key figures that businesses must monitor for growth include:

- Sales volume of products and services
- Other revenues (all items)
- Cost of goods sold (all items)
- Expenses (all business costs)
- Wages (usually the highest cost per unit)

- Lead generation costs (people who might convert into customers)
- Conversion rate (from lead to customer)
- Average sales volume
- Average gross profit per sale
- Average gross profit margin percentage
- Average net profit per sale
- Average cost per sale
- Average number of purchases per customer
- Customer lifetime value
- Average sales per employee
- Daily, weekly, and monthly sales
- Sales per specific product or service
- Up-selling and Cross-selling volume.
- The average return rate
- Return on investment (ROI)
- Capital cost
- Net profit (profit after expenses)
- Number of receivables and overdue payments
- Paid amounts and due dates
- Bank capital balance
- Available credit balance
- Total debt or business liabilities
- Overall sales statistics trend
- Number of future orders
- Number and volume of overdue debts and overdue payments
- Inventory by product grouping
- List of tangible assets
- Depreciation costs of assets and capital

Answer the following questions:

What are the three most important statistics you pay attention to in your business?

....

....

....

....

What is your average sales volume?

....

....

....

....

What is your gross sales profit?

....

....

....

....

What is your average sales cost?

....

....

....

....

How often does your typical customer purchase from you?

....

....

....

What are your main resources and costs for l prospect generation?

....

....

....

What are your most profitable products or services?

....

....

....

....

Which products or services are the least profitable for you?

....

....

....

....

What are your most profitable activities and tasks?

....

....

....

....

Which of your activities and tasks yield the least profitability and efficiency?

....

....

....

....

Which sales and marketing activities are the least profitable and efficient for you?

....

....

....

....

Who are your most profitable employees? Whose contributions have the greatest value?

....

....

....

....

Who are the least profitable individuals in your organization? Whose contributions provide the least value?

....

....

....

....

What are your most profitable marketing and sales activities?

....

....

....

....

....

Looking closely at the statistics provided helps managers and business owners make more informed decisions about:

- Financial planning

- Raising capital

- Improving profitability, creating economic stability, and ensuring investment security

- Optimal resource utilization and capital allocation

- Increasing budgets

- Enhancing company value

- Increasing savings

- Maintaining liquidity

- Asset management

- Managing operational costs

- Fund management (organizational reserve fund).

▶ Financial Software to Overcome Manual Records

In our country, there are two discrepancies regarding the use of financial software:

1. Some businesses still do not use financial software for accounting purposes and rely on manual record-keeping or general programs like Excel, which is not much different from traditional manual accounting.

2. There are companies that, in addition to financial software, keep part of their accounts elsewhere, often due to tax concerns. They try not to register all information in one place, using manual records, Excel files, or second accounting software.

Do not shrink your business because of taxes!

These two discrepancies, rooted in market norms, interaction with technology, and financial literacy levels in business, have caused business owners not to fully understand the benefits of using financial software.

Advantages of using accounting software instead of manual accounting for a financial unit:

- **38%:** Recording and searching for sales documents

- **70%:** Understanding the profitability or loss of the company

- **31%:** Tracking cash flow and decision-making

- **60%:** Preventing bankruptcy and identifying break-even points

- **44%:** Avoiding manual and human errors

- **65%:** Generating reports and searching for documents

- **65%:** Saving time for the accountant

If even one of the checklist questions below is answered with "yes," you need accounting software, and if you already have software, you need to upgrade it.

Checklist for Assessing (and Troubleshooting) the Need for Accounting Software in Your Business:

1.Do you lose suppliers due to late payments?

Yes ☐ No ☐

2.Do you have unpaid invoices from customers that you forget to follow up on?

Yes ☐ No ☐

3.Have you noticed repetitive and time-consuming tasks in your manual accounting processes?

Yes ☐ No ☐

4.Do you use reports and financial statements to make major business decisions?

Yes ☐ No ☐

5.Have you ever lost a receipt, invoice, or any financial document?

Yes ☐ No ☐

6.Do you refer to financial records from the start of your business?

Yes ☐ No ☐

7.Are you unable to track cash flow in your business?

Yes ☐ No ☐

8.Does your business experience waste, product returns, or customer dissatisfaction?

Yes ☐ No ☐

▶ Are Financial Software Programs Merely Data Storage Tools?

Financial software is a tool for data storage in businesses, but the method of entering and utilizing this data varies depending on the type of business. Data entry into software is often a time-intensive process, and companies typically aim to integrate software or link systems via APIs to save time on data input. Financial software is often the primary database for the business. Modern financial and accounting software automates much of the data entry process. For example: With payment gateways, customer payment information is automatically recorded in the software and Barcode scanners enable automatic entry of product or service information.

This automation reduces both the need for manual input and human errors in data entry.

However, in some cases, customer data in financial and accounting software may be confused with data stored in phonebooks or CRM systems. For instance, payment patterns and purchase dates may be used by marketing teams for tracking purposes. This could compromise the primary purpose of accounting software.

The key advantage of stored data in financial software is that the history of all transactions is automatically saved without the need for separate manual records. This feature: Saves time and eliminates manual entry errors. This is the distinct advantage of using accounting software for financial operations and other business processes.

▶ The Role of Software in Accounting and Auditing

Both **accounting** and **auditing** are essential for any business, and financial software plays a vital role in enhancing the accuracy and speed of these processes. **Accounting** is an ongoing process managed by accountants using software. **Auditing** is periodic and typically conducted by an external company at the end of a month, quarter, or year.

Accounting software serves as a common language between **accountants** and **auditors** for document recording, ensuring optimized reporting. Accountants can also learn from auditors to improve their processes and make better use of the software's features.

It is recommended to audit your business's entire accounting system at least once a year to ensure the accuracy of processes.

▶ Impact of Financial Software Features on Managerial Reporting

Imagine a company faces a cash flow issue and is struggling to provide funds for a check due the following day. The source for this check lies in receivables from customers, recorded in the company's financial software as checks or installments. The company manager needs to make an immediate decision but has little time to follow up on receivables. This is where the importance of financial software features becomes evident. If the company's financial system is integrated and up-to-**date**, and the accountant can easily generate a receivables report within seconds, the manager can solve the problem much faster.

In today's business environment, managerial decisions rely on accurate and analyzable information, which requires proper data entry into financial software. This software helps managers by categorizing and segmenting information, enabling deeper and more fundamental analysis while reducing reliance on surface-level insights.

With the establishment of **new tax systems** in the country, such as **Article 169 periodic reports, insurance listings**, and the **Taxpayers' System**, the importance of financial software for reporting has increased significantly. Modern accounting software compliant with tax and insurance standards can provide accurate financial information for managerial reports.

▶ Requirements for Implementing Financial Software

Financial software can be divided into two categories based on access methods: **web-based** and **network-based**. The type of software a business owner chooses influences how it is implemented.

Network-Based Software   Web-Based Software

● **Network-Based Software**

Network-Based Software These are software programs that run on a **local area network (LAN)**. The database is installed on a primary system equipped with a Windows server, and other computers in the network connect to it. Each computer operates independently but shares a common database.

● **Web-Based Software**

These software programs operate over the **internet**, functioning like websites. They are more robust and up-to-date than network-based software. In this method: The accounting software is installed on a **server**, not individual computers. The main database is also stored on the server.

One key reason for the popularity of web-based software is its **infrastructure flexibility**. When a business uses web-based software, it can be accessed **anytime** and **anywhere** as long as there is an internet connection and Vendors of such software offer solutions for server space, ensuring users can easily access the system. While web-based accounting software has gained popularity, many Iranian businesses still rely on network-based software for their accounting needs.

To set up accounting software, the following hardware is necessary: A suitable monitor, preferably large, Dedicated memory storage for continuous data backup, Printers for issuing invoices and documents, Barcode scanners, scales, and other essential devices.

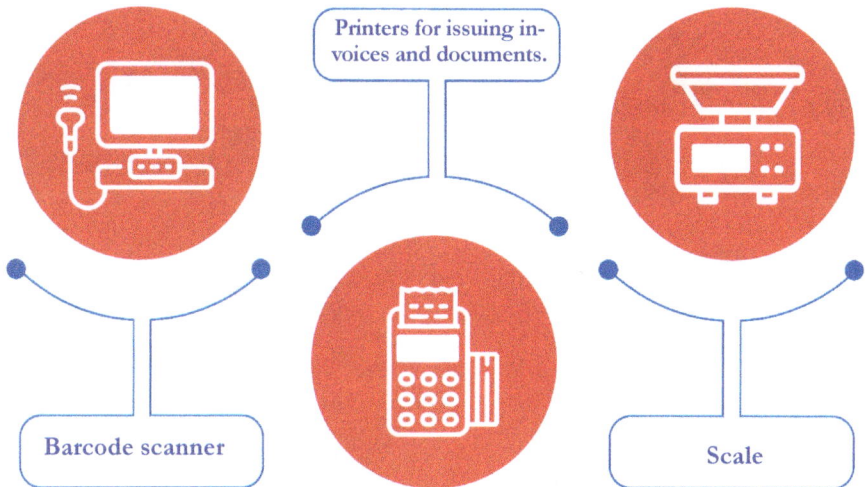

Printers for issuing invoices and documents.

Barcode scanner

Scale

▶ Questions to Consider Before Purchasing Accounting Software

Keep in mind that these questions differ from those mentioned earlier under the "Checklist for Assessing Accounting Software Needs in Business." These questions apply once you've decided to purchase the software and implement a system. Consult your business partner or the person responsible for accounting in your business before answering.

What budget have I allocated for purchasing accounting software and implementing the system in my business?

Guidance for Response: Some business owners prefer to spend the accounting software budget on store décor instead and opt for the most basic and cheapest version of the software. However, the heart of a business is its financial department, which can undoubtedly recover décor costs later.

Your Answer:

....
....
....
....
....
....

Who should I consult before purchasing the software?

Guidance for Response: It's best to seek advice from financial and tax experts.

Your Answer:

....
....
....
....
....
....
....

Will I need training after purchasing the software?

Guidance for Response: Everyone in a business is involved with accounting and its concepts. It's better to provide relevant training to them so they can work more efficiently and with greater awareness.

Your Answer:

....
....
....
....
....
....

Will implementing accounting software improve other departments in my business?

Guidance for Response: Consider a workshop with two workers and one supervisor that only handles packaging lamps. All workshop tasks, such as recording workers' attendance, their performance, and the count of packaged and broken lamps, are done manually. By implementing an accounting system connected to an attendance device, the workshop can calculate workers' wages and manage lamp inventory within minutes.

Your Answer:

....
....
....
....
....
....
....

● Questions to Ask the Software Vendor Before Purchase

Detach the form below and send it to the company you're considering purchasing accounting software from. Alternatively, share an image of these questions via social media if that's how you're in touch with them. Use the same questions whether you already have accounting software or are purchasing it for the first time.

To: ....[Name of the Accounting Software Company] ....

From: Hossein Taheri

Subject: Questions Regarding Accounting Software

Dear Sir/Madam,

I respectfully submit the following questions regarding your accounting software for review and assessment of needs in my business. A detailed response will assist in making a more informed decision and fostering better collaboration.

List of Questions:

1. How is the software implemented and set up?
2. What is the maximum time required for initial setup and support?
3. Which software modules are most relevant to our business?
4. Is it possible to transfer data from other departments or previous software via APIs or file imports like Excel?
5. Does the software receive updates? When was the latest version released?
6. Does the software handle all statutory requirements (e.g., quarterly reports)?
7. Are software support fees annual or on a per-case basis?
8. What is the cost of adding users over time?

Kindly send your responses to the above questions via.................. [communication channel] to.......................... [contact number].

Thank you.

Best regards,

[Your Name]

▶ Sample Accounting Coding System Aligned with Financial Statements

Accounting coding refers to categorizing and organizing titles related to accounting activities that create order in these operations. In this categorization, financial operations are arranged based on the activity subject and at various levels of accounting operations in different formats.

Accounting coding is one of the specializations every accountant should have. A business owner must think and act like a manager in their financial transactions. This means they must decide and act in a manner that aligns with the accounting coding specific to their business.

▶ Financial thinking

● Business Master Glossary in Financial and Tax Accounting

You may have encountered various financial and tax-related terms and concepts without knowing their exact meanings. This section familiarizes you with practical concepts to help you interact effectively with your accountant and financial manager as a business master.

Accounts Receivable	Money to be received in the future from customers for the sale of goods or services. If its collection is doubtful, it is reported as "doubtful receivables" in audit reports.
Notes Payable	Written documents representing a business's debts that it is obligated to pay.
Notes Receivable	Revenue committed to being collected in the future by the seller, such as interest on participation bonds.
Accounts Payable	Accounts that must be settled in the future.
Capital	Tangible items like goods or intangible items like shares representing a business's worth.
Assets	The sum of liabilities and equity.
Long-Term Assets	All assets except current assets.
Long-Term Liabilities	All liabilities except current liabilities.
Liquidity	The ability of a business to convert goods or services into cash.

Revenue	The increase in capital resulting from the sale of goods or services.
Liabilities	Obligations a business has to individuals or legal entities.
Balance Sheet	A financial statement presenting the assets, liabilities, and equity of a company over a specific period. It does not always reflect reality.
Management Accounting	Preparing financial statements for the senior management of a business.
Financial Accounting	Providing a business's financial information for external parties.
Financial Statements	Specifying information about a business's performance and its profit and loss statements in a documented and substantiated manner.
Accounting Principles	Guidelines defining the preparation, reporting, and disclosure of financial statements.
Prepaid Expense	An asset that will be consumed or used in the near future, such as third-party certifications for vehicles.
Unearned Revenue	A liability where the recipient of funds (seller or business) commits to delivering goods or services to the payer (buyer or customer) in the future, such as pre-sales of cars.

Accounting Cycle	The accounting process for financial statements over a defined period.
Accounting Period	The time frame in which a business's profit or loss is determined, with financial reports prepared at the end.
Fiscal Year	The annual period for calculating a business's financial status.
Depreciation	The process of an asset losing value over time.
Fixed Assets	Long-term assets, such as property.
Current Assets	Assets convertible to cash or saleable within 12 months, including cash, accounts receivable, inventory, and matured securities.
Closing Temporary Accounts	Transferring the balances of revenue, expense, and withdrawal accounts to permanent accounts at the end of the financial period, leaving these accounts with zero balances.
Accrued Expenses and Revenues	Costs and revenues postponed to the future, not yet paid or received.
Income Statement	Details operational and non-operational costs, revenues, profits, and losses over a specified period.
Net Profit	The surplus of income over expenses, also known as net income.

Gross Profit	The difference between revenue from selling goods or services and their cost of sales (revenue minus the cost of goods sold).
Operating Profit	Gross profit minus operational expenses.
Inventory Turnover	The ratio of the cost of goods sold to the average inventory.
Net Purchases	Purchases of goods or services minus discounts.
Non-Core Costs and Revenues	Costs and revenues not related to a business's primary activity, such as the profit or loss from selling a fixed asset.
Net Loss	The surplus of expenses over income.
Current Liabilities	Liabilities expected to be settled within 12 months or less.
Current Ratio	The ratio of current assets to current liabilities, indicating a company's ability to repay its debts.
Debt Ratio	The ratio of total debt to total assets. A number greater than one indicates high investment risk, while a number less than one reflects a company's assets exceeding its liabilities.

▶ TDA Canvas / Hossein Taheri in Business

Thinking, Decision, Analysis (TDA)

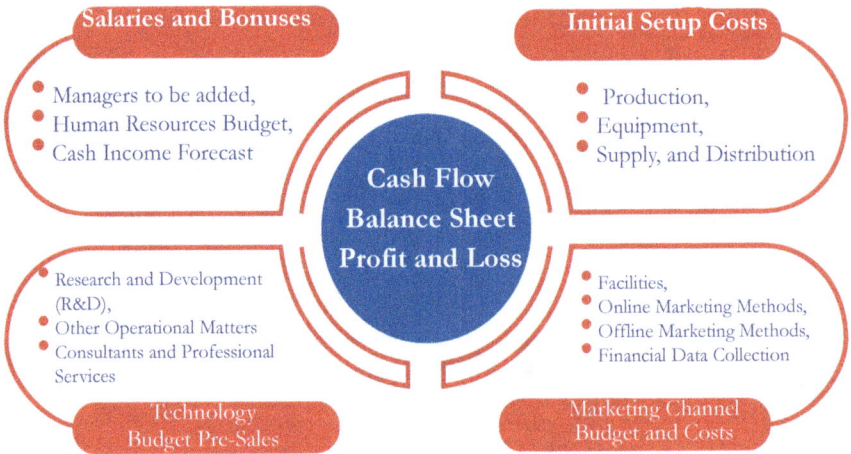

Salaries and Bonuses

- Managers to be added,
- Human Resources Budget,
- Cash Income Forecast

Initial Setup Costs

- Production,
- Equipment,
- Supply, and Distribution

Cash Flow Balance Sheet Profit and Loss

- Research and Development (R&D),
- Other Operational Matters
- Consultants and Professional Services

Technology Budget Pre-Sales

- Facilities,
- Online Marketing Methods,
- Offline Marketing Methods,
- Financial Data Collection

Marketing Channel Budget and Costs

▶ Financial Models

Complete the worksheet below using the common financial standards in your field of work.

Financial Models:	
Percentage Price Increase for Retail Goods	
Percentage Price Increase for Distributors:	
Percentage Commission for Sales Representatives:	
Credit Terms:	
Minimum Inventory Required (in Days):	
Average Sales Return Percentage:	
Other Financial Considerations:	

| Contribution of Different Factors in Final Pricing: | Labor Costs: |
| Fixed Costs: |
| Raw Material Costs: |
| Transportation Costs: |
| Energy Costs: |

Tool	Details	Number of Uses	Annual Cost
Purchasing Professional Thoughts (Consultants)			
Marketing Consultants Public Relations Advertising Agencies Social Media Experts SEO Specialists Web/Graphic Designers			
Brochures Flyers			
Billboards and Signs			
Trade Shows			

Product Samples Awards			
Media Advertisements			
Television Radio Online Ads Other Media			
Advertising Specialists			
Email Newsletters			
Postage			
Website			
Development-Programming Maintenance-Hosting			
Trade Exhibition			

Registration Setup Costs Travel Transportation Trade Show Signs/Supplies			
Public Relations Content and activities			
Informal Networking and Marketing			
Membership Meetings Entertainment			
Other			
Total			

Offline Marketing Methods

Customer-Based Marketing:

How do you increase sales to your current customers?

....
....
....

Strategic Partnerships:

What relationships do you have with other companies to help promote sales or distribute your product or service?

....
....
....
....

Promotional Activities Special Offers:

What types of discounts do you use to increase your sales?

Gifts/Prizes: What kind of gifts or prizes do you offer to show goodwill and drive more sales?

....
....
....
....
....

Other Methods:

....
....
....
....

Online Marketing Methods

Website:

How does your website promote your products or services or enhance the credibility of your business?

....
....
....
....

What are the main marketing and sales goals of your website?

....
....
....
....

SEM/SEO:

Do you use search engine marketing (paid or organic) to drive traffic to your website?

If yes, how do you implement it?

....
....
....
....
....
....
....

Email Newsletter:

Do you create email newsletters to communicate with current and potential customers?

....
....
....
....

What type of content do you use?

....
....
....
....

How frequently do you send newsletters?

....
....
....
....

How do you build your email subscriber list?

....
....
....
....
....

Weblog:

Do you engage in blogging?

....

....

....

....

In which blogs do you actively participate to increase your visibility?

....

....

....

....

Social Media:

Do you use platforms like Facebook, Twitter, YouTube, LinkedIn, Pinterest, etc., to provide information about your products/services and engage with current and potential customers?

....

....

....

....

....

....

....

Other Online Advertising:

Do you advertise on other websites or platforms?

....
....
....
....
....
....
....

Other Online Methods:

Do you use other online tools such as podcasts, daily trading videos, or review sites?

How do you use these tools?

....
....
....
....
....
....
....

Collecting of Financial Data	Month 1	Month 2	Month 3	Month 4	Month 5	Month 6
Professional Assistance						
Marketing Consultants						
Public Relations, Branding, etc.						
Advertising Agencies						
Social Media Experts						
SEO Experts						
Web/Graphic Design						
Brochure/Flyer/Ads						
Signage/Billboards						
Product Exhibitions						
Sample/Giveaways						
Media Advertising						
Print (Newspaper, etc.)						
TV and Radio						
Online						
Other Media						
Advertising Experts						

Month 7	Month 8	Month 9	Month 10	Month 11	Month 12	Total

Sales Forecast	Month 1	Month 2	Month 3	Month 4	Month 5	Month 6
Item Number 1						
Unit Volume						
Unit Price						
Gross Sales						
Commissions						
Returns & Discounts						
Net Sales						
Cost of Goods Sold (COGS)						
Gross Profit						
Item Number 2						
Unit Volume						
Unit Price						
Gross Sales						
Commissions						
Returns & Discounts						
Net Sales						
Cost of Goods Sold (COGS)						

Month 7	Month 8	Month 9	Month 10	Month 11	Month 12	Total

	Month 1	Month 2	Month 3	Month 4	Month 5	Month 6
Gross Profit						
Item Number 3						
Unit Volume						
Unit Price						
Gross Sales						
Commissions						
Returns & Discounts						
Net Sales						
Cost of Goods Sold (COGS)						
Gross Profit						
Total Unit Volume						
Total Gross Sales						
Total Commissions						
Total Returns & Discounts						
Total Net Sales						
Total Cost of Goods Sold (COGS)						
Total Gross Profit						

Month 7	Month 8	Month 9	Month 10	Month 11	Month 12	Total

Lease Contract Details

Duration of the Contract	
Rent and Lease Terms	
Other Terms	
Additional Aspects	
Privileges	

Preparation

Existing Facilities	
Facilities to Be Provided	
Landlord's Payment Responsibilities	
Company's Payment Responsibilitie	

Utilities (Water, Electricity, Gas, Maintenance)

Average Monthly Cost

How is Seasonal Changes in Costs?

How is Correlation Between Costs and Production Levels?

Is there any Methods for Energy Savings

How much Average Maintenance Costs?

Do Maintenance Costs Fluctuate?

Other Notes

Key Factors in Producing Your Goods or Services (Excluding Machinery and Equipment):

Processes	
What Are the Main Stages of Production?	
How Does the Product Move Between Stages?	
How Are New Technologies Incorporated into Processes?	
What Are the Advantages of the Production Process?	
What Are the Disadvantages of the Production Process?	
Which Parts of the Production Process Are Outsourced?	
What Are the Costs of These External Services?	
Provide a Brief Overview of Contracting Companies:	
What Other Costs Are Related to the Production Process?	

Workforce

Total Number of Workforce	
Permanent	Full-time ☐ Part-time ☐
Temporary	Full-time ☐ Part-time ☐
Under What Circumstances Are Part-Time Workers Hired?	
Number of Shifts	
Duration of Each Shift	
Working Hours	
What Are the Initial Requirements for Hiring Employees?	
How Is the Workforce Organized?	Team-Based Approach (Production Line) Other ☐
Who Is Responsible for Supervising Employees?	
Other Workforce Issues	

Productivity

For producing each unit of a product or service, how much time and how many workers are required?

....
....
....
....
....

How many products does each worker produce daily?

....
....
....
....
....

What methods do you use to reduce the production time without compromising quality?

....
....
....

What methods do you use to improve productivity?

....
....
....
....
....

Capacity

With the current resources, how many products or services can you produce or offer daily, weekly, and monthly?

How many products or services does each worker produce daily, weekly, and monthly?

With the current workforce, machinery, and facilities, at what percentage of capacity are you operating?

How are you utilizing your excess capacity at present?

How will you increase your capacity to achieve your desired growth?

Quality Control

Who is responsible for overall quality control?

....

....

What actions do you take to inspect the final product or service?

....

....

What measures do you take throughout the process to ensure quality?

....

....

Are products and services evaluated for quality?

....

....

How do you motivate your employees to ensure quality?

....

....

What additional steps do you take for quality control?

....

How do you gather customer feedback?

....

....

What additional steps do you take for quality control?

....

....

Existing Equipment				
Description (Name/ Model)	Condition	Date of Purchase	Cost	Payments Made

Future Equipment				
Description (Name/ Model)	Condition	Date of Purchase	Cost	Payments Made

These questions help supplier and distribution to evaluate their needs:

Suppliers

Who is responsible for your purchasing decisions?

....

....

What are the main goods or raw materials you require?

....

....

What is the average cost of these items?

....

....

What are your primary sources for raw materials?

....

....

What are alternative sources for these materials?

....

....

Do you need any specific inputs that are provided by only one or two suppliers?

....

....

If yes, how reliable are these suppliers?

....

....

Suppliers

Can your suppliers provide the requested goods or materials immediately or within a short period of time?

....

....

What are the additional costs incurred for such immediate supplies?

....

....

Do you have reorder point contracts with your suppliers?

....

....

What are the credit terms offered by your suppliers?

....

....

What is your average credit cost?

....

....

What factors influence your choice of suppliers?

....

....

....

Mention any other supplier-related issues.

....

....

....

....

Distributors

How does your product or service reach consumers?

....

....

Are there wholesalers or intermediaries between you and the consumers?

....

....

If yes, how many wholesalers or distributors do you work with?

....

....

What are the terms and benefits of working with these companies?

....

....

What are the disadvantages of working with these companies?

....

....

If you work with only one or two distributors, how reliable are they?

....

What is the reputation of these entities among consumers?

....

....

How are payments or commissions to these intermediaries structured?

....

....

Describe any other distribution methods you use.

....

....

Describe the method your company uses to process orders and provide customer services.

Customer Orders and Services

Who is responsible for processing orders?

How are orders communicated from the sales team to the orders department?

How are online orders routed to the orders department?

What is your process for ensuring the accuracy and timeliness of order processing?

What percentage of processed orders encounter issues?

How are goods prepared for shipment?

What methods do you use for shipping goods?

What is the average cost of shipping an order?

Do orders reach customers promptly or within the shortest possible time?

Customer Orders and Services

Who bears the shipping costs? You ☐ Customer ☐
....

What alternative shipping options do you have?
....

What service programs do you offer your customers?
....

What maintenance programs do you provide for your customers?
....

What percentage of orders require repairs?
....

What is the average cost of repair per instance for the company?
....

What is the company's return policy?
....

How many returns are processed on average?
....

What is the average cost of processing a return?
....

Do you have a customer complaints or service department?
Yes ☐   No ☐
....

How do you collect feedback from your customers?
....

This worksheet helps evaluate research and development (R&D) activities and the costs associated with them.

Research and Development (R&D)

Describe the new products you want to develop.

....
....
....

Describe the new services you want to offer.

....
....
....

Which employees are responsible for R&D?

....
....
....

How do you involve employees in R&D efforts?

....
....
....

What percentage of your employees' time is allocated to R&D?

....
....
....

Costs associated with R&D efforts:

....
....
....
....

Research and Development (R&D)

What newspapers and journals are required for R&D?

What equipment and tools are needed for R&D?

Costs:

What conferences do employees attend for R&D purposes?

Costs:

Describe any other R&D activities within your company.

Costs:

▶ Other Operational Matters

The questions below highlight some key concerns regarding your plans and company. These questions also encompass other related operational topics:

Safety and Health

What measures have you implemented for worker safety and health?

....

....

What programs do you have in place to encourage safety compliance among employees?

....

....

Other safety-related matters:

....

Insurance and Legal Issues

What types of insurance does your business need? (e.g., fire, accident, liability, negligence, vehicle insurance)

....

What coverage amount is required for adequate protection?

....

....

What legal issues does your business face?

....

....

Does your company require legal counsel or advisory services?

....

Other legal matters:

....

....

Regulations and Environmental Issues

What licenses or permits are legally required for your business?

....

....

What regulations specifically govern your type of business?

....

....

Which environmental regulations impact your business operations?

....

....

....

What voluntary actions does your company take to protect the environment?

....

....

....

How does your company ensure products and processes support animal rights?

....

....

....

Other legal or environmental issues:

....

....

....

Other operational issues:

....

....

▶ Initial Startup Costs

Detail the cash requirements for launching your business. Remember, these are the expenses incurred before your business operations begin. Startup costs are reported in the income statement.

	Costs	
Facilities	Purchase of land	
	Purchase of building	
	Initial rent	
	Deposit (for guarantees/ utilities/others)	
	Preparation/renovation	
	Other	
Machinery and Equipment	Furniture and fixtures	
	Production machinery and equipment	
	Computers/software	
	Payment counters	
	Telephone Telecommunication	
	Vehicles	
	Other	

Costs	
Raw Materials and Office Supplies	
Office items	
Stationery business cards	
Brochures/flyers/other promotional items	
Other	
Other Costs	
Licenses and legal permits	
Business or professional memberships	
Legal fees	
Accounting fees	
Insurance costs	
Managerial and marketing consultancy	
Technical and design consultancy	
Advertising and promotional activities	
Other	

Total:

▲ Technology Budget:

Use this worksheet to determine the costs of your ongoing technology needs.

	Year 1	Year 2	Year 3	Year 4	Year 5
Accounting					
Customer Relationship Management					
Human Resource Management					
Inventory Management					
Office Software					
Custom Software					
Desktop and laptop computers					
Tablets and mobile devices					
Servers					
Backup Systems					

Software

Hardware

	Year 1	Year 2	Year 3	Year 4	Year 5
Hardware — Printers					
Networking Equipment					
Others					
Remote communication — Mobile Phones (Telecommunication)					
Landline Phones					
Fax Machines					
Internet Services					
Others					
Consultants — System Design and Maintenance					
Technical and Informational support					
Others					
Total					

Description of Salary and Bonus for Key Staff Members:

Chairperson of the Board / CEO

Salary:	
Bonus:	
Other Incentives:	

Executive Manager

Salary:	
Bonus:	
Other Incentives:	

Chief Financial Officer (CFO)

Salary:	
Bonus:	
Other Incentives:	

Marketing/Sales Manager

Salary:	
Bonus:	
Other Incentives:	

Production Manager

Salary:	
Bonus:	
Other Incentives:	

Human Resources Manager

Salary:	
Bonus:	
Other Incentives:	

Technical/Technology Manager

Salary:	
Bonus:	
Other Incentives:	

Other Key Staff Members

Salary:	
Bonus:	
Other Incentives:	

Lawyer

Institution Name:	
Lawyer Name:	
Consultation Field:	
Consulting lawyer's fees	
Annual Fee	

Accountant

Institution Name:	
Accountant Name:	
Details:	
Field of Work:	
Annual Fee	

Management/Marketing Consultant

Institution Name:	
Consultant Name:	
Details:	
Consultation Field:	
Annual Fee:	

Industry Specialist

Institution Name:	
Lawyer Name:	
Details:	
Field of Work:	
Annual Fee	

Technology Consultant

Institution Name:	
Lawyer Name:	
Details:	
Field of Work:	
Annual Fee	

Other

Institution Name:	
Specialist Name:	
Details:	
Field of Work:	
Annual Fee	

▶ Managers to be Added

Describe the details of the managers you intend to add.

Managers to be Added		
Position:	Required Skills/Capabilities:	
	Approximate Date of Addition:	
	Other Benefits:	
Position	Required Skills/Capabilities:	
	Approximate Date of Addition:	
	Other Benefits:	
Position	Required Skills/Capabilities:	
	Approximate Date of Addition:	
	Other Benefits:	
Position	Required Skills Capabilities:	
	Approximate Date of Addition:	
	Other Benefits:	

Human Resource Budget	Month 1	Month 2	Month 3	Month 4	Month 5	Month 6
Management						
Salaries						
Employee Benefits						
Payroll Taxes						
Total Cost						
Administrative and Support						
Salaries						
Employee Benefits						
Payroll Taxes						
Total Cost						
Sales and Marketing						
Salaries						
Employee Benefits						
Payroll Taxes						
Total Cost						

Month 7	Month 8	Month 9	Month 10	Month 11	Month 12	Total

Human Resource Budget	Month 1	Month 2	Month 3	Month 4	Month 5	Month 6
Operations & Production						
Salaries						
Employee Benefits						
Payroll Taxes						
Total Cost						
Other						
Salaries						
Employee Benefits						
Payroll Taxes						
Total Cost						
Total						
Salaries						
Employee Benefits						
Payroll Taxes						
Total Cost						

Month 7	Month 8	Month 9	Month 10	Month 11	Month 12	Total

Cash Income Forecast	Month 1	Month 2	Month 3	Month 4	Month 5	Month 6
Product 1 Sales Cash Received — Sales Current Month						
Sales 30 Days Before						
Sales 60 Days Before						
Sales 90 Days Before						
Sales 120 Days Before						
Total Cash Income (P1)						
Product 2 Sales Cash Received — Sales Current Month						
Sales 30 Days Before						
Sales 60 Days Before						
Sales 90 Days Before						
Sales 120 Days Before						
Total Cash Income (P2)						
Product 3 Sales Cash Received — Sales Current Month						
Sales 30 Days Before						
Sales 60 Days Before						
Sales 90 Days Before						
Sales 120 Days Before						
Total Cash Income (P3)						
Product 4 Sales Cash Received — Sales Current Month						
Sales 30 Days Before						
Sales 60 Days Before						
Sales 90 Days Before						
Sales 120 Days Before						
Total Cash Income (P4)						
Total Cost						

Month 1	Month 2	Month 3	Month 4	Month 5	Month 6	Total:

▶ Financial Ratios for the Balance Sheet

Financial ratios are a key tool for assessing the financial position of a business. By creating relationships between important financial indicators, financial ratios provide a strong and accurate understanding of the financial condition and operational outcomes of your business over a specific time period. Many business owners use financial ratios as a first step in **diagnosing** the health of their business. In the first phase, the business owner works with financial advisors and managers, followed by input from marketing, production, and human resources consultants, to analyze different types of financial ratios and review past performance as well as future strategies.

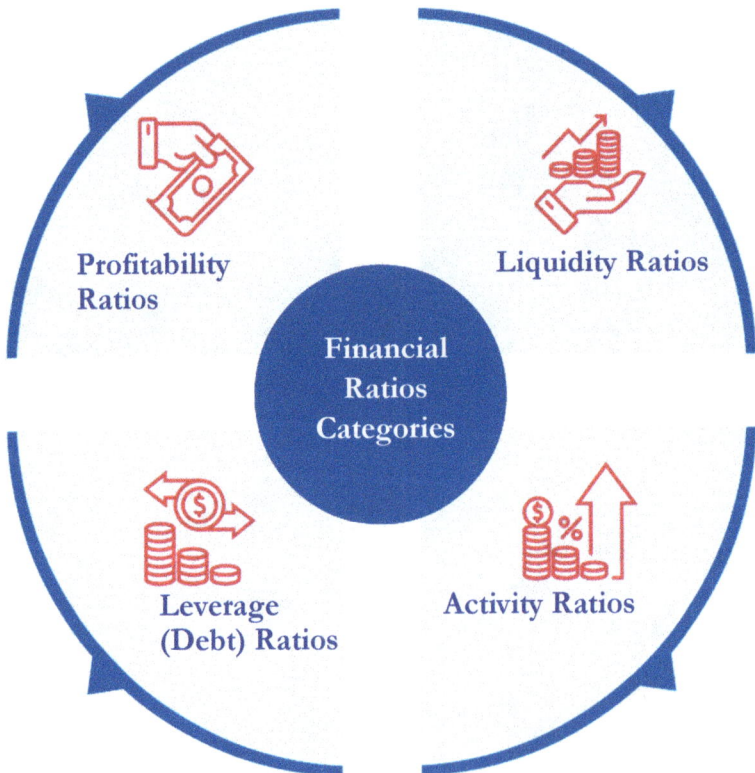

Profitability Ratios

Liquidity Ratios

Financial Ratios Categories

Leverage (Debt) Ratios

Activity Ratios

- **Liquidity Ratios**

  Indicators of a business's ability to meet short-term obligations:

  - Current Ratio

  - Quick (Fast) Ratio

  - Cash Ratio

- **Profitability Ratios**

  Indicators of a business's return on sales and assets:

  - Net Profit Margin

  - Operating Profit Margin.

  - Gross Profit Margin

  - Return on Equity (ROE)

  - Return on Assets (ROA)

- **Activity Ratios**

  Indicators of efficient use of business assets:

  - Receivables turnover ratio

  - Payable Turnover Ratio

  - Inventory Turnover Ratio (Average Inventory Age)

  - Asset Turnover Ratio

● Leverage (Debt) Ratios

An indicator to show the proper utilization of a business's assets:

- Debt ratio;

- Interest coverage ratio;

- Total debt-to-equity ratio;

- Current debt-to-equity ratio;

- Long-term debt-to-equity ratio;

- Fixed assets-to-equity ratio;

- Equity ratio;

- Equity-to-total debt ratio;

- Equity-to-fixed assets ratio.

▶ **Liquidity Ratios**

By dividing current assets by current liabilities, the current ratio is calculated, and both figures are obtainable from the balance sheet. Current liabilities include obligations that are due within the current financial period and must be repaid within this timeframe. Current assets are highly liquid assets that can be converted into cash within the next year.

If the current ratio is less than one, it implies that the company's current assets cannot cover its short-term obligations, which can be considered undesirable. However, it should also be noted that an excessively high current ratio is not necessarily favorable because profits are fundamentally generated from long-term assets. If a company has an excessively large current ratio due to focusing solely on current assets, it may harm its long-term profitability.

Thus, a fluctuation around one, or slightly above one, is generally considered favorable.

$$\text{Current Ratio} = \frac{\text{(Current Assets)}}{\text{(Current Liabilities)}}$$

The quick ratio considers more liquid assets, subtracting inventory and prepayments from total current assets due to their slower liquidity and then dividing by current liabilities. A quick ratio above one indicates the company is well-positioned to meet short-term obligations.

$$\text{Quick Ratio} = \frac{\text{Current Assets-(Inventory+Prepayments)}}{\text{(Current Liabilities)}}$$

The cash ratio is calculated by dividing the sum of cash and short-term investments by current liabilities. It's important to note that a high cash ratio is not always desirable for a business, as efforts should be made to utilize cash in a productive manner. Therefore, a balanced target should be set for this ratio, which is also important for investors.

$$\text{Cash Ratio} = \frac{\text{Cash+ Short term Investments}}{\text{(Current Liabilities)}}$$

▶ Activity Ratios

The accounts receivable turnover ratio shows the average number of days it takes for the company to collect receivables. Typically, "sales" is used instead of "credit sales" to calculate this ratio. **A higher ratio implies the company is leaning toward credit sales, which can impose cash flow pressures if excessive.**

"A 100-day receivables collection period means that, on average, the company can collect its receivables 100 days after selling products on credit."

$$\text{Average Daily Credit Sales} = \frac{\text{Annual Credit Sales}}{365}$$

$$\text{Accounts Receivable Turnover Period} = \frac{\text{Accounts Receivable}}{\text{Average Daily Credit Sales}}$$

The accounts payable turnover period indicates the average number of days it takes for the company to pay its suppliers. **A lower ratio suggests the company is moving toward cash purchases, which can exert cash flow pressures.** However, it improves bargaining power and allows goods to be purchased at lower costs.

$$\text{Accounts Payable Turnover Period} = \frac{\text{Average Accounts Payable}}{\text{Credit Purchases}} \times 365$$

Inventory turnover (average inventory age) shows the time taken for raw materials to be converted into goods and sold. **A longer inventory turnover period indicates extended production and sales processes.**

$$\text{Inventory Turnover Period} = \frac{\text{Average Inventory}}{\text{Cost of Goods Sold}} \times 365$$

The asset turnover ratio demonstrates the revenue generated per unit of the company's assets. **A higher ratio indicates better efficiency and productivity of the company's assets.**

$$\text{Asset Turnover Ratio} = \frac{\text{Sales Revenue}}{\text{Average total assets at the beginning and end of the period}}$$

▶ Profitability Ratios

The net profit margin shows the profitability per unit of sales. For example, a 10% net profit margin indicates the company earns 10 cents in profit for every dollar of sales. Note that all revenues and expenses, including operating and non-operating, are **included in the calculation of net profit.**

$$\text{Net Profit Margin} = \frac{\text{Net Profit}}{\text{Sales Revenue}}$$

The operating profit margin demonstrates the profitability from a company's core operations. **It's a stronger measure for evaluating profitability and sales because non-operating items, financial expenses, and taxes are excluded.**

$$\text{Operating Profit Margin} = \frac{\text{Operating Profit}}{\text{Sales Revenue}}$$

Gross profit margin is calculated by dividing gross profit by sales. A gross profit margin of 20% means that after deducting production costs, the company earns **20% profit from its sales revenue.**

$$\text{Gross Profit Margin} = \frac{\text{Gross Profit}}{\text{Sales Revenue}}$$

Return on Equity (ROE) indicates the success of management in maximizing shareholders' return. For instance, an ROE of 30% signifies that shareholder earn **30 units of profit for every 100 units of capital invested in the company.**

$$\text{Return on Equity} = \frac{\text{Gross Profit}}{\text{Total Shareholders' Equity}}$$

Return on Assets (ROA):is derived by dividing net profit by total assets and serves as a better measure of profitability compared to net profit to sales or operating profit ratios. **It reflects management's efficiency in utilizing assets to generate net profit.**

$$\text{Return on Assets} = \frac{\text{Net Profit}}{\text{Total Assets}}$$

▶ Leverage (Debt) Ratios

Debt Ratio indicates the proportion of economic resources financed by entities other than shareholders. For example, a 40% debt ratio means that for every unit of economic resources owned by the company, 0.40 units are financed by creditors, such as banks.

$$\text{Debt Ratio} = \frac{\text{Total Liabilities}}{\text{Total Assest}}$$

A higher Debt Ratio signals greater ability of the company to repay its bank loans. This ratio is crucial for banks, influencing their decision to extend or withhold credit. Ideally, this ratio should be greater than one. An Interest Coverage Ratio of three indicates the company can pay three times its current interest expense to the bank.

$$\text{Interest Coverage Ratio} = \frac{\text{Earnings Before Interest and Tax}}{\text{Interest Expense}}$$

The Debt-to-Equity Ratio serves as an indicator of the company's ability to meet its debt obligations. The smaller this ratio, the lower the financial risk, making lenders more willing to provide loans.

$$\text{Total Debt to Equity Ratio} = \frac{\text{Total Liabilities}}{\text{Total Shareholders' Equity}}$$

Current Debt-to-Equity Ratio measures the company's ability to repay short-term debts, usually settled from current assets. **A high ratio may strain the company's liquidity, affecting working capital and possibly hindering operations.**

$$\text{Current Debt to Equity Ratio} = \frac{\text{Current Liabilities}}{\text{Shareholders' Equity}}$$

Long-Term Debt-to-Equity Ratio evaluates the company's ability to meet long-term debt obligations. A higher ratio indicates greater financial risk and may deter lenders from providing long-term loans.

$$\text{Long-Term Debt to Equity Ratio} = \frac{\text{Long-Term Liabilities}}{\text{Shareholders' Equity}}$$

The Fixed Assets-to-**Equity** Ratio indicates how much of the shareholders' equity is allocated to the purchase of fixed assets.

$$\text{Fixed Assets-to-Equity Ratio} = \frac{\text{Fixed Assets}}{\text{Shareholders' Equity}}$$

The Equity Ratio (or Equity-to-Total Assets Ratio) shows the proportion of the company's assets financed by shareholders' equity. **The larger this ratio, the stronger the company's asset structure. An important point to note is that the sum of the Equity Ratio and Debt Ratio always equals one.** Therefore, the larger the Equity Ratio, the smaller the Debt Ratio, reducing reliance on credit and loans in the company's asset structure.

$$\text{Equity Ratio} = \frac{\text{Shareholders' Equity}}{\text{Total Assets}}$$

The Equity-to-Debt Ratio reflects **the weight of shareholders' equity relative to the company's borrowed funds.**

$$\text{Equity-to-Debt Ratio} = \frac{\text{Shareholders' Equity}}{\text{Total Debt}}$$

The Equity-to-**Fixed Assets Ratio measures the proportion of shareholders' equity** relative to the company's fixed assets.

$$\text{Equity-to-Fixed Assets Ratio} = \frac{\text{Shareholders' Equity}}{\text{Fixed Assets}}$$

▶ Key Points in Financial Management and Profitability

● Creating Effective and Proper Financial Habits

A significant portion of your expenses often stems from incorrect behaviors and habits in financial management. Everything depends on your ability to control your spending. Establishing internal financial protocols, even if it only involves reviewing and updating your financial information, greatly contributes to maintaining your business's financial health.

● Pay Yourself

Small business owners should value their own work. They should set salaries and benefits for themselves proportionate to their responsibilities and efforts. It is also important to regularly review both personal and business financial situations to ensure stability. Many business owners neglect their roles because they prioritize business growth or paying employees first. Remember, you are part of the business, and your salary deserves as much attention as others'.

● Invest in Growth

In addition to paying yourself, you should save some money and look for growth opportunities. This ensures your business continues to grow and moves in the right financial direction. Owners must always plan for the future. All businesses aim to grow, innovate, and attract top talent. Investing is a vital skill that, over the long term, shows its benefits and helps managers plan for future needs, including retirement. Saving 10% of your monthly income as soon as it enters your account should be a priority.

● Focus on Return on Investment (ROI)

Measuring costs and ROI provides a clear picture of investment goals and identifies investments that should be discontinued. Business owners must carefully allocate their resources to each expense. Ignoring this step could lead to financial waste in irrelevant areas. Know where your money goes and ensure every investment is profitable. If it isn't, shift your focus to areas that bring greater returns.

● Budgeting is Your Best Friend

The budget is the cornerstone of financial management. Use it as a guide, and make changes when necessary. Budgets must be flexible, but they should not be ignored. Always track cash inflows and outflows to ensure overhead costs are covered. While some issues require immediate resolution, financial planning must always anticipate the future.

● Manage an Emergency Fund

An emergency fund is a type of quickly liquidatable asset (within three days) designed to address unexpected financial challenges. Such a fund can help you navigate tough situations. Determine your monthly expenses and multiply them by six to calculate the required emergency fund balance. Always ensure this amount is available to safeguard against unforeseen events.

During downturns or unexpected expenses, the emergency fund is there to help. However, it must be replenished promptly to protect against future unpredictabilities.

● Keep Things Professional

Attempting to save costs by handling everything yourself can increase expenses in the long run. Hiring an experienced accountant or financial manager can reveal strategies to save money and prevent tax penalties. Moreover, accounting software can significantly aid this process.

● **Ensure Customer Payments**

When running a business, customer payments are like a lifeline. If invoices aren't paid, your bills won't be either, putting your business at risk. Establish a clear payment system with precise due dates and methods. Set a payment schedule to avoid missed payments and follow up on late invoices. Unpaid customer invoices can lead to cascading financial problems, including your inability to meet your own obligations, ultimately leading to debt and business failure.

● **Don't Downsize Your Business Because of Taxes**

Taxes are a critical source of government revenue and essential for public administration and social services. However, in some regions, insufficient emphasis on taxation has led to reliance on unstable revenues, increasing non-compliance rates.

Businesses should not reduce their income just to avoid taxes. Learning to handle taxes appropriately ensures growth.

Maintaining financial records is crucial, especially during tax seasons. Losing a single receipt can severely impact your tax file. While no one enjoys paying taxes, it is an obligation no business can escape. Always set aside a portion of your revenue specifically for taxes.

▶ **Forecasting**

Financial forecasting is akin to accounting and often involves professionals in the organization. Managers who utilize forecasting gain better financial control and make more informed decisions. Forecasting uses historical organizational data to predict future sales and profitability, preparing managers for unexpected events and helping them select the best growth strategies.

▶ **Write Your Five Key Takeaways from This Chapter:**

1. ....

2. ....

3. ....

4. ....

5. ....

▶ **Three Steps I Will Immediately Start:**

1. ....

2. ....

3. ....

▶ **One Golden Lesson to Share with Others:**

....

....

....

....

Download all the tables and exercises of this chapter from the following website.

https://hosseintaheri.ir/bmg/